"Lucid and thought-provoking, *Miracles in the S*[...] [...]ual awakening and remarkable communication with t[...] other side. Science cannot explain all the strange and wondrous phenomena that occur every day in this world. But science and technology can still be important tools in creating those miracles, as author Mark Macy and his colleagues have shown. In telling his personal story, Macy bridges a crucial gap between science and the spirit."

—Uri Geller, www.uri-geller.com

"From his perspective [as] a key insider and participant, Mark Macy in his book *Miracles in the Storm* provides the definitive story [of] the small band of courageous explorers who, during the last twenty years, have been using modern technology to receive apparent communications from human spirits who have survived physical death. Loud and clear throughout this fascinating book, he carries home to the reader . . . that we do not die. . . ."

—Jon Klimo, author of *Channeling: Investigations on Receiving Information from Paranormal Sources*

"The unfolding of the ITC (Instrumental Transcommunication) story by Mark Macy in this book reveals a heroic struggle by a relatively small number of sincere, dedicated, and properly motivated people attempting to forge a reliable linkage and communication pathway into the unknown and cognitively unseen domains of our Earth world. I found it to be an excellent read and potentially very enlightening for both the general public and many of today's scientists who may be open to the larger wonders of nature's expression."

—William A. Tiller, Professor Emeritus
Department of Material Science and Engineering
Stanford University

MIRACLES IN THE STORM

Talking to the Other Side with the
New Technology of Spiritual Contact

Mark H. Macy

NEW AMERICAN LIBRARY

New American Library
Published by New American Library, a division of
Penguin Putnam Inc., 375 Hudson Street,
New York, New York 10014, U.S.A.
Penguin Books Ltd, 80 Strand
London WC2R ORL, England
Penguin Books Australia Ltd, Ringwood,
Victoria, Australia
Penguin Books Canada Ltd, 10 Alcorn Avenue,
Toronto, Ontario, Canada M4V 3B2
Penguin Books (N.Z.) Ltd, 182–190 Wairau Road,
Auckland 10, New Zealand

Penguin Books Ltd, Registered Offices:
Harmondsworth, Middlesex, England

First published by New American Library, a division of Penguin Putnam Inc.

First Printing, November 2001
10   9   8   7   6   5   4   3   2   1

REGISTERED TRADEMARK—MARCA REGISTRADA

LIBRARY OF CONGRESS CATALOGING-IN-PUBLICATION DATA:
Macy, Mark, 1949–
Miracles in the storm : talking to the other side with the new technology
of spiritual contact / Mark H. Macy.
p.   cm.
ISBN 0-451-20471-9 (alk. paper)
1. Spiritualism—Case studies. 2. Radio in parapsychology—Case studies.
I. Title.
BF1261.2 .M32 2001
133.9—dc21   2001032629

Set in Adobe Garamond
Designed by Leonard Telesca

Printed in the United States of America

BOOKS ARE AVAILABLE AT QUANTITY DISCOUNTS WHEN USED TO PROMOTE PRODUCTS OR SERVICES.
FOR INFORMATION PLEASE WRITE TO PREMIUM MARKETING DIVISION, PENGUIN PUTNAM INC.,
375 HUDSON STREET, NEW YORK, NEW YORK 10014.

ACKNOWLEDGMENTS

I extend my deepest gratitude (1) to my twin soul and best friend, Regina, whose inner voice I've come to trust; (2) to the folks on Earth who made it possible for me to immerse myself in ITC miracles because their minds and hearts were in the right way—George W. Meek, Hans Heckmann, and Maggy and Jules Harsch-Fischbach; and (3) to the folks in spirit, especially those good souls associated with Timestream and our ethereal friends who have brought the miracles to our world—Konstantin Raudive in particular. (Sincere thanks also go to spirit friends Isar, Arthur Beckwith, Bill O'Neil, my father, Blair Macy, and others who have dedicated their efforts to my project.)

Very special thanks go to two kindred spirits whom I admire deeply—Juliet Hollister for opening the door to miracles, and Willis Harman for taking a sincere interest in my work and extending a helping hand while on Earth and Beyond.

Heartfelt thanks go to all of my many ITC friends and colleagues around the world—Ernst Senkowski, Fritz Malkhoff, Nils Jacobson, Ralf Determeyer, Sonia Rinaldi, Hans Luethi, Theo Locher, Guenter Emde, Claudius Kern, Irma Weisen, Adrian Klein, Alison van Dyk, Paola Giovetti, Jacques Blanc-Garin, Marcello Bacci, Peter Ledermann, Cristina and Luciano Rocha, Maria Saraiva, Hernani Andrade, Siyoh Tomiyama, Ludwig Schoenheid, Elisabeth Berneck, Monique Simonet, Monique Laage, Hans Schaer, Franco Tellarini, François Brune, Wilma Stein, Pierre Thery, Silvana Pagnotta, Paolo Presi, Gerrit Westera, Alfred Zogg-Meier, and others whose names (please forgive me) I have left out.

Kay, Rich, Judy, and Bram: Your commitment over many months helped open the bridge in Colorado. Your friendship is deeply appreciated.

Last but not least, I thank the two bright, intuitive women who gave this book the chance it deserves to help the world in a big way: First and foremost, my agent, Sandra Martin. The advice you gave on how to heal relationships within world ITC, simply as a step toward making the book successful, shows me what a great agent can really do when she or he is also a great human being. And second, my editor, Cecilia Oh: Your resonance with the book has added life to it, as well as greater cohesion and readability. Your suggestions were right on. Thank you.

CONTENTS

The storm, March 5, 1998—Healing the world and me, late 1980s—
To the threshold of death, the summer of 1988—Clearing my spiritual
path, the early 1990s—Meeting my spiritual mentor, the autumn of
1991—My private course in miracles—Getting started in Luxembourg,
1985—Our extraterrestrial home; long, long ago

Voice of authority, February 1987—Making plans to spread the miracle,
1988—New bridges to other worlds, 1988–89—Storms of the ego,
the summer of 1989—Broken dreams and darkened hearts, the fall of
1989—On deaf ears, 1989–91—Getting started in Colorado, the winter
of 1991–92—Jeannette settles into Wonderland, 1992—A world of
infinite possibilities, timelessness—Surprise call from a musician, August
11, 1992—Angel wings and a fork in the road, 1992–93—Note from
a nineteenth-century chemist, summer of 1992

History is made, April 16, 1993—The media catch wind of ITC, the
fall of 1993—My guardian angel, Juliet in the East, November 1993—
Bridge opens to the States, January 1994—Another media dead end,

PREFACE

While some situations in this report have been dramatized to make the events more interesting to readers, I have made serious efforts to ensure that the information throughout the book is conveyed as accurately as possible. While I created some incidental dialogs based on my recollections of conversations, the crucial dialogs that represent researchers' perspectives were quoted accurately based on transcripts and other reliable documents.

This book is about ITC, or Instrumental Transcommunication—the use of technology to get information directly from the worlds of spirit in the form of voices, images, and text. The miraculous ITC contacts documented in this book—are they the genuine result of interchange between the Earth and other realms of reality? I'm confident that all the transcontacts do indeed originate from sources beyond the Earth. Plenty of good evidence supports their legitimacy. Is the information contained in those contacts factual? While there's no way for us on Earth to be certain about the accuracy of various details pertaining to spirit world descriptions and the personal experiences of those who contact us from beyond our world, I can safely say that since I got involved in ITC in 1991, our spirit colleagues have always communicated to us in a reasonable, wise, and empathetic manner. We humans come to trust the opinions of people on Earth who exhibit those qualities consistently over a long period of time, and it is natural, then, for us to extend the same trust to our spirit friends.

Of the large amount of information that has been sent to us from our invisible friends and departed loved ones through receiving equipment, this book includes only a glimpse at a cross section of contacts. I published most of the miraculous contacts in a journal between 1992 and 1999, then the publication halted when the contacts dried up for stormy reasons that are described in this book. When contacts resume on a worldwide basis in the early years of the twenty-first century, I may resume publishing an ITC journal. Meanwhile, I anticipate the complete documentation of those miraculous contacts in book form, hopefully around the time of this book's publication. When the main researchers, especially Maggy Harsch-Fischbach of Luxembourg, make that happen, I hope the material is embraced by the world as a miraculous gift. Those who sent the information to our world intended it as a gift.

Contacts from spirit are printed in *italics* in this book. Some of the contacts are printed verbatim, and those are enclosed in *"quotation marks."* Contacts that are paraphrased are *italicized without quotation marks.*

After the publication of this book, approximately half of all author's royalties will be used to help worldwide research—especially ITC research—that is focused on resonance among researchers, with the intent of establishing a fruitful, endurable relationship between Earth and the light, ethereal realms of existence.

—*Mark H. Macy*

PROLOGUE

A miracle of profound possibilities was brought to Earth in the closing years of the twentieth century, as people in various countries began to receive information through their televisions, telephones, radios, and computers from spirit colleagues. With the support of ethereal beings, or angels, an international team of scientists and researchers came together to nurture the development of Instrumental Transcommunication (ITC), under an umbrella of love and morality. Properly nurtured, the miracle could bring reassurance and understanding to our troubled world as we step into a new millennium.

But alas, negative human tendencies began to leak into the work, threatening to destroy the miracle and to trap humanity in its present state of uncertainty. The researchers must find a way to remove the threat.

Miracles in the Storm is a factual account of the author's role in sustaining the international, interdimensional research and documenting the amazing results over a nine-year period. During that time, he and his colleagues worked alongside some of the most powerful forces of Light involved with our world, and they confronted various influences of negativity and darkness on both sides of the veil which nearly destroyed their valuable work.

Miracles in the Storm is the first book that takes a close, compelling look at the fragile, young field of ITC research from the eye of the storm that nearly tore it apart. Since 1991 the author has been a key figure in world ITC—documenting the results of the most prolific receivers of ITC contacts, funding and organizing annual research seminars on both sides of the Atlantic, and opening the first enhanced ITC bridge in the States.

Currently, in the year 2000, the author is experiencing unprecedented miracles in his lab as he completes this book. The miracles include color images of spirit beings on a reliable basis and steady improvement of radio contacts toward loud, clear dialog. This book could play an important part in the resurrection of world ITC by putting things into clearer perspective. That is the author's hope.

Chapter 1

THUNDER AND RAINBOWS

THE STORM, MARCH 5, 1998

This was *not* a pleasant phone call. I glanced out the window. The moon was moving behind a cloud and the trees were waving their branches wildly as winds from the north brought a chill to the air.

"I'll tell you something, Mark. You need to get some advice, and I'm talking about legal advice," said Dale Palmer.

He was telling me to get a good lawyer! An uneasiness stirred in the pit of my stomach; I sensed a battle coming. "Why do you say that?" I asked.

"I think you're terribly naive sometimes," Palmer replied. "When you get stuff like that, and you reproduce that, and you send it through the United States mail, and then you use that to raise money, do you know what they call that in the United States, Mark?"

Was he accusing me of fraud? I couldn't believe it. Dale Palmer was a lawyer—a retired district attorney for the State of Indiana. The job of a DA is to prosecute criminals, and I was starting to feel like a criminal, even though I knew I'd done nothing wrong.

I'm involved in a controversial field of communication research called ITC, or Instrumental Transcommunication. It's not your normal, everyday type of communication; it involves the use of technical instruments to get information from the worlds of spirit in the form of voices, images, and text. Effectively, my fellow researchers and I are in contact with departed colleagues and loved ones by various means—primarily telephone, radio, television, computer, and camera.

At the time of my phone conversation with Dale Palmer, I was part of a group of scientists and researchers calling ourselves INIT (the International Network for Instrumental Transcommunication), and we were dedicated to the spread of ITC around the world in an ethical way. I was in charge of compiling the contacts from the various research stations and publishing them in a journal.

Now Palmer seemed to me to be suggesting that my journal carried false information. I wondered if he really believed that, or if it was just a case of sour grapes. He had been voted into our research group a couple of years earlier, then was asked to leave a couple of months ago as a terrible conflict raged among several members, including him.

I didn't like the idea of someone implying I was involved in fraud, but ITC researchers such as myself had heard empty accusations before, and we would likely hear them again and again until the notion of ITC became more widely accepted. It was a real mind-boggler to many people—the idea that we were talking, as some would say, to "dead people" on the phone. Still, hearing those words coming from Dale Palmer—a man I'd considered a friend and colleague—was especially troubling. I thought he really should have known better.

Palmer's main contention seemed to be with the research results of a European couple who were friends and colleagues of mine at that time—Maggy and Jules Harsch-Fischbach of Luxembourg. Maggy was reporting by far the most miraculous contacts in the world. She was enjoying not just phone conversations, but also computer contacts, voices through radio speakers, images flashing across TV screens, and even faxes—all purportedly coming from sources beyond the Earth.

Palmer said, "One of the things that bothers me a great deal is that you really don't know whether this dialogue that's coming out of Luxembourg is valid or not, and yet you reproduce that and send it out to hundreds of people."

I asked, "You're referring to the contacts they receive?"

"The contacts they *say* they receive," he replied. Again, it seemed to me he was suggesting my friends were involved in some kind of a hoax, which I knew was not true.

"Of course they're valid!" I said, and I explained in some detail why I believed so.

I was not alone in that belief. Many other discerning researchers and scientists who had witnessed the couple's miraculous experiments had walked away believing that amazing and wonderful things were under way in the life of this woman who claimed to be in touch with "Timestream," a team of several thousand spirit beings who worked with the support and guidance of angelic beings to choreograph contacts with the Earth. Palmer had never witnessed those experiments, so if he was skeptical, as he seemed to me to be, then perhaps his skepticism was understandable.

I thought that if we could now go our separate ways in peace, that would be fine. But it was not to be. We debated for more than an hour. I felt like a falsely accused criminal, defending the legitimacy of the research and the character of my friends and colleagues against what seemed to me like a pointed attack. When our conversation ended, neither of us having budged on our positions, I placed the receiver back on the hook and shook my head.

It was dark and still outside now, but the rumble of distant thunder could be heard. A storm was approaching.

Our story begins a decade earlier—a time when the world was preparing for a spiritual renaissance. In the 1980s, a few scientists and researchers claimed to be enjoying long dialogs with spirit colleagues by telephone and radio, and they began to report images from Beyond through TVs and computers. Those events apparently were being made possible by the collaboration of ethereal beings, or angels, and I have to make it clear that they were miracles, not phenomena.

Phenomena and miracles are those extraordinary things that happen in our world which can be observed, but not necessarily understood. Nor can phenomena and miracles be explained completely by conventional science, as a rule. According to Webster's Dictionary, what sets miracles apart from phenomena is divine intervention. Miracles involve the influences of higher spiritual powers.

Back in the 1980s when all those miracles began, I didn't believe in any sort of higher spiritual powers, so I would have rejected such claims outright. Now, as I write this book, having been immersed in this new field of spirit communication through technology for more than a decade, not only do I *know* the miracles are genuine, but I believe that those same miracles could conceivably usher our world into a whole new era of peace and understanding as we enter a new century. We could be on the threshold of a complete spiritual transformation. That's how I see things today.

In the late 1980s it was a different story. At that time, I was on the threshold of my own spiritual transformation, and spirit communication was the farthest thing from my mind.

HEALING THE WORLD AND ME, LATE 1980S

In the fall of 1987 I started to feel occasional twinges just below my rib cage on the left side. I hardly noticed them at first and paid little attention. One evening after dinner I was relaxing on the couch when one of the twinges occurred, and I mentioned it for the first time to my wife, Regina, who was still at the table going through the mail.

"There it goes again," I said with mild surprise.

"What's that, honey?" she asked.

"I've been having these strange little feelings lately," I replied, rubbing my upper abdomen.

"You mean like butterflies?"

"Not really . . ."

"Nausea?"

"No," I said. "I get a little twinge now and then. It's like something is grabbing me from the inside."

"Maybe you're pregnant," she joked. I smiled. Then, more seriously she said, "Maybe you should go see a doctor."

"No, I'm sure it's nothing."

Looking back now, I realize the twinges were like that pesky little voice in *Field of Dreams* that kept telling Kevin Costner, "Build it, and they will come." The voice whispering to me was more ominous, and I believe it was saying something like, "Time is short. Find the path."

I started having strange dreams at that point in my life too. In one dream that was especially vivid, I was in a large building with offices, conference rooms, and a large theater. A lot of people, some with familiar faces, were busy performing various technical tasks. As I came into their presence, they would look at me, and although we said nothing, I knew what they were thinking, and they knew what I was thinking. They were wondering why I was there. We all knew I was an outsider, and I had a feeling that I was supposed to give a talk or presentation in one of the conference rooms, so I started wandering about, trying to find it, encountering people along the way, all of whom regarded me as a visitor. Then I woke up with a confused, why-am-I-here?, what-am-I-supposed-to-be-doing? sort of feeling.

I had been a technical writer for more than a decade, working with computer programmers and engineers in high-tech corporations. It brought in a good, steady income, but lately I had been growing weary of that career. I assumed the dream had something to do with my mixed feelings about technical writing, since some of the people in the dream reminded me of engineers I'd been working with.

In another lucid dream I was among a small group of people standing around a shoebox-sized electronic device sitting on a table. Two transparent cables were attached to the device, and rainbow-colored light was streaming to and from the unit through the cables. I leaned forward to get a closer look, resting my hands on the table, and they stuck there. It felt as though my hands were glued or powerfully magnetized, fixed solidly to the table.

I exclaimed, "Wow! These are no ordinary energies!"

The others all glanced at me with looks on their faces that could best be interpreted as, "Well, duh." Again, I felt like an outsider.

At the time, I could only guess at the meaning behind those and many other strange dreams having to do with busy, high-tech places, but eventually it would be made clear to me that I was being recruited and trained at some subconscious, spiritual level for a project that would bring me closer in line with my life's purpose.

As months passed, the twinges beneath my rib cage slowly grew into spasms that felt like someone was reaching inside of me to give a firm twist to the muscles and ligaments. It was a strange feeling but not painful, so having no prior experience with serious illness, I wasn't worried. I didn't know about the malignant tumor that had been growing in my colon, probably for more than a year, and now must have been about the size of a child's fist. I had cancer and didn't know it yet.

At that time, I was deeply immersed in a book project. Whenever I wasn't at the office writing technical manuals, I was usually at home or in a forest cabin somewhere laboring on a series of books—typing at the computer or talking on the phone. I was contacting bright, innovative people from around the globe, discussing the world situation with them, and gathering their best ideas for achieving sustained peace, prosperity, and happiness in the world. I was contacting those people with letters and phone calls, and I was publishing the results of our discussions and correspondence in a series of books.

My colleagues came from all corners of the world:

- Dutch economist and Nobel laureate Jan Tinbergen offered a revolutionary solution as to who in the world—at what level of government or society, from the personal level to the global—should be deciding what: Every decision should be made at the lowest possible level, but high enough so that the interests of everyone affected by the decision are represented fairly. According to Professor Tinbergen, the idea that one overall leader or one overall government could effectively run society like a puppeteer was dangerously naive; also the other extreme, the notion that an unregulated group of people left to their own devices could achieve any semblance of order in today's world, was also dangerously naive.
- Futurist Hazel Henderson of Florida warned that the world economy was flying blind and would eventually crash if outdated economic indicators in use today (such as Gross National Product) were not replaced by more modern tools such as environmental impact statements and cross-impact studies.
- UN Assistant Secretary-General Robert Muller provided blueprints for an overhaul in global education, noting that the four elements of human nature, in descending order of importance, are the spiritual, social, mental, and physical elements, but Western education virtually ignores the two most important elements—the human spirit and appropriate social interactions! An immersion in spiritual understanding would be the most important step toward a healthy future.
- Physician Bernie Siegel isolated love as the most potent healing agent not only for cancer patients, but maybe for a troubled world as well.
- Two Chinese population officials reported in great detail how good planning would bring their crowded country into a new era with a flourishing social structure and economy, and how a good population plan

could do the same for other struggling countries. The article suggested that appropriate regulation at all levels of society could help to ensure right moral decisions among individuals and groups.

Scores of authors from scores of countries provided thoughtful solutions for our troubled world. For me, one of the most memorable authors was Dr. Willis Harman, president of the Institute of Noetic Sciences (IONS). IONS was one of the best-known research facilities involved in what might be called the "frontier sciences," especially such areas as consciousness study and energy healing. Conventional scientists ignored those subjects because there were no instruments or concepts with which to observe and measure them, but frontier scientists like Willis Harman knew that those troublesome issues would have to be patched into the scientific worldview eventually—and the sooner the better.

When I initially contacted Dr. Harman by phone and told him I would like to include some of his ideas in a book, he expressed interest. "Can you tell me a little bit more about the project?" he asked.

"Okay." I paused for a moment to gather my thoughts. "I want to create a series of books that take a fresh look at the world situation and help to create a better way of looking at things."

"That's a pretty broad field," he chuckled. "Can you be a little more specific, or narrow it down a bit?"

"What I'm really looking for are a few key principles of health and happiness that apply to all levels of humanity, from the personal to the global."

I had read a number of his articles in various journals, and I felt confident that a project of this type would be right down his alley. I asked if he would write a chapter for the book, and he agreed. Willis Harman's chapter was built around the idea that the most profound changes in history come about not when a few leaders made big decisions, but when vast numbers of people changed their minds just a little bit. (A decade later, with any luck, I would try to put that theory to the test with this book.)

A highly regarded scientist, Willis Harman was the founder of the Futures Research Group at the Stanford Research Institute, a famous think tank in California. He had become a champion in applying steady pressure on conventional science to broaden its worldview, and though he rarely used the word "spirit" in his writing, what he was doing, as I would determine later, was building a bridge between science and spirit. His article was a cornerstone of my first book in the series, *Solutions for a Troubled World*.

TO THE THRESHOLD OF DEATH, THE SUMMER OF 1988

The gruesome details leading up to my rush to the hospital in July 1988 and the persistent efforts of the staff to get me, bloated, groaning, and greenish in hue, to grope my way through a series of tests, are better left to myself.

They finally found the tumor, by then the size of a baseball, completely blocking the colon. It was removed along with much of the surrounding tissue, leaving me (as a writer, I found it ironic) with a semicolon.

My surgeon, John Day, was familiar with my recent book. When he visited me in my hospital room after the surgery, he said, "Mark, you better heal yourself before you try to heal the world."

At first I balked at the suggestion that I had some sort of flaws that needed healing, but as the weeks and months passed, I took his advice to heart. I'd always had a difficult time with addictive substances, but now I decided to give up alcohol, nicotine, and caffeine completely until I was fully recovered. I made appointments with a nutritionist, who convinced me to acquire a taste for greens, grains, and legumes; a deep body masseuse, who dug way down into my muscles and connective tissues to release tensions that had been buried since childhood; a spiritual career counselor, who tapped into my spirit guides to see what kind of work I *really* wanted to do in life; and a psychologist, who helped me dredge up and heal old childhood wounds. A lot of the things these professionals were doing to me were completely alien to me, but I decided to go along for the ride, even if I didn't understand at the time. It was like a journey into the unknown aboard a mystery train.

Regina would support me, even guide me to some degree, in my arduous transformative healing. She had been through serious healing cycles in her own life before I'd met her, and so she had deep empathy for my pains. Also, she knew that the processes would bring me greater balance of body, mind, and spirit, and that would strengthen our family considerably.

It all began on the morning she drove me home from the hospital. I'll never forget her words.

"Mark, you know I love you, and our marriage is the most important thing in my life, but if you need to get away for a while, I'll understand. Even if you decide that marriage is not . . ."

I knew what she was going to say, and I didn't want to hear it. It was obvious to me that she had cried a lot in the past few days, and maybe even blamed herself unjustly at some level for my illness. Apparently her tears of the previous days allowed her now to say all that without wavering. So it was my turn.

"Let's just go home so I can heal," I interrupted, my voice shaky. I looked out the window so she wouldn't see the tears streaming down my cheeks. They mixed with her brave words and formed a cement that would hold our marriage together through the challenging times that lay ahead.

CLEARING MY SPIRITUAL PATH, THE EARLY 1990S

Eventually my agnosticism would slowly fade away while firm beliefs in God and spirit would ease their way into my life, but it would be a long and formidable process. The two techniques that would take me for a quantum leap in my spiritual search, as well as in my healing, would be breathwork to release blockages, and heart meditation to find that place of peace within.

I was typical of many men: Throughout most of my adult life I had difficulty trying to express emotions. I kept things bottled up inside. Breathwork involved lying on my back with feet flat on the floor and knees up, breathing as quickly and as deeply as I could. After about five minutes, the breathing would take on a life of its own, and in ten or twenty minutes intense, long-buried emotions would start to pour out. The tears, the rage, and the intense resentment from long-forgotten situations startled me at first, but the more I did this breathwork process, the more welcome they became, because very often when the process was finished, I felt as though a ten-ton weight had been lifted off my mind and spirit! All my organs and tissues were completely relaxed. If I had trouble sleeping on a particular night, a session of breathwork would let me fall into a deep slumber.

Heart meditation came later. I learned to clear my mind and focus my awareness on the seven chakras, or energy centers, that are located in a line from the top of the head to the tailbone. I wouldn't just stay in my head thinking about each chakra; I would actually move my self, my awareness, so that it felt as though I were thinking from that energy center instead of from the brain.

Being present in each separate chakra had unique sensations, but the most profound experience for me was to move into my heart and remain there, sometimes for an hour or longer. For centuries, mystics have called the heart the seat of the human soul. I was learning from my research that the soul is a piece of God, or the sacred source, so it stood to reason that if I stayed in my heart, I would be as close as possible to a complete oneness with God. That seemed to be the case as my body would go through a series of gentle jerks as though I had been plugged into some form of pleasurable electricity. The more I did my heart meditations, the more blissful and less stressful my life became.

As I did breathwork and heart meditations on a fairly regular basis over a period of several years, my life came into greater balance than I could ever have hoped a decade earlier. I found happiness that I thought was reserved only for others. Negative spiritual influences would seem to be repelled by the positive feelings that were becoming a constant part of my life.

But that process would take several years. Meanwhile, early in my recovery stages my psychologist showed me a book by Dr. Stephen Levine, *Healing into Life and Death,* to see if I wanted to read it, and I think he was surprised by my reaction.

"What the hell is that?" I demanded. "A book on dying? Who said I'm going to die? Where do you get off suggesting I read a book on how to die!"

I was just starting to tap into my emotions after many years of repression, so I was still a little clumsy at it. The psychologist seemed to understand. He put the book away and I never saw it again. It's too bad my fear of death was so strong; I learned later that it is an excellent book, and I would have benefitted from reading it at that point in my life.

When you're gripped by a chronic fear of death, it creates many imbalances in your life. As months passed after the removal of the malignant tumor from my colon, I came to realize that I was in a quandary; my mind was entwined with my body, and it assumed that the body was the source of life and security. If the body died, the life and security would be gone. That's what I had always believed, but as months passed, I realized I would have to question that belief if I wanted to come to terms with my fears. If there were a higher spiritual self within me, as many people suggested, it was apparent that I had somehow severed ties with it. I was living in a society whose collective worldview had been reduced by science to a comprehensible picture of material existence. What if there were more to the picture than just the material world? What if we, as a society, had severed ties with a higher reality?

Those questions began to consume me as I healed. But the biggest question of all was, What happens to us after we die? For I now had a personal, immediate stake in the answer to that question.

I started reading books that approached the subject from various angles—Christian, Buddhist, metaphysical, and Yogic—but nothing resonated within me. All these explanations, while appealing, seemed like wishful thinking, and I couldn't buy them. They all required faith, but what I needed was hard evidence.

MEETING MY SPIRITUAL MENTOR, THE AUTUMN OF 1991

I was still a recovering agnostic in search of meaning in this fleeting life on Earth. I *wanted* to believe in life after death, but the whole notion seemed like wishful thinking to me. Those who believed in it—regardless of whether they were Christians, New Agers, Moslems, Hindus, or Buddhists—based their beliefs either on faith or on personal experience. I had never had an out-of-body experience, nor had any departed loved ones ever come to me in the middle of the night to stand smiling radiantly beside my bed to assure me that life goes on. I had read about such experiences, and I *wanted* to believe them all, but a skeptical little voice inside refused to take it on faith alone. I needed hard evidence.

That's when I crossed paths with George W. Meek. George was a retired industrialist who had revolutionized the air-conditioning industry and had made a small fortune on a series of patents. With a commanding presence at six-foot-three, he possessed a powerful intentionality that was apparent whether watching him march straight to the podium for a speech or whether observing him quickly chunk down a complex research project into tasks that he could delegate to his staff. Like all men of good character, George had learned to still that little inner voice that advocates bad choices from day to day, until the voice had become weak and ineffective. He had learned to make the right choices again and again until they had become habit. I would get to know him well, and he would become a role model for me. Over the years his intentionality had shaped a comfortable and pleasant lifestyle for his family. It had also spurred the creation of the Metascience Foundation, Meek's highly regarded, nonprofit enterprise to explore the human spirit from a scientific angle.

As he had planned for many years, George retired on his sixtieth birthday to fulfill a lifelong dream. He began traveling the world with his wife Jeannette to explore the deepest and richest spiritual truths hidden along the backroads of the twentieth-century world. Something inside him was driving him to get to the bottom of life's mysteries. He organized and funded research teams of medical doctors and scientists to travel to the forests of Southeast Asia, to crowded hospitals in China, and elsewhere to observe such phenomena as energy healing and the use of acupuncture as a sole painkiller during major surgery. He had written two pioneering books that had opened up new markets and blazed the way for a new breed of writers on spiritual matters. George Meek's two breakout books were *Healers and the Healing Process,* published in the 1970s, and *After We Die, What Then?,* published in the 1980s.

When I met George Meek in 1991, I was well on my way to healing from cancer. I was giving a small address to the International Association for New Science at their annual fall conference in Fort Collins, Colorado. I was introducing principles of healing that could be applied at all levels of humanity, from the personal to the global. About thirty people attended my talk and found it interesting.

George Meek delivered a keynote address, which drew a standing ovation from a crowd of hundreds, and for good reason. He had come to the end of twenty years of tireless investigation into the true nature of man. He had traveled around the world forty times, and from his massive collection of research data he shared the kind of evidence that minds like mine were craving. His beloved wife Jeannette had died within the past year, and George had received a letter from her, via computer, which she had sent from her new home in the spirit worlds. She missed him and awaited his arrival in the coming years, but emphasized that there was no hurry. Life there was absolutely beautiful, she wrote, and she had much to keep her busy. It seemed that she had just arrived, and she was already acting as a guardian angel of kindness for victims of war—men, women, and children who were coming across the veil in terror from the Persian Gulf Crisis. Jeannette's job was to calm them and get them settled into their new lives. This was not just channeled information; it was the result of objective reports from a woman who had died, then found a way to deliver clear, unfiltered messages to her husband through a computer on Earth.

The information in George Meek's lecture resonated so deeply within me that I was overwhelmed. It was the kind of hard evidence I had been craving, and I sat with tears in my eyes through much of the presentation. Afterward I approached the man and introduced myself.

"Mr. Meek, what you're doing is amazing. It's going to change the world!" I effused.

With a little smile and knowing eyes, he said, "I think you're right. At least I *hope* you're right. The research is very important, but there are many obstacles standing in the way right now. We'll just have to see how things unfold in the coming years."

I wanted to ask him about the obstacles—certainly they were not insurmountable!—but George Meek was a much-sought-after man for the remainder of the conference, and I had no further opportunities to talk to him.

I returned home from that conference a changed man. I immediately wrote a long letter to George Meek telling him of his profound effect on me. To my delight, he sent back a scrawled note along with a 90-minute cassette tape called "Spiricom." I read the note, which stated, simply: "I'm glad you enjoyed my talk. I think you might enjoy this tape as well. Let me know."

The Spiricom tape contained the most incredible sounds I had ever heard in my life—two voices emanating out of a loud buzzing monotone. One voice was fairly clear; it was the voice of Meek's colleague, Bill O'Neil. The other voice was hard to understand, and no wonder! It was the voice of a deceased man named Doc Mueller, a former NASA engineer. Somehow this "Spiricom" device was allowing O'Neil to converse with an invisible friend on a wide range of subjects.

In one dialog, Doc Mueller was giving O'Neil technical advice on how to improve the Spiricom equipment: *"William, I think the problem is an imped-ance mismatch into that third transistor."*

O'Neil replied slowly, as though studying the circuitry. "Third transistor."

"Yes, the transistor that follows the input."

"I don't understand," replied O'Neil.

"The pre-amp, the pre-amp!" Doc Mueller stated emphatically.

"Oh, the pre-amp."

"Yes, I think that can be corrected by introducing a one-hundred-fifty-ohm, half-watt resistor in parallel with a point-double-oh-four-seven microfarad ce-ramic capacitor. I think we can overcome that impedance mismatch."

Obviously baffled, O'Neil lamented, "Oh boy, I'll have to get the schematics."

The Spiricom tape contained dozens of such high-tech dialogs between Heaven and Earth. I listened to the complete tape several times, and each time I felt my mind being stretched into new shapes and sizes, until this miraculous new information could fit in. After digesting the information, I placed a phone call to North Carolina.

"Hello, this is George Meek," said a voice that sounded warm and some-what raspy with age.

"Mr. Meek, this is Mark Macy." I began, "You probably don't remember me, but . . ."

"Oh yes, the fellow from Colorado. It's good to put a voice with the letter I got from you two weeks ago. Did you receive the Spiricom tape? It should have arrived last week."

He had understandably forgotten about our brief encounter at the crowded New Sciences Conferences. Still, I wasn't expecting such a sharp mind for an eighty-year-old man! "That's what I'm calling about," I said. "That tape was the most amazing thing I've ever heard, and I want to thank you for sending it."

We talked for about twenty minutes. He seemed particularly interested in my writing background. Then he stunned me. "You know, Mark, I've been toying with the idea of starting a new research project, and I'd like to talk to you about it. Is there any chance you could come to Franklin for a few days?"

Good thing I was sitting down. I exclaimed without hesitation, "I'd love to!" It was one of those rare occasions when I made a decision like that on the spot, without first consulting Regina.

I had discussed this new technology with Regina quite a lot since the conference, and she had mixed feelings. On one hand, she could feel my excitement about this new spiritual connection I'd made, but on the other hand, she sensed that it might not be a very high level of spiritual pursuit. She loved the idea of praying to Christ and God and soliciting help from compassionate spirit guides and guardian angels, but she didn't seem that keen on the idea of collaborating with discarnate human beings. If the various aspects of my wife's personality could have voted, I suspect they would have been about seventy-five percent in favor of my new interest, and about twenty-five percent opposed.

MY PRIVATE COURSE IN MIRACLES

Two weeks later I was sitting in George Meek's living room. I had flown into Asheville, North Carolina, and rented a car for the ninety-minute drive through richly forested hills past mist-covered rivers to the town of Franklin. Now I was sitting face-to-face with the man whose ideas had changed my life, virtually overnight.

George talked a lot about Jeannette. He obviously missed her very much. He said he still remembered their world travels together as though it were yesterday. Whenever they returned home from those trips, George said he would spend a lot of time in his lab doing experiments, for example capturing on film spiritual energies emanating from his physical body, or observing how his emotions could affect the growth of plants. The results of his plant experiments were especially fascinating. Plants which he lavished with love would flourish. Other plants were not so lucky. Early in their growth cycle he would hold a hissing blowtorch menacingly in the air above his head, direct anger, contempt, and other negative feelings toward the poor seedlings, and shout in a threatening voice, "If you grow so much as a centimeter, I'll *burn* you to a crisp!" Those plants would grow weak and small.

"I hope you didn't do those experiments outside where the neighbors could see," I quipped.

George laughed. "They all know the sort of research I'm involved with. I don't think it would have raised any eyebrows."

When the Meeks had moved to Franklin from Fort Myers, Florida, George had purchased a large tract of land on the side of a forested hill and developed it into a small housing subdivision. He dreamed that the research of his Metascience Foundation would burgeon in the coming years, and the cozy neighborhood would become a thriving community inhabited by his staff of scientists, spiritual adepts, engineers, and researchers, all collaborating to uncover the mysteries of the human spirit.

The dream only partially materialized, as human egos and troubled personalities chipped away at the Metascience projects to the point where George, advancing in years and his wife ailing, could no longer manage things. One by one he had sold the houses and the lots until, by the time I met him, his only property left on the hillside was the cozy house that he shared with his housekeeper Loree. A beautiful view of the Smoky Mountains rising through the mist to the northwest greeted George in the evenings on his front porch where he enjoyed glorious sunsets.

Meek told me he had spent many hours in his large basement office piecing together road maps of the spirit worlds from the vast knowledge he had gained from his research. He had discovered that the actual locations of Heaven and Hell were not somewhere out there in distant space nor hidden away deep inside the Earth, but right here, all around us. He told me that mystics over the centuries have had an intimate knowledge of the fact that many universes interpenetrate our own physical universe, but they didn't know how to explain it to the world; humanity until now had always lacked the technological background to understand how this interpenetration worked. Mystics would say simply that the path to God and higher spirit lies within, which makes no sense to most people, who would argue that the path within leads only to organs and tissues, blood and bones. Now George could employ our understanding of radio technologies and electromagnetic energies to explain the true location of the spirit worlds in a way that human beings alive today could easily understand.

"Now, you know this room is filled with radio signals, right?" George quizzed me.

"Of course," I muttered. Just about everyone was aware nowadays that wherever you went in the world, hundreds of radio stations in the region were constantly broadcasting hundreds of radio signals through large transmitting antennas, and the signals in the form of vibrating energy were filling

18

the air, getting all jumbled together, and passing through houses, trees, and other solid structures.

"And you know that each signal remains distinct by its frequency. That's why this radio can tune separately to each signal," he added, pointing to the clock radio on the table beside him.

"That's right."

"Well, all the spiritual universes—and there are hundreds of them—they're all sharing this space with our physical universe, like radio signals sharing this room."

I nodded silently, not wishing to interrupt.

In a similar way, he explained, all the universes are "broadcast" by a central source which religions typically call "God" or "Allah" or "Yahweh" or "Brahman." These universes are all jumbled together in the same space as they are sent out by God, yet each universe remains distinct by its frequency or rate of vibration. The frequencies of the spirit worlds are much finer than the energies we are familiar with here on Earth, such as electricity, radio signals, and light. Most of these spirit-world energies are imperceptible not only by our physical senses, but also by modern scientific equipment.

"Hence Jesus' passage in the Bible, 'My Father's house has many mansions,'" George continued. "I learned about these interpenetrating worlds about thirty years ago. My first thought was, if we can use a radio to tune into each radio signal, maybe we could find a device that would let us tune into the spirit worlds and talk to their inhabitants. That's how Spiricom came together."

According to George Meek's model of the multidimensional universe, there are many, many levels of spiritual existence, from the rather dense astral planes which are a lot like the Earth, to the light, ethereal realms where angels and Light beings live a formless existence of pure, loving thought. Spiricom was in contact with the astral worlds where people from Earth wake up after they die. As such, those worlds are filled not only with the good qualities of mankind, but also with many of the troubled thoughtforms and strange behavior patterns that people from the Earth carry with them into the next life. So I asked George if he had ever thought about contacting the higher or finer spiritual worlds with technical equipment, where love and wisdom are the rule.

"We tried for a few years after the Spiricom project," George replied with a hint of disappointment still in his voice, "but nothing ever came of it."

He said it was called "Project Lifeline." George had hired a staff of technical experts who had developed elaborate transmitting and receiving devices and antennas operating with the highest frequencies they could achieve, but they were unable to make spirit contact. He had employed an entire staff of psychic channels who used their mediumistic skills to get technical advice from the other side in developing the equipment, but to George's great disappointment, no technical contacts were ever made. The only spirit communications received by Project Lifeline were boxes upon boxes of transcribed messages coming through the psychic channels.

"There seemed to be limits as to how far into the spirit worlds we could reach with our electronic equipment and electromagnetic energies," George said. "The only way we could tap those very light and subtle realms was with psychic channeling, and that method has its limitations."

Meek explained to me that psychic channeling involves a blending of minds of the spirit communicator and the human channel. As a result, the message received has been "filtered" by the mind of the channel. Very rarely does a message come through a human channel in a pure and unfiltered form. With ITC, on the other hand, messages from spirit can come through the equipment virtually unfiltered by the minds of the experimenters. So, ITC allows a more reliable means of communication with the worlds of spirit. Project Lifeline was an unsuccessful effort to tap into the highest spiritual levels with technical equipment.

"That's too bad," I said philosophically. "There's so much we could learn instantly if we could just talk to an angel."

"Interesting you should bring that up," George said. "I have some colleagues in Europe who are doing just that." He told me about a schoolteacher named Maggy Harsch-Fischbach whose research results in Luxembourg were causing quite a stir among those involved in spirit communication through technology. She and her husband Jules were in contact with a dedicated team of spirit colleagues calling themselves Timestream, who had opened the communication channels wide. Timestream members were calling Maggy on the phone, speaking to her through radios, sending live, moving images of themselves and their world through her television, and lately even planting large files of text and images on the hard disk of her computer. It was all made possible by the intervention of highly intelligent, loving beings from light, ethereal realms of existence—angels.

I felt tingles along my spine. If this were true, it would change the world! A team of highly competent spirit colleagues—folks who once had lived on Earth—called themselves "Timestream" and were working in close collaboration with angels to open communications with our world. My mind raced. Such communications would ease the suffering of those grieving over loved ones who had died. It would transform religions, replacing faith and belief with knowledge and understanding. It would allow science to move beyond its material-world confinements that have severely limited its vision since the days of Isaac Newton. It would allow humanity to get in direct touch with its ancestral roots. My mind was dashing from one possibility to the next as excitement welled up inside.

"Follow me," he said, pushing himself up slowly from his favorite chair in the living room. "I have something to show you."

He led the way down the stairs to the office, where he walked to a file cabinet, pulled open a drawer, and removed a large stack of papers. It was a series of rough translations of a research bulletin coming out of Luxembourg—the experimental results of Maggy Harsch-Fischbach. She seemed to be carrying on the legacy of George Meek's Spiricom and Lifeline research, penetrating the finer dimensions of the spirit worlds with technology.

I stayed up most of the night in my motel room, reading through the fascinating experiences of the Luxembourg schoolteacher whose part-time experiments had converted her home into what might well qualify as the eighth wonder of the world. The documents were works of art. Maggy herself had written them. Even after being translated from German to English, the words painted magical images, showed life from a heightened perspective, and stirred the hearts of readers like me. What an amazing person this Maggy Harsch-Fischbach must be. The miracles under way in her life were unprecedented, if the reports were true.

The next day over breakfast, my incredulity was obvious as I recounted some of the things I'd read during the night. For example, the folks at Timestream claimed to be living in a riverine world very much like the Earth, complete with forests, waterways, and towns full of houses where the spirit people resided. They called their world "Marduk" and reported that it had three suns.

At the breakfast table I shook my head and said with some exasperation, "George, I have friends and family members who are solid Christians. I've been telling them for years that I don't believe in any sort of heaven, and they've gotten used to that. What do you think would happen if I changed my story now and start saying, 'When people die, they don't go to Heaven . . . they go to Marduk!'?"

George chuckled but had no comment. He listened with mild amusement. He apparently enjoyed seeing my frustrating assimilation process going on. He'd no doubt observed it before with other colleagues and friends whose minds were being stretched by his research findings.

I would learn some years later, through deeper research, that "Marduk" was not just some arbitrary name pulled out of thin air. It was a crucial key for modern man in understanding his ancient heritage and his emergence on Earth. In time it would allow me a most amazing, wonderful, and insightful view of mankind, but for now it would remain a funny-sounding name of a spirit world, nothing more.

That was just one of many items in the Luxembourg reports that baffled me. There were others. In one transmission received in 1987, the nineteenth-century English explorer Sir Richard Francis Burton had found his way to the Timestream spirit group at a time when the group had been displaced from their sending station—a high-tech communication center in the spirit worlds from which they made contact with ITC experimenters on Earth. The sending station had been wrestled away from the Timestream group by a negative spirit group calling itself Group 2105. The negative spirit group had been occupying the place, disrupting communications, and upsetting the Harsch-Fischbach couple until Burton and his new friends recaptured Timestream.

"George, that sounds like something out of a science fiction novel. What do you make of it?" I asked.

He laughed and replied, "You'll find that a lot of the stuff they're dealing with in Luxembourg sounds like science fiction."

"Are you sure it's not just a hoax?"

"To tell you the truth, I wasn't sure what to believe until I visited the couple," George said. He moved his gaze to the woods outside the window, and a thoughtful look came over his face as he remembered his experiences with the Harsch-Fischbachs.

"I visited their lab in February of 1988. Well, it wasn't really a lab; it was their living room. They had an old black-and-white TV set and a brand-new video camera set up, along with all the radio equipment they were using."

George said he had been traveling around Europe with Dr. Ernst Senkowski, a retired physics professor from Mainz, Germany, and a well-known ITC expert who was a friend of the Harsch-Fischbachs. The two retired men had been visiting researchers in various countries, covering 2,000 miles in 50 hours. He laughed at the memory. "I don't know how a couple of old guys like us did it. We hardly slept, and neither of us ever got tired!"

I said nothing. It was my turn to listen and enjoy as George told his story:

When he and Dr. Senkowski arrived in Luxembourg on that winter day in 1988, the Harsch-Fischbachs told them that the TV they'd be using for experiments once belonged to Jules's grandfather, but it had been sitting on a shelf in the closet for years, collecting dust. The spirit team had suggested they use that TV and a video camera during Meek's visit. Jules and Maggy were skeptical. The TV had no antenna and didn't function at all. They didn't own a video camera, couldn't afford to buy one, and wouldn't know how to use it anyway. Still, Timestream told them to acquire a video camera, so they borrowed money from the bank and bought one the day before the two researchers arrived.

Under the circumstances, by all rational thought, the couple should have been skeptical about getting any results with their visitors present that day, but they were accustomed to the miracles which their spirit friends were able to accomplish. They had come to realize that almost anything is possible if you keep your mind and heart open, have faith, and tap into the finer spiritual forces.

The TV was plugged into the wall current, and when Jules turned it on, it worked. A screen full of "snow," or static, appeared. The video camera was pointed at the TV. Moments after it was turned on, a three-second sequence of images flashed by on the screen: mountains, a forest, a building, and most impressive, a couple walking hip-deep out into a lake or ocean—holding hands, then releasing hands, then joining hands again. A high-pitched voice, which Maggy said was the voice of an angel, broke through the TV static to announce the end of this successful experiment—the transmission of pictures "live" from the astral world Marduk.

As Meek's story ended, I asked him, "How did it feel to see history being made right there in front of you?"

"It was humbling," he replied quietly. Tears welled up in his eyes, and his voice broke as he said, "It was the culmination of all my years of research. My greatest dream was coming true right there in front of me."

We spent a lot of time talking about the Luxembourg miracles throughout the day, and that evening we decided we would try to arrange a visit with the Harsch-Fischbach couple. George and I decided we would be stronger if we joined forces, so the two of us established Continuing Life Research to explore consciousness and the afterlife. The new research firm would become the cornerstone of our collaborative efforts.

In the coming weeks, George contacted the couple by letter and succeeded in finding a place in their busy schedule in the late summer of 1992, the same week that an esoteric conference was to be held in Dusseldorf, Germany. It would be my first trip to Europe, and it would be a busy one.

GETTING STARTED IN LUXEMBOURG, 1985

It had all started for Maggy Harsch-Fischbach in 1985, a few years before my own life-changing experience had gotten under way. Maggy had been inspired by recent breakthroughs. The Spiricom experiments of George Meek and Bill O'Neil had ended in 1982. In 1983, a German experimenter named Hans Otto Koenig had successfully demonstrated his "Ultrasound" device to an audience of millions during a live television show broadcast from Station RTL (Radio-Television Luxembourg). Koenig and the program's host, Rainer Holbe, stood wide-eyed as loud, clear voices were conveyed through the device—voices that technicians and engineers could not explain by any normal means.

Inspired by Meek and Koenig, Maggy had received her first tiny voices on tape right away, and before long a rather strong, high-pitched voice became an integral part of the work. It was a very precise voice, crisp and clear, and it announced the beginning and end of all the sessions. At times it would surprise Maggy with words of wisdom that suggested vast knowledge on a wide array of subjects—math, science, relationships, religion, history, and even events that were supposed to have occurred many thousands of years before recorded history. It soon became clear that he or she—the wise, incredibly knowledgable being behind the voice—was not only allowing Maggy to make unprecedented progress in the development of her ITC receiving station, but was actually guiding and protecting that development. Often Maggy would ask the brilliant being about himself, or herself, and over time she received the following information in reply:

Our existence is beyond your comprehension. It's easier for us to explain to you what we are not. We are not human, nor animal, nor male, nor female, nor Light being, nor, of course, God. There are seven of us, and although we are individual beings with individual natures, we are fused together. Many beings such as us live together closely in small groups, or clusters, as we exist in subtle realms where such boundaries as skin and ego, which separate physical beings in your world, do not exist. We are in ethereal realms of spacelessness and timelessness where beings who resonate with one another can join together in common existence, if they so choose. Many of the great beings who have walked your planet, such as Jesus Christ, Mohammed, and Gautama Buddha, return home to live in ethereal clusters in our realm which, from your perspective, is very close to God.

Names are of no importance to us. As they are important to you, you may call me Technician, as my role in this project is that of a technician to facilitate contact between worlds. Our group you may call, simply, The Seven. We, The Seven, are assigned as a Gatekeeper between Heaven and Earth, between time and space. For us it is only an assignment, while from your perspective we have accompanied your world for many thousands of years.

We have provided humanity with guidance and protection, and we have moved particularly close to the Earth during seven crucial periods of climactic growth, your current civilization being the seventh. We are here to assist you.

There is a widely known picture in your world of two children crossing a bridge, accompanied by a being who protects them. That is our role in your work, but we have no wings.

Maggy was in close cooperation with seven angels. As I would come to understand, it was her dedicated efforts, and especially her sincerity, which had attracted the help of this group of seven ethereal beings into her life and into her work at this pivotal point in the development of mankind. Apparently it was time for ITC to unfold in our world, and it would become evident to me later on that the home of Maggy and her husband, Jules Harsch—who by now was working with Maggy in her experiments—had been selected as a sort of test site for the first fully functional ITC receiving station.

* * *

Ethereal beings such as The Seven are the beings of love, compassion, and wisdom which people throughout history have reported encountering at key moments in their lives—so-called angels, or divine guardians. These are the beings who manifest miracles around the Earth. They have subtle, radiant bodies when they move in close to work with the Earth, emitting ribbons of rainbow light reminiscent of wings and ethereal robes.

Ethereal beings can come into the lives of us humans at times when all shreds of deception and insincerity have been stripped away, such as in a time of severe crisis or during the moments before death of the physical body. Insincerity is alien to these beings, and it keeps them away.

People who live in a sincere and trusting way on a daily basis, whether through inner work or by their basic nature, are blessed with ethereal presence. There is an aura of bliss around these individuals, and their lives are synchronistic; they seem always to be in the right place at the right time.

Perhaps many years of teaching young children had helped to hone Maggy's sincerity, thus allowing a group of these ethereal beings to commit themselves to assisting her efforts, and soon she was taking quantum leaps in ITC research. Strange beeps and whistles emanated from her radios, produced by spirit-world apparatuses. The music on a radio station would suddenly disappear, to be replaced by voices of departed loved ones and other helpful astral beings.

These astral beings are the folks whom we sometimes call "spirits of the dead." They inhabit our ancestral planes—the so-called "astral" regions of the spirit worlds where people still think and behave as they had on Earth. There are many astral realms ranging from the hellish to the divine, depending on the attitudes and thought patterns of the departed people who inhabit them.

When people on Earth die and shed the physical body, they awaken in an astral body in an astral world. The new body is a replica of the body they had enjoyed in the prime of life—organ for organ, maybe even cell for cell—and their new world is very much like our world. The main difference is that everything is subtler, less dense, and easier to shape and change by intention. The astral planes, where most people wind up after death, are more of a paradise than is the Earth. Most of the astral beings are a bit more elevated than we physical beings, since some of our troubled emotional patterns and our conflicting personality quirks that make our lives difficult here on Earth are left behind when we die and move on to the next life.

The ethereal beings are more elevated still, or of finer vibration, than the astral beings, who sometimes refer to their ethereal brethren as "rainbow people." That seems to be an appropriate term, because when the ethereal beings show themselves in the astral worlds, they glow and pulsate in magnificent colors reminiscent of a rainbow.

A team of astral beings—deceased relatives, scientists, celebrities, and others—were coming together around the work of Maggy Harsch-Fischbach to assist in the new and exciting project of opening channels of communication with their old home, Earth. The group of seven ethereal beings were moving in also, to provide guidance and protection.

As one of the rainbow people, the Technician, began to work directly with Maggy, the being's high-pitched voice began to come through the radios to introduce all the sessions. The voice reflected incredible knowledge and wisdom about the equipment and this new communication process between Heaven and Earth.

In a few short years, Maggy and Jules were capturing pictures from the spirit worlds on their television; long, clear messages were coming through their radios; and they would even get phone calls, usually from the researcher Konstantin Raudive, who had died in 1974.

Konstantin Raudive had been a leading authority on spirit communication before his death, and he had chosen to continue the work from the other side of the veil. Now he was making it clear to Maggy through phone calls as well as through radio contacts that it was his calling to help open the doors of clear communication between Heaven and Earth.

Konstantin Raudive and the higher beings soon began to stress to Maggy a message with growing urgency. The message was stated on various occasions with various wordings, and warned as follows:

Humanity is at a crucial stage in its development. This is the seventh time that humanity has reached this crucial stage, and the results were devastating during the six preceding eras, some extending back in time far beyond recorded history. ITC is the most important means of waking the human consciousness out of its sleep, and in that way will play an important role in getting you through the coming "End Time," but in order for ITC to further develop on Earth, it must involve an effort of many unified minds representing many countries. It cannot be centered around any one country, and especially not around any one individual.

So, the overall goal of ITC development was set: Researchers would be able to work miracles if they could learn to work together. A resonance among researchers on Earth would attract ethereal influence into the work.

OUR EXTRATERRESTRIAL HOME; LONG, LONG AGO

If we could hop aboard a spaceship today and head away from the Earth and away from the sun, in a straight line through the orbits of the other planets in our solar system, we would first cross the orbit of Mars, then Jupiter, then Saturn, Uranus, Neptune, and Pluto, then off we'd sail into "outer space." We would face the most hazardous part of the journey in the large gap between Mars and Jupiter. Millions of rocks and boulders of various sizes form a belt between those two orbits and could easily rip open the side of any spacecraft trying to pass through.

Astronomers have known of the presence of the asteroid belt between Mars and Jupiter for about 150 years, but why it's there they can only speculate. Many scientists think the asteroids are debris left over from a former planet that circled the sun in an orbit between Mars and Jupiter—a planet that was somehow destroyed many thousands of years ago.

Through ITC contacts we have been told that those scientists are correct; there was indeed a planet between Mars and Jupiter. It was called Marduk, and it was no ordinary planet. It was the jewel of the solar system, thriving with life and supporting a civilization that would make modern humanity seem like a pack of gifted apes by comparison.

Our ITC contacts of recent years suggest that the people of Marduk enjoyed an Eden-like experience and a highly advanced culture in which science and technology far surpassed anything on Earth today. With an ability to move among worlds, the people of Marduk established colonies on nearby planets, including Earth.

The destruction of Marduk and the fate of its marooned colonies provide a vital missing link to our understanding of the human heritage, which has been coming together like an elaborate puzzle through ITC contacts received in recent years. We are told that the trials and tribulations of the stranded survivors trying to carve a paradise in the primitive and barbaric environs of Planet Earth comprise the true fall of Man.

So our present story *really* begins more than 25,000 years ago, when things were a lot different in our little corner of the physical universe.

Chapter 2

STORMY BEGINNINGS

VOICE OF AUTHORITY,
FEBRUARY 1987

There were a number of researchers around the world who were studying the miracle of ITC to try to understand it. The man considered by many people to be the leading European authority on the subject was a German physicist and university professor named Ernst Senkowski. He theorized that ITC technology was a blending of forces such as electricity, nerve impulses, emotions, and attitudes. The respected, well-known doctor founded a research group called the Association for Psychobiophysics through which to study the miracle of ITC.

A warm, delightful man with sparkling eyes, Senkowski was admired as much for his good nature as he was respected for his keen intellect. When he was invited to observe the experiments under way in the Luxembourg home of Maggy and Jules Harsch-Fischbach, he was excited. Such results were unprecedented. He had studied the "Spiricom" project of George W. Meek in the States, which had provided the first electronic dialog in history between Heaven and Earth in 1979. He had listened to long, clear radio voices received, apparently from the spirit worlds, by German experimenter Hans Otto Koenig and by Italian researcher Marcello Bacci, and he had seen the video images that had emerged out of the boiling clouds of static on the television screen of Klaus Schreiber of Germany, all in the early 1980s. All these breakthroughs were major steps in the development of enhanced technical spirit communication—miracles in their own right—but none of them compared to the results rumored to be coming out of Luxembourg.

Over the years, Senkowski had seen his share of hoaxes as well, so he entered the lives of the Harsch-Fischbach couple with a discerning eye. What he found was amazing. Video images of forests and mountain ranges in the astral worlds came through the television. Long messages by well-known historic personalities, late scientists, and ethereal beings broke through the radio sounds.

When Senkowski visited Maggy on February 8, 1987, the high-pitched voice of Technician came through:

Dr. Senkowski, we are glad you have found your way to this bridge.

Senkowski was startled, but he quickly gathered his thoughts. It was an ideal opportunity to get confirmation on some of his theories. He asked the ethereal being, "Do experimenters' coworking brainwave patterns make these contacts possible?"

Yes, that is true.

Senkowski was delighted. He had long assumed that the mind of the experimenter was a key factor in ITC contacts and that there was some sort of interplay between the minds on both sides of the veil. His assumptions were apparently correct. "Are these patterns something you can perceive?" he asked.

Yes, I can also impress them, came the high-pitched reply.

So, thought Senkowski, the higher beings not only could *read* our minds, but could actually help *shape* them! Amazing, he thought. "Burkhard Heim suggests that communication is facilitated by five-dimensional field pulses. Is that correct?" Senkowski asked.

Yes. Heim is brilliant.

The contact ended a few minutes later, after Senkowski had asked several questions relating to technical equipment which went unanswered, and the Technician announced that energy for the contact was running out, explaining:

For you, the principal energy is electricity. For us it is consciousness, which sends out much finer vibrations than you are able to perceive with your five senses.

Over a period of several years, Senkowski studied the Luxembourg experiments closely and found no traces of foul play. Maggy's sincerity and honesty were obvious. The messages from Beyond were often profound. Senkowski quickly became a friend of the Harsch-Fischbach couple and an advocate of their work, but the friendship was destined not to last.

MAKING PLANS TO SPREAD
THE MIRACLE, 1988

The ethereal beings were applying pressure on Maggy to spread the miracle from her living room out into the world, for without widespread collaboration, they reiterated, the miracle would not take root on Earth at this time. There was a problem. Maggy and Jules Harsch-Fischbach led very busy lives—she as a schoolteacher, he as a bureaucrat in the Luxembourg national government—and whatever time they had after work they spent experimenting, fostering ties with the spirit friends, and publishing their research results. They had no time whatsoever to organize an international research panel, but perhaps their new friend Ernst Senkowski did.

Every year in Europe there was a conference called "PSI Days," where thousands of Europeans would experience the latest results of paranormal and esoteric research from around the world. The 1989 conference was to be held in Basel, Switzerland, and it was quickly approaching. Maggy asked Professor Senkowski to announce at the Basel PSI Days conference that a new international research association was being formed. The miracles surrounding the lives of the Harsch-Fischbach couple would be the nucleus of the group, and through the dedicated, united efforts of serious researchers and scientists from around the world, those miracles would spread to all parts of the globe. It was a beautiful dream.

Several months before the conference, Maggy's plans were announced to a small circle of international researchers, and they found almost unanimous approval. The association at first would cover all German-speaking areas, then expand. There would be a journal published, and all groups involved in technical spirit communication would be represented.

The fact that there was little time to plan the details of an association and no money available to get it on its feet didn't slow Maggy down. Her spirit friends were making miracles happen in her life. With their help, perhaps, such details would come together behind the scenes.

But other problems began to develop. The opinion evolved among researchers that Maggy intended to be president of the association, and her husband Jules would be general secretary. Some researchers felt that it was only right, considering that the couple were the source of the whole idea in the first place, and they had a direct link to higher spiritual sources. Others, however, began to feel left out. Such human feelings and motivations are largely beyond the control of higher beings. The group of experts on Earth were seeing a rift developing now between the human spirit which yearns for one mind, and the human ego which demands recognition, power over others, and independence. It's a rift that has followed humanity throughout history, and it would cause a serious division in world ITC in the coming years. And it would have disastrous consequences during the upcoming Basel PSI Days conference.

NEW BRIDGES TO OTHER WORLDS, 1988–89

Friedrich (Fritz) Malkhoff lived in Schweich, Germany, a village sitting on the banks of the beautiful River Moselle, which forms part of the border between Germany and Luxembourg. He was about ten miles from the ancient city of Trier.

Fritz had spent most of his life working on the German railroad. Now in his forties, he was already retired and living on a meager disability pension which supported his wife Erika and himself and their teenage son Markus in a small, two-story flat. He was known by friends as a rather uncomplicated man, clean and pure inside and out, handsome of appearance, and a loving and supportive husband and father who was completely devoted to his family.

Schweich residents received clear broadcasts from Radio-Television Luxembourg (RTL), which for many years aired a series called "Unbelievable Stories," first on radio, then on TV. The series gave a rather serious look at paranormal phenomena. Fritz and Erika followed the series with mild interest until the autumn of 1987, when commentator Rainer Holbe hosted a program about spirit voices on tape. According to the program, people from many walks of life were busy taping various sounds with the intent of capturing short, faint spirit voices on tape. And some of those people were having an astonishing degree of success.

Something inside Fritz was stirred, and he became excited as the program went on. By the time it was over, he had decided to do some taping of his own.

After acquiring the necessary equipment he started experimenting, at first with a great deal of uncertainty. To his great surprise, he very soon captured easily discernible voices on tape, and as his confidence grew stronger, so did the contacts.

Meanwhile, a man named Adolf Homes of Rivenich, Germany, was also having good results capturing spirit voices on tape. There were few similarities between the two men beyond their common interest in spirit communication. Two main differences could be lumped under the heading "Spirits." Adolf Homes was psychically sensitive; he picked up thoughts and impressions from spirits rather routinely. Fritz Malkhoff was more absorbed in the physical world and, like most people alive today, had little conscious awareness of influences of spirit beings in his life. Fritz had both feet planted firmly on the ground, while Adolf had only one foot on Earth while the other was often testing the waters in the spirit worlds.

Adolf Homes also indulged in liquid spirits, as millions of people do. From personal experience I knew that alcohol numbed the mind and eased some of the pains that life on Earth deals us. Looking back, though, I believe it also made my connection to the spirit worlds rather cloudy and unpredictable over a period of many years. Overall it weakened my mind-body-spirit connection. I wondered if it might be bearing the same bittersweet fruits for Adolf Homes and other researchers who consumed alcohol.

The fact that these two German men—the clean-cut Fritz Malkhoff of Schweich and the psychically gifted Adolf Homes of Rivenich—got good spirit voices so quickly was like a billboard along life's highway that read: "Miraculous opportunities ahead for all sorts of people of good intention! Next exit." The two men were about to take the same detour on life's highway.

Adolf Homes became rather excited about the field of research called EVP, or electronic voice phenomenon. At last he could capture on tape the voices that he had been hearing in his head most of his life. He placed advertisements in newspapers to find others of like interest, and in the spring of 1988, Fritz found one of those ads, he called Mr. Homes by phone, and they set up a meeting. Sometimes opposites don't attract, but in this case, the two men got along together like brothers, and from that moment on, their contacts began to improve steadily. It was as though their combined energies were immeasurably stronger than just the sum of their individual efforts.

The two men began recording together every day during sessions lasting up to two hours. They found that they made a good team and complemented each other. Fritz was more comfortable dealing with the technical equipment, while Adolf employed his unusually strong psychic gifts. Also, Adolf had never known his mother, who had died when he was just an infant, and that lack had left a big hole in Adolf's life that he hoped ITC would fill. Such burning desire to share loving thoughts with departed family members, it was starting to become apparent through the experiments of other researchers, could provide an important fuel to contacts with the spirit worlds.

Fritz and Adolf began to present their results at ITC congresses, and they attended public conferences. At a meeting held in Darmstadt, Germany, they learned of the work being done by Maggy and Jules Harsch-Fischbach of Luxembourg, who were in touch with a team of exceptionally capable spirit beings calling themselves Timestream.

The two men started to focus their attention on the Timestream spirit group. They made a copy of the equipment which had provided some breakthroughs for the Luxembourg experimenters, and it also worked for them.

In Rivenich it was not Timestream that contacted the two men, but a group that identified itself as "Centrale." Adolf's deceased mother and Fritz's father belonged to that group, so the two men were delighted by this new development.

Initially, their friends from beyond contacted them only through their radio speakers, but before long they began receiving phone calls as well. In 1988 Fritz read reports about other experimenters in Europe having some success with computers. They would type a question into a computer, and eventually an answer would appear.

These reports began to preoccupy Fritz's mind, so before long he decided that he and Adolf should try computer experiments. He suggested that they install Fritz's old Commodore C64 in Adolf's home in Rivenich to see if the Centrale group could come through the computer to communicate. At first Adolf balked at the idea because of his total unfamiliarity with computers. He wanted to stick with what he knew best—voice contacts—and he felt certain computer contacts were not for him. After much discussion, Fritz finally convinced him by telling Adolf he need not worry. Either it would work, or it would not. Adolf shrugged and resigned himself to the fact that it was time to enter the computer age.

Once the computer was installed, the two men composed a short letter comprising a single question. They left the computer running, and two days later an answer appeared on the screen. They knew then that a strong contact field had been firmly established at the Rivenich station.

They assumed that building up a station in Schweich would run as smoothly as in Rivenich, but they were wrong. Try as they did, contacts were not springing forth in the Malkhoff home as they were in Adolf's home in Rivenich.

When they posed the question of what Fritz could do in Schweich to duplicate the terrific results of Rivenich, the reply was vague, but disappointing. It said Fritz did not have any more influence. The two men interpreted the message to mean that there was nothing left for Fritz to do at this time, but that the spirit team would try to get through there too. Still, Fritz was eager to get things moving ahead.

July 5, 1989. Group Centrale informed the two men:

Wernher von Braun is trying to make contact in Schweich; disturbances unknown to you still hinder the efforts.

STORMS OF THE EGO, THE SUMMER OF 1989

It was at this time that the idea of an international ITC association was being bandied about by researchers in Germany with a growing upsurge of mixed feelings. Malkhoff and Homes had no desire to get involved in the politics of an organization; they wanted only to be left alone to experiment and get contacts. Unfortunately, it is impossible to remain truly isolated in this world or in any world. The thoughts, words, and actions of other people in many worlds boil over into our lives in every waking and nonwaking moment.

In this case, various conventional researchers were having difficulty accepting the kinds of miraculous breakthroughs that had been coming out of Luxembourg in the past few years, and which were now starting to be reported by Malkhoff and Homes. Some well-known researchers had worked diligently for many years to gather large collections of tiny spirit voices on tape. For newcomers simply to begin experiments and to get results that made the work of established researchers pale by comparison, was a hard pill for many people to swallow.

Perhaps in another world where the higher human spirit prevails, all people would embrace the miracles that had been granted to their world through the Harsch-Fischbachs and other young researchers such as Malkhoff and Homes. But it was a world driven largely by the human ego, and it was not always easy to embrace the good fortunes of others.

Longtime voice experimenter Fidelio Koeberle operated one of the largest organizations for technical spirit communication, publishing a widely circulated newsletter that focused almost exclusively on the subject of EVP research—the capturing of short, faint voices on tape. After the more elaborate forms of ITC contact began to occur, his journal began to carry articles suggesting that these contacts (such as the miracles being experienced by the Harsch-Fischbach couple, by his onetime friend Hans Otto Koenig, and by such upstarts as Malkhoff and Homes) were impossible, and therefore must be a hoax.

Such words and actions by Koeberle and others were starting to muddy the waters. Enhanced ITC contacts were made possible by a "contact field," or a pool of attitudes, thoughts, and desires of the experimenters on Earth and their spirit friends. These thoughtforms existed as vibrations, and if there was a resonance or harmony among all the vibrations, then information could be sent across the veil through electronic equipment. If there was dissonance, the veil was difficult to penetrate from the other side. The skeptical opinions being published by Fidelio Koeberle were beginning to harm the contact field that was making enhanced ITC possible in Europe.

The young experimenters—the Harsch-Fischbachs of Luxembourg, and the Germans, Fritz Malkhoff and Adolf Homes—all sensed that they could overcome the dissonance and strengthen their contacts by working together, so they forged an alliance.

Working in close collaboration had a magical effect. In the coming months, the station at the Fritz Malkhoff home began to open up, and the three stations began to receive cross-contacts. For example, two or three stations might receive identical contacts at the same time. Or in other cases of cross-contacts, one station might receive, say, a phone call, then another station would receive shortly thereafter another contact—perhaps a message planted in a computer—which verified the phone contact. Such cross-contacts provided solid evidence that the ITC contacts were genuine.

BROKEN DREAMS AND DARKENED HEARTS, THE FALL OF 1989

Ernst Senkowski, who was in charge of organizing all the details and co-ordinating the efforts in the formation of an international research association at the quickly approaching Basel PSI Days conference, was getting a little concerned. There still were many unresolved factors regarding such matters as funding, organization, and interest among researchers. While interest had seemed great when the idea was first announced, it was now starting to wane. So Dr. Senkowski had mixed feelings. On one hand, there would be tremendous benefits if a tightly knit association would foster the spread of these unprecedented miracles. On the other hand, the most rapid progress is made when many independent minds explore many paths at the same time. Ernst Senkowski was a free thinker who enjoyed figuring out the mysteries of life. Being guided or directed to bring people into unified thinking was an uncomfortable position to be in. Dr. Senkowski had earned a reputation as a discerning scientist, but now he was in a position that could make a person feel a bit like a disciple. He was in a difficult position, to say the least.

At the same time, some of the other established, well-known researchers were getting nervous, starting to feel that they would be playing only minor roles in the association, and they were not accustomed to minor roles. Hans Otto Koenig and Fidelio Koeberle were presidents of the two largest organizations for technical spirit communication in Germany, and they had decided not even to attend the conference.

Perhaps Maggy could not see the underlying current of dissonance that was brewing beneath the surface, or maybe she was ignoring it, assuming it would be resolved in time. In any event, she did not foresee the terrible disappointment that would soon send her reeling.

The conference arrived, and on the last day most of the PSI-Days visitors had already gone home. Those who remained had only the desire to say good-bye to friends and to enjoy the warm glow that had been kindled by the conference. Few people, if any, were interested in hearing about the founding of a new research association. After all, some of the best-known researchers had already turned their backs on the proposed association. By now Ernst Senkowski's initial enthusiasm had run out of steam, so the message he delivered that day was quite the opposite of what Maggy had initially intended. Senkowski announced that the time was not yet ripe for an international association. Each researcher should pursue his or her own path for the time being.

Maggy had built a beautiful dream as fragile as a perfect sphere of thin glass, and when she heard the news, her dream shattered. Suddenly she was left standing before a pile of broken pieces that she and her husband Jules would have to clean up painstakingly with great care, tremendous effort, an investment of their savings, and a great deal of kindness and understanding from friends and close supporters.

Name-calling and accusations were exchanged among the key figures involved in the fiasco, and within weeks a deep chasm grew between the Harsch-Fischbach couple and those who had broken their dream—Fidelio Koeberle, Hans Otto Koenig, and especially Ernst Senkowski. The dark division within ITC in Europe would last more than a decade, despite the efforts of good souls on both sides of the veil to heal the wounds.

ON DEAF EARS, 1989–91

As the storms raged among ITC researchers, efforts were made beyond the veil to help calm those storms. Timestream spirit group contacted Maggy Harsch-Fischbach by computer on May 10, 1990, to give her a peace offering which she could extend to Ernst Senkowski. Obviously both researchers were highly regarded by the other side—Maggy for such qualities as sincerity and diligence, and Ernst for his knowledge, wisdom, and reputation. If they could work together in peace and mutual respect, they would be a powerful force in world ITC.

The peace offering from Timestream was in the form of a vital insight into the true nature of ITC contacts. For years researchers had assumed, falsely, that technology would provide the needed breakthrough in communication across the veil, just as it had provided a breakthrough in communication across the oceans with the invention of radios and telephones.

Senkowski himself had a lab in his attic filled with custom-made converters, generators, transmitters, and receivers that he and his colleagues had spent years developing and using, with only modest results.

Timestream quietly planted a letter in Maggy's computer hoping to point Ernst Senkowski, as well as world ITC, in the right direction:

As difficult as it may be for you to believe or understand, the most important factor in successful ITC is people's interest.

So, it was not technology, but people's thoughts and attitudes, which enabled contacts.

Just as you form us with your thoughts and attitudes, and we seem to be the object of your dreams, you, likewise, exist primarily in our dream world. If there is widespread interest in us on your side, we become real to you and can participate in your activities. Likewise, our widespread interest in what is happening in your world allows you to become more real to us.

Timestream was telling Ernst Senkowski, through Maggy, a basic truth about spirit-world physics: It is the awareness and rapport between beings in two different realities which build the bridge for collaboration. Without the awareness—if ITC researchers on Earth focus only on themselves and their equipment, for example—the bridge cannot be built.

One problem with ITC is that there never seems to be enough proof to satisfy those on your side. In other studies, a fraction of the proof is convincing. There is more than twice the statistical evidence to support the reality of spirit communication than Freud had to support the existence of the subconscious, or than Einstein had to hypothesize the structure of the atom. In any other scientific field, the statistical evidence alone would shatter the opposing views.

As science branches out to explore an unknown field such as gravity or time or space or spirit, more and more evidence is gathered about the nature of each mystery, and at a certain point a theory or law is postulated. The scientific model is then rebuilt to incorporate the new "truths." To the dismay of the spirit worlds, up to the end of the twentieth century, scientists on Earth were still ignoring the massive evidence that supported spiritual reality. Perhaps the reason is that scientists had developed processes and instruments to measure gravity, time, and space, but had never yet figured out how to measure spirit.

You continue to argue about the evidence supporting the legitimacy of spirit communication through technology. Your efforts would be better spent studying ITC to understand in what tremendous ways your world could be transformed by it.

In other words, from the view of Timestream, scientists on Earth were spinning their wheels. They were ignoring the sources of vast wisdom flourishing in the unseen worlds around them. Rather than being fully absorbed in the physical universe, they should have been charting a course for future collaboration between our world and the invisible realms.

For example, if humanity could accept the idea of morphogenetic resonance as proposed by Sheldrake, you would be closer to understanding the way things really are. Indeed, similar life forms can be in contact with each other beyond space and time by means of what Sheldrake calls "morphogenetic fields."

Rupert Sheldrake, the frontier scientist in England, was at that time bringing humanity closer to reality with his assertion that living beings everywhere are like antennas; they resonate to similar vibrations, or "structures of activity," of other living beings from the past and present. While antennas resonate to radio signals and TV signals, humans and other living things resonate to thoughts and feelings—or "consciousness"—of other living beings. It is that resonance among living things that opens the channels of communication.

Then, on a personal note to Maggy and her husband, Jules, Timestream concluded their message, *By the way, how can you take ITC seriously without fostering human communication? Give your heart a tug, and send this information to Ernst Senkowski. Allow him to decide how he wishes to use it. We all have made mistakes, after all. We on our side, you on your side, all of us! Let's begin anew. We are ready. But please don't be harsh; be gentle! An eternity awaits us.*

Ideally, the above message would have resonated with the Harsch-Fischbach couple and with Ernst Senkowski, and it would have closed the chasm between them. Sadly, that did not happen. There apparently were some inner blockages that would have to be penetrated before the needed resonance could be achieved among them, and among various other independent researchers.

GETTING STARTED IN COLORADO, THE WINTER OF 1991–92

It was around this time that I had met George Meek. After my first life-changing visit with George in North Carolina, I returned home to Colorado, where I started dialogs by fax with Maggy Harsch-Fischbach that would continue for the next seven years. I soon became completely immersed in the experiences of this Luxembourg woman whose life had been touched in a most dramatic and wonderful fashion.

At the same time, I set about opening an experimental station for ITC communications. By then my goal was becoming crystal clear to me: I wanted more than anything else to be fully immersed in the miracles of ITC. I wanted to help share with the world the gift that had been shared with me—the solid, undeniable evidence that life continues after we shed the physical body. In my lifetime I wanted to hear humanity issue a collective sigh of relief as people everywhere released the ages-old fear of death. It was that fear of death, boiling over into our social systems, that had shaped our businesses, nations, and sciences into materialistic and hostile life forms that were wearing heavily on our planet. ITC research could help undo the damage by helping people realize that we are not alone in our struggle to find peace and happiness in our troubled world. We have powerful allies beyond the Earth if we but acknowledge their presence and ask for their help. But they won't help unless we ask.

From my many visits with George Meek, it had become clear that a habit of daily prayer was a vital first step toward successful ITC research. I reflected back on the Spiricom device that had opened up the field in 1980. On the surface it seemed that Bill O'Neil's personal qualities had been responsible for the breakthrough—specifically his strong psychic skills that had kept him attuned to spirit friends, and his radio expertise that had guided the actual development of the Spiricom tone generators. But as I thought more deeply on the situation, it became obvious there had to be more. Various people had tried to replicate the work of O'Neil, building systems according to the wiring diagrams and schematics used in Spiricom, with no success.

There was obviously something missing, and I became convinced that the missing ingredient was what we on Earth often call "divine intervention." George Meek's spiritual attunement, his good character, and his powerful dream to improve the world through the spread of spiritual understanding all had attracted ethereal beings into the work. *They* were the forces responsible for the quantum leap from tiny spirit voices on tape to audible dialog between Heaven and Earth. The reason that other experimenters could not replicate the Spiricom results is that they all took a purely technical or material approach to the work. They ignored the spiritual. I became convinced of that as I delved more deeply into the research. A few people, inspired by the Spiricom breakthrough, had taken a spiritual approach to the work, and some of them were getting results that far surpassed the results of Spiricom. Maggy Harsch-Fischbach was a good example of these young pioneers.

I was not interested in phenomena such as tiny voices on tape; my interest was in the more miraculous forms of contacts that allowed long, clear messages and images to be delivered to our world from Beyond. If such miracles required the intervention of ethereal beings, then I would simply have to find a way to attract angels into my work and into my life.

Various experts advised me that I probably would have to begin my experiments with tiny voices on tape, and then let things evolve from that point. The birth of an ITC receiving station seemed to be a bit like the birth of a child: there were stages of evolution that couldn't be avoided in the early development. Just as a fetus evolves from gilled creature to human in the womb, an ITC receiving station apparently has to begin with tiny voices on tape before it can evolve into a full-blown receiving station.

Reading about the miracles in Europe, I thought it might not be too difficult to start getting enhanced ITC contacts, but it would be one of the most challenging things I'd ever done.

I assumed that prayer was the only link I would need to open myself to ethereal collaboration and miracles, but in the coming years I would learn that prayer was just the beginning. There would be so much more.

In the meantime, I set up a basic spirit communication system, patterned loosely after the equipment being used successfully in Europe for voice contacts with spirit. I purchased a couple of broadband radios and a cassette tape recorder with a built-in microphone. I positioned the recorder about a foot from the two radios and began experimenting periodically. I would adjust the two radios to frequencies between stations, so that a soft hiss of static filled the air. At first I tried frequencies popular among European researchers—around 87 MHz on the FM band, and about 1490 KHz on the

AM band. During each experiment, I would start with a prayer, then pose a series of six or seven questions to any invisible friends who might be with me. I would space out the questions over a session that might last anywhere from fifteen to forty-five minutes, depending on how tired I was and how much blank tape was on the cassette. Between questions I would remain silent, waiting for them to answer. I realized that most spirit voices couldn't be heard until playback, so I wasn't expecting any audible answers to my questions during the recording session.

After a few weeks of experiments, finding no spirit voices on the tapes, I sought the advice of experts. Sarah Estep of Maryland had been taping for many years. As founder and president of the American Association for Electronic Voice Phenomena (AAEVP), Sarah published a newsletter on her own experimental results as well as those of her network of readers, many of whom also experimented with the tiny voices. She suggested I purchase a small "electret" microphone from Radio Shack. Some of her readers were reporting good results using the frequencies that pilots and air-traffic controllers used—the so-called airband—so I switched one of the radios over to those frequencies. As I experimented with these changes, I heard occasional voices breaking in, but they sounded to me like the voices of pilots or air-traffic controllers. Some of them might have been spirit voices, but I couldn't be sure. The airband frequencies didn't feel right for me. I was beginning to understand what more experienced researchers had told me: Successful experimenters follow their intuition to customize their equipment while establishing a rapport with spirit friends.

Following my gut feelings, I switched the airband radio to the shortwave band, around 11 MHz, while the other radio was still tuned around 1490 AM. I found that if I moved the radio dials closer to a station, I could hear voice fragments in the soup of static. Someone told me that spirits could sometimes use those voice fragments to create their own voice messages, so I began to keep the radios tuned near distant radio stations—preferably foreign broadcasts—so that radio voices would fade in and out during my experiments, and if any spirit voices came through in English, I would be able to distinguish them from the foreign radio voices.

I was now well into my fourth month of experimenting, with no good results. I was starting to get a little discouraged, and I had to remind myself that some of the most famous and prolific tapers had had a very hard time getting their first voices. Probably the most famous of them all was Dr. Konstantin Raudive, a European psychologist back in the 1960s. Raudive had heard stories about tiny spirit voices being captured on tape, but being a well-grounded man, he had a hard time believing them. After visiting some experimenters and listening to the voices they'd gathered, Raudive had been overwhelmed. He started experimenting right away with tremendous enthusiasm, but got rather dismal results. He had no luck whatsoever for several months, but once he got his first voice, he went on to capture more than seventy thousand tiny voices on tape, many under strict laboratory conditions, before his death in 1974. He continued the work after his death, but instead of *receiving* spirit voices, he now began to *deliver* them to experimenters around the world. The deep, distinctive spirit voice of Konstantin Raudive had become familiar to many tapers. I had even heard the voice a number of times myself on recordings from other experimenters.

So, even the famous pioneer Konstantin Raudive had overcome early failures to achieve success. I kept my hopes up.

Usually I would work with the radios around three in the morning. We lived in a rather small house at the time, and I had my radios set up in the living room. My mother-in-law lived with us and was home all day, so the only time the living room was sure to be isolated was in the early morning hours.

In the summer of 1992, I woke up one morning in a bit of a daze. I climbed out of bed and went to the kitchen for a bowl of fruit and a glass of water. My mind was still in a fog when I turned on the radios, did a short prayer, and began experimenting. About twenty minutes into the session I was getting tired.

"Please," I said, "can you tell me about any breakthroughs that will happen in my experiments?"

I waited a moment, asked a couple more questions, and then turned the system off. I brought the tape over to the couch, where I would lie down and try to stay awake long enough to listen to the entire forty-five-minute session. As I listened, the soft radio voices recorded on tape faded in and out of the static. Several times I drifted off into light sleep for a few seconds, then awakened. It was all rather surreal and dreamlike. Then I heard my question, "Can you tell me about any breakthroughs . . . ?"

Suddenly my eyes bolted wide open as I heard a loud whisper:

"*. . . minds . . . much . . . term.*" I played it back numerous times, and each time the message became a bit clearer, and the voice became a familiar one. It was the unmistakable voice of Konstantin Raudive conveying an unmistakable message:

"*Your mind's too much in turmoil.*"

It was my long-awaited breakthrough. At last I had gotten my first voice, and it was advice from the other side on how to improve my techniques for better results. Progress would accelerate in the coming months as I learned to focus my thoughts and clear my mind.

I kept Maggy Harsch-Fischbach abreast of my progress, and although my breakthrough was but a small step by her standards, she encouraged me to continue.

JEANNETTE SETTLES INTO WONDERLAND, 1992

In the spring of 1992, a few months before my planned trip to Europe, Maggy sent me exciting news: She had just received a message from Timestream spirit group indicating that Jeannette Meek was now residing in higher levels of spirit. While studying under higher beings, George's wife had advanced quickly, and she had developed a large circle of friends, including Eleanor Roosevelt and a well-known musician.

"What musician?" I asked, fascinated.

"Unfortunately I misplaced the man's name," Maggy replied apologetically. "All I remember is that he is a famous black musician. I think he played jazz."

In any event, Jeannette was enjoying a new life very much like life on Earth, but much more of a paradise. She had grown young again and looked very much as she had looked at the prime of her life with George.

Maggy added, "Timestream is trying to send a picture of Jeannette through to George, but they're having tremendous difficulties."

So within months of making her transition to the astral planes, Jeannette began ascending to higher levels and forging important new friendships.

* * *

A picture of life on the other side was starting to emerge with increasing clarity. Our invisible friends were sending reports of a world very much like our own. Many people, after death, would awaken in that world amid familiar faces, forms, and structures—for example, comfortable, familiar homes. For some people their home in the next world would be like the family home they'd grown up in. For others it was more like a home they had built or acquired and spent many years in, raising a family of their own. More adventurous people found themselves suddenly in an exotic and beautiful temple or mansion suitable to their active imaginations. People fell smoothly into lifestyles that made them comfortable and happy, with all the trappings. The following story is a composite of several reports that were received through ITC systems. It is assembled with the intent to give a rather clear and accurate view (according to ITC reports) of the outcome awaiting many people on Earth who lead a wholesome life and die a natural death.

An old man was lying in a hospital bed, near death, and the slightest movement was difficult and painful. He was aware of his family at the foot of the bed. His wife was crying and being comforted by their daughter while the two sons stood off to the side, talking quietly.

Suddenly the wall across from the old man began to shimmer, reminding him of heat waves rising from hot pavement. A hole the size of a bowling ball opened up in the wall, and it grew quickly to the size of a doorway. An intense white light poured into the room. The man was in awe as a head popped through the doorway to peer in. He lifted a feeble hand and pointed at the strange scene; he wanted his family to see what was going on. The family members didn't notice the old man's gesture, and they certainly didn't see the three beings who had entered the room through the portal and were now gathering around the bed.

The old man was deeply moved by the beauty of these three glowing beings, and he was overwhelmed when he realized that one of them was his mother, who had died many years earlier. She was young and beautiful. He reached his hand out to his mother, and this time his hand moved smoothly and easily with newfound strength. His mother took his hand and helped him sit up, then stand up.

The old man looked back, saw his lifeless body on the bed, and was mildly puzzled. He noticed his family becoming agitated, one son running out into the hall to find a nurse, but all this activity in the room was beginning to seem surreal and dreamlike. It was his mother and the other two visitors who now seemed vital and real. As the four entered the portal, he noticed that the walls of the tunnel pulsated in rainbow colors.

The small group moved quickly through the tunnel and emerged in a breathtaking meadow filled with flowers that glowed from within. The vivid colors and iridescent hues were of such otherworldly diversity as to make the colors on Earth seem like shades of gray by comparison. Majestic mountains rose in the distance, and heavenly fragrances filled the air.

The man looked down and was amazed. His hospital slippers suddenly turned into patent leather shoes—the most comfortable shoes he'd ever worn. He began running through the meadow, then stopped, turning around and around with outstretched arms, trying to absorb all the beauty. As the other three caught up to him, he took his mother's hand again, and they came to a small community where a crowd of people with familiar faces cheered and welcomed him home as he approached. Most of them were neighbors and friends who had preceded the man in death. His mother led him to a house that was exactly like the home he'd grown up in, and in the house was a big, comfortable sofa.

Suddenly the old man felt very tired and decided to lie down for a short nap. He awakened six Earth weeks later. Looking in the mirror, he saw the face of a young man with thick, black, wavy hair instead of the balding, gray-haired face he was expecting. He was in the prime of life again, and his face was as smooth as a baby's butt. No stubble. He found a wardrobe in the house, opened it, and found a beautiful sport coat, which he put on. He felt that a red tie would go perfectly, but he couldn't find one. He closed the wardrobe, opened it a moment later, and there was a perfect red tie! In the coming days he felt pressure in his gums, and strong, new teeth emerged.

A WORLD OF INFINITE POSSIBILITIES, TIMELESSNESS

The many possibilities awaiting us all are beyond what we can imagine. Shoes appearing suddenly on feet, ties manifesting magically in wardrobes, and many other similar incidents have given many ITC researchers pause for thought. Our invisible friends of ITC tell us they have no idea how these things happen, but they are very much a part of their world. They tell us it is a completely different physics from what we on Earth have gotten used to.

Trying to judge or to understand their world from our scientific or familiar worldview would be futile.

As we get settled into our new lives, we can expect to find ourselves in or migrate into communities of people who think the way we do. Devout Christians, Moslems, or Buddhists find themselves in communities of people who share the same beliefs and attitudes. People in spirit with common interests, like birds of a feather, do indeed flock together.

Then, a variety of things can happen. Some people enjoy the astral planes so much that they spend many decades of Earth time there, even centuries, drinking in the wonders of paradise that only a fortunate few could ever hope to taste briefly here on Earth.

Other people are called back to Earth by an inner voice saying there is more to be learned. These people reincarnate.

Still other people yearn to move closer to God, and a teacher comes into their life to help them raise their vibration and ascend to brighter, more loving environs where forms and structures become wispy and ethereal, or even fade away completely into a timeless, spaceless realm of pure consciousness. People learn to shed most of their negative thought patterns before they can ascend in vibration to these levels of spiritual existence.

Some of these deceased individuals become what we on Earth might call angels. It is a life of peace and beauty beyond worldly description. The garments worn by these angels are white, but with a whiteness of a soft, ethereal quality nowhere to be found on Earth. They are immersed in Light that makes the brightest lights on Earth seem like darkness. When people on Earth or in the astral worlds see a group of angels, they are almost stunned by the magnificence of the sight. The angels seem clothed in golden plates with winglike ribbons of white or rainbow-colored light emanating from their bodies. They are moving about like so many glorious suns.

The path chosen by Jeannette and her new circle of friends had landed them in a spirit world close to this angelic realm. They had found an existence somewhere between the Earth-like home of Timestream and the light, ethereal realm of angels. They had washed many of the material-world thoughts from their minds. Now they thought, behaved, and communicated more as angels did—with greater love and understanding.

Inhabiting higher levels of spirit, Jeannette and her friends either had to be sought out in order to participate in the activities of Timestream, or else they had to lower their vibration so that their spirit bodies became denser and more solid. In this way they could interact with the extremely dense instruments and energies of Earth. When they descended in vibration to work with Timestream, they stood out from the astral residents. There was a purity and brightness in their countenance which made it clear they were visiting from higher levels. At the same time, some of the patterns of Earthlike thought and behavior returned to them. Remnants of the personalities and egos that had guided much of their behavior on Earth faded back into their minds.

SURPRISE CALL FROM A MUSICIAN, AUGUST 11, 1992

Maggy Harsch-Fischbach had friends visiting in her Luxembourg lab, fascinated by the radio equipment under development and asking lots of questions. One of those friends was Hilde Schwickerath of Saarbruecken, Germany, whose husband Otto had died twelve years earlier.

Suddenly the phone rang. When Maggy answered, she was surprised to be greeted by the voice of Scott Joplin. It immediately occurred to Maggy that Scott Joplin was the friend of Jeannette Meek, the black musician who was living at a higher level of spirit.

"Ah, Mr. Joplin!" Maggy exclaimed.

Mr. Joplin had made a name for himself as "The King of Ragtime" before he died in 1917. One of his compositions, "The Entertainer," was resurrected in the 1970s for the popular movie *The Sting*. Scott Joplin spoke quickly in a Black American dialect that Maggy struggled to follow, with only partial success. Mr. Joplin said he was in the company of Otto Schwickerath, as well as Jeannette Meek and Maggy's grandfather.

Maggy heard two dogs barking in the background, and when she mentioned that, Mr. Joplin identified the dogs by name—Terry and Cookie. When she heard Scott Joplin mention the name "Otto Schwickerath" a second time, she turned the telephone over to Hilde Schwickerath, who listened to the dogs barking and immediately identified the distinctive yelp of her dog Cookie, who had died in 1985.

Although Mrs. Schickerath spoke fluent English, it was difficult for her to grasp all the information being conveyed by the fast-talking Mr. Joplin amid the sounds of dogs barking excitedly. Somehow, Scott Joplin managed to convey a message to Hilde Schickerath from her husband Otto—a message that contained information known only to the Schwickerath couple. It involved an incident that had occurred forty years earlier.

This fella' here wi' me goes by the name "Otto Schwickerath," Mr. Joplin said quickly. *He talks about a place in Saarbruecken called Saint Johanner Mark't, and a bause, or somethin' like that?* (A *bause,* pronounced "bow-zuh," is a bump on the head in a dialect of southern Germany.)

"Yes, yes," acknowledged Mrs. Schickerath, partially absorbing the message. "Saint Johanner Market is in Saarbruecken."

Yeah, okay. He talks about a "bause," whatever that is. You got me? said a somewhat befuddled Scott Joplin.

Mrs. Schwickerath was confused by the message. "Bowser?" she asked. "Is that a name?"

No! exclaimed Mr. Joplin, somewhat exasperated now. *It's a BAUSE!* He spelled the word.

"A *bause!*" repeated Mrs. Schickerath as though a light had clicked on in her head. She eventually absorbed the complete message and testified in a signed letter that the incident at Saint Johanner Market had occurred forty years earlier, just as Mr. Joplin had said, and was a very private matter known only by Otto and Hilde Schwickerath. Apparently, not even Scott himself knew the details of the message he was conveying to Mrs. Schwickerath. Nor was her dog's name "Cookie" known by anyone else present in the Harsch-Fischbachs' lab that day. This was one more shred of good, hard evidence that Maggy's link to Timestream spirit group was solid and true.

Our spirit friends planned such elaborate contacts for just that reason: To help convince a skeptical humanity of the reality of timeless spiritual existence.

ANGEL WINGS AND A FORK IN THE ROAD, 1992–93

When I received a fax from Luxembourg containing the news about Jeannette's friendship with Scott Joplin and her ascension to higher spirit levels, I immediately called George Meek to share my excitement. I assumed he had received the fax as well.

"Did you get the news about Jeannette?" I asked.

I expected him to be as excited as I was, but I was greeted by an uncertain voice of someone who was a bit ill at ease, as though he were talking to a bearer of false information. "Yes, I got it."

"Wonderful news, isn't it?" I exclaimed.

"Well, yes and no," George said coolly.

I paused, waiting for an explanation as to why the mixed feelings. There was no explanation, so I said, "George, the contact confirms what Loree has been telling us: Jeannette has moved to higher levels of spirit."

That information not only confirmed some of the channeled information of the housekeeper Loree, but also verified much of Meek's most important research findings—that there are many levels of spiritual existence which can be contacted and even visited by people who know how to move among those levels.

"That's correct," George replied, "but I'm a little leery about some of the information."

"Like what?" I asked, a little concerned now.

George said that, for one thing, Loree had never mentioned anything about Scott Joplin being a friend of Jeannette. That made George suspicious of the Timestream contacts.

"But my main concern about all this is how they describe Jeannette," he continued. "When Loree is in trance, she reports that Jeannette is definitely an angel. Loree can see the wings clearly."

There, it was out. George questioned the validity of the Timestream contacts because they contradicted the information he was receiving via his housekeeper Loree. The Timestream folks reported that George's wife was advanced spiritually, but still human in form—no wings. In fact, Timestream had stressed on several occasions that angel wings were a myth, the product of ancient misconceptions. That contradicted George's beliefs about angels, and it contradicted the visions of the housekeeper Loree.

It occurred to me then that George Meek would need time to sort out the contradictory information, decide for himself what was correct and incorrect, and reformulate his mental picture of reality, if necessary.

Meanwhile there would be obstacles to ITC contacts involving Jeannette.

It was becoming clear to ITC researchers that contacts depended on resonance of minds on both sides of the veil, and that had profound implications. If our spirit friends saw Jeannette as a spiritually advanced woman in spirit, and if they tried to convey that image to George, who saw his wife as a winged, celestial being, the image would not come through.

On Earth it is very easy to communicate misconceptions—even lies— from one person to another because our lives are guided by our egos and brains, which cannot always discern what is true and what is false. On subtler levels of reality, communication involves a merging of resonant minds. Once two minds have merged, information compatible with both minds can flow instantly between them. If minds are not resonant, they cannot merge very easily, and so there is a gap in communication.

That was the problem faced by Timestream in sending a picture of Jeannette to Earth. There first had to be a resonance between George and Jeannette about her true appearance, and Loree's perception seemed to be making that resonance impossible. If he wanted a picture of Jeannette to come through, George would have to adjust his view. Perhaps Western civilization would have to do the same thing someday, if there was to be any chance for the miracles of ITC to spread on Earth.

Ironically, ITC's solid evidence of life after death, which had pulled me onto the same spiritual path with George Meek in 1991, would also cause us to start diverging onto separate paths the following year. George Meek had accumulated a broad range of information about life after death during his twenty years of research, and while his most important findings—for example, that a human being is not just a physical body, but a composite of five overlapping bodies—were now being supported by the information received through advanced ITC systems in Europe, some of the less significant information, such as the notion of angel wings, was in dispute. The contradictions clearly made George uncomfortable, and from that moment on, our paths began to diverge. We would continue to correspond as friends for years, but our close collaboration would cease.

Our book project was the first victim of the division that came between us. Shortly after my initial visit to his home in Franklin, I began compiling three large volumes about George and Jeannette Meek, putting in several hours a day on the project. It included some historical information, some information from ITC contacts that pertained to Jeannette, and a substantial amount of channeled material, mostly from the housekeeper Loree. Various discrepancies began to appear, which made the book project increasingly difficult.

Even so, throughout 1992, from my home in Colorado I worked closely with George Meek in North Carolina. Also, through correspondence, I was starting to get to know a fellow named Hans Heckmann in Pennsylvania, as well as the Harsch-Fischbach couple in Luxembourg. George's many years of research provided rich soil for my spiritual growth. Maggy and Jules kept very busy receiving unfiltered information directly from the spirit worlds. Their unprecedented doorway to the Beyond would soon be showering me with new insights into life, death, and afterlife that would completely transform my understanding of the larger world. Hans Heckmann had been translating into English some of the reports from Luxembourg which were received in German.

It was plain to see that ITC could someday tranform humanity as it was now transforming me. I found myself frequently wondering, was humanity ready for a spiritual transformation? It was a vital question which to this day I hope to see answered positively in my lifetime.

NOTE FROM A NINETEENTH-CENTURY CHEMIST, SUMMER OF 1992

George Meek was not up to traveling, so I went to Europe with his close colleague, Hans Heckmann, instead. Hans had worked on Project Lifeline as part of Meek's Metascience team, and he had done the translations of the Luxembourg reports from German to English, so few people knew more than Hans about the evolution and current state of world ITC. Hans and I attended the esoteric conference in Dusseldorf, where I met Dr. Ernst Senkowski, Dr. Nils Jacobson of Sweden, Fritz Malkhoff of Germany, and various other ITC researchers. After the conference we visited the Harsch-Fischbach couple in Luxembourg, where we were greeted by a message appearing on a computer screen:

This is Henri Sainte Claire de Ville, member of the Scientific Group. We were unable to link Timestream and Centrale in joint efforts for a successful cross-contact last weekend. It's a vibrational problem that will require a minor adjust-

ment to your device. We warmly greet Mark Macy and Hans Heckmann. Please tell George Meek that I am no longer with Project Lifeline, but work with Marie Curie, who is in charge of the Scientific Group.

Over dinner, the four of us decided to collaborate on publishing the couple's research results. Maggy would continue to document her work in German, a good technical language. Hans would translate the German to English, and I would take care of editing, assembling, printing, distribution, and subscription lists in the English-speaking world.

With flourish, Jules presented me with an official-looking document giving me full permission to publish and discuss any CETL materials in articles, books, and conferences. I'd begin by establishing a journal.

I had no idea at that time how I would get a list of people interested in subscribing to a journal on such an unfamiliar topic, but shortly after I returned home, I received a call from Willis Harman at IONS. He invited me to write an article for his journal, the *Noetic Sciences Review*. ITC had been a subject of interest to him for several years, thanks to frequent updates he had received from George Meek. He had always been leery of getting the Institute involved in fields such as ITC that were so far out there beyond the fringes of science that they might reduce the credibility of IONS. When he had found out that I had gotten involved in the work, he decided to take a chance. From our collaboration on the book *Solutions for a Troubled World* a few years earlier, he regarded me as a well-grounded individual. He would clearly be sticking his neck out by including an ITC article in his journal, but he felt it was a vital subject well worth the risk, and so we went ahead with the plans. It was a giant step in moving spirit and science closer together, much appreciated by our spirit colleagues, we were told afterward.

When my article on ITC came out the following spring, hundreds of readers of the *Noetic Sciences Review* were excited by the article and contacted me in the ensuing months. Nearly two hundred signed up for subscriptions to my ITC reports, thanks to the synchronistic help of Willis Harman.

Chapter 3

BATTLING THE ILL WINDS OF SKEPTICISM

In the early nineties, storm clouds were still hovering over ITC research in Europe. Since joining forces in 1990, Luxembourg experimenter Maggy Harsch-Fischbach along with German experimenters Adolf Homes and Friedrich Malkhoff had been enjoying miraculous contacts. There were cross-contacts among the three in which Timestream spirit group would send the same messages or the same images to two stations at the same time, or sometimes to all three stations. In some cases the information came through computers that were not connected to the public networks, reassuring the researchers that these were indeed contacts from beyond the Earth.

However, as the months passed, Adolf Homes began to feel stifled. All the decisions about the work seemed to be originating in Luxembourg, and with every passing month he felt more and more as though his only purpose in the collaborative effort was to support the Harsch-Fischbach couple.

A friendship was developing quietly between Homes and physicist Ernst Senkowski, who had visited Homes on several occasions and was impressed by his experimental results. On January 12, 1993, Homes severed collaborative ties with Malkhoff and the Harsch-Fischbachs in order to pursue ITC research with Senkowski, leaving Maggy once again to pick up the pieces of a broken relationship.

HISTORY IS MADE, APRIL 16, 1993

Maggy and Jules Harsch-Fischbach left for work early in the morning, unaware that a historic event was about to unfold in their empty apartment. They had received their first loud, clear spirit voices through radio sounds in 1985, their first spirit telephone call in 1986, their first clear television images from the astral worlds in 1986, and computer contacts beginning in 1988. While miraculous, these contacts did not break new ground; other experimenters in various parts of the world had already received voices, images, and text through these types of electronic devices.

Today was different. The couple had installed a new fax machine a month earlier, and since then their spirit friends of Timestream had been studying the new device and assembling an interactive apparatus in their world.

At eight forty-five that morning the telephone circuits in their small condominium were activated, not by a signal coming through the public telephone network, but by signals created by invisible hands operating invisible devices. The new fax machine rang once, then began receiving data. In a moment a sheet of paper with a typed message came grinding slowly out of the machine, and a loud, sharp ripping sound emanated through the empty apartment as the paper was cut. Then all was still.

That evening when the couple arrived home, they were delighted to find the gift in the fax machine. Their spirit friends had come through with yet another miracle. They read the letter:

"This is the first contact attempt through FAX. We now have all the information we need to continue our treatment of the diseases in their totality. The analysis of the five bodies will take about a week of your time, whereupon we'll give you more details about further treatment.

"Please thank Mark Macy for his excellent article which has met with great approval here. At this time we also want to thank Hans Heckmann. Although we all speak the Language of the River of Eternity here, we appreciate his talent of finding the right words. Great things are in store for him here, but all in good time. We don't want to divulge any details yet. May he enjoy the company of his family a long time to come, as they enjoy him.

For me, committing to a close collaboration with the couple from Luxembourg was like opening a doorway to paradise. The good folks of Timestream spirit group, and especially The Seven higher beings who monitored and guided the work from their lofty perspective, had committed themselves to a working relationship with Maggy, and from my perspective the couple's lives seemed blessed as a result of that commitment. Physical ailments and fatigue could be alleviated by the spirit team, who could work not just on the physical body but also on the subtle inner bodies where many of our human ailments originate.

To me the couple seemed to be in an energized, blissful state much of the time, as though extra energies streaming through them from higher spiritual levels gave them the stamina to juggle superhuman schedules of full-time jobs and nearly full-time ITC research. Accidents could be foreseen by Timestream and prevented. The spirit colleagues actually warned the couple of negative or disruptive thoughtforms being generated by other researchers, so that steps could be taken to minimize the harm to the delicate contact field.

In the coming years I would see letters from The Seven that had been delivered directly to Maggy's computer—letters warning about doubts or fears being experienced by some of her colleagues. Or worse, envy and resentment on the part of researchers who were opposed to her work. The Seven would report that such negative emotions were disrupting the contact field. Eventually, those emotions would strain ITC to the breaking point, despite the early warnings by our spirit friends.

In the spring of 1993, shortly after my article in *Noetic Sciences Review* was published, Maggy wrote a letter of gratitude to her friends in the States— Hans Heckmann, George Meek, and me. She said she was convinced that the miraculous new breakthroughs being experienced in her ITC work were being made possible by George's many years of pioneering research; Hans's selfless efforts to translate from German into English the steady river of information pouring across the veil from Timestream into the computers, radios, and telephones of the Luxembourg couple; and my ability to spread that information to the public in a positive way, especially with the recent article in Willis Harman's *Noetic Sciences Review.*

It was becoming clear to us that an ITC contact was the product of collaborative efforts—not at all like a phone call between two friends on Earth. During an ITC contact, the spirit team were in telepathic communication with each other, forming a pool of consciousness among them. Likewise, the attitudes and feelings of the experimenters on Earth blended together, mostly at a subconscious level, with each other and with the minds of their spirit friends, into a soup of consciousness that spanned dimensions. Cooperation among researchers helped unify their thoughts and feelings, having an effect like wiping fog off a window to let light shine through more clearly. Teamwork on Earth allowed better ITC contacts to come through by clearing away the fog of conflicting emotions and confused thoughts.

While my efforts were helping Maggy get better contacts, I discovered to my gratification that when I committed to work with the Luxembourg couple, I automatically came under the umbrella of Timestream and The Seven. Discomforts in my abdomen—remnants of my earlier illness and surgery—gradually disappeared. My entire digestive system began to function better than ever before. Aches and pains became a thing of the past, and a sense of enthusiastic appreciation pervaded my day-to-day disposition.

Later I would learn that one needs to be mindful and cautious of these gifts; taking them for granted can lead to various imbalances. For example, when I felt great most of the time through spiritual intervention, it was easy to start neglecting such principles of good physical health as wholesome nourishment and regular exercise.

Nonetheless, the rewards of a close collaboration with Maggy were profound, if intangible at first. There was a subtle glow about my life from the omnipresence of positive spiritual support.

Before long the rewards became tangible. I received a fax from Luxembourg on October 29, 1993, a Friday. Maggy reported receiving a note from Timestream spirit group. She had discovered it in her computer upon arriving home from work. The message from Timestream had arrived in German, so I immediately called Hans Heckmann, who translated it as follows:

"Louise C— T— arrived here two weeks ago and is going to help Bill to reach the ITC group around Mark Macy. The higher being Isar will monitor and facilitate the group's progress."

This was the first I had heard of the higher being Isar. I was absolutely delighted to be getting ethereal assistance in our project. It was a crucial step toward enhanced ITC contacts.

In the coming weeks I got a call from a Minnesota man who was a subscriber to our ITC journal. He informed me that Louise C— T— was his late wife, but that was the last I heard from him. I heard no further mention of Louise either.

It was not unusual for people to become immersed in the miracles of ITC—to soak up the wonderful and exotic information into their mind to the point it became boggled. Then the mind would shut down, and the person would turn his or her back on ITC. ITC had that effect on some people, and there was not much I could do about it. That might have been the case with the man from Minnesota.

"Bill" referred to Bill O'Neil, the man who had developed the Spiricom device in 1980. He had died in 1992 and was now working with me. As a matter of fact, thanks to the efforts of Bill O'Neil, I was now starting to get some encouraging results in my experiments. A new sound was coming through the radio noises. It was a loud, incessant buzzing, reminiscent of the old Spiricom sounds. I could hear Bill O'Neil trying to talk through the loud sounds, but it was extremely difficult to decipher what was being said.

At one point I began asking him to focus on the vowel sounds—A, E, I, O, and U—since it seemed to be those sounds in particular that were getting lost in his efforts to talk to me. After several days of asking him to say the vowel sounds, I began to hear efforts in that direction, and then one morning, suddenly, they broke through loudly and clearly:

Ay—eee—ah-e—oh-h—you-u-u-u-u.

For several weeks, O'Neil would enunciate the vowel sounds from time to time during our experiments, and then the efforts ceased. He continued to work diligently to break through with clear voices, but it was frustratingly difficult. Many of our sessions lasted between forty-five minutes and two hours, and of the many dozens of comments O'Neil spoke during a session, maybe only one or two would be comprehensible to some degree.

THE MEDIA CATCH WIND OF ITC, THE FALL OF 1993

In November 1993 I received a phone call from a TV producer named Lisa Lew who had learned of ITC and said she was fascinated.

"I heard about the work you and George Meek are doing with spirit communication, and I'd like to include you guys on a segment of our show," she said.

"What show is that?" I asked. I had no idea at that point whether I'd want to be on TV. The thought hadn't really crossed my mind.

"It's called 'The Extraordinary.' Have you heard of it?"

"Uh, no," I said almost apologetically. "I haven't watched much TV lately."

She described the show—a typical program on paranormal subjects. I, in turn, described ITC research, mentioning that I had some old file footage of the Spiricom device being operated by Bill O'Neil. "But the real story's in Europe nowadays," I said, "especially in Luxembourg. There are some real miracles under way over there."

I told her about the Harsch-Fischbach couple, their computer contacts and TV images, and I could feel her excitement level rising.

"Listen," she said, "I want to talk to the other producers. If possible, I'd like to fly a crew over to Europe to get some footage. Do you think that's possible?" she asked.

"I don't know," I said. "I'll contact Maggy and Jules and see what they say."

Later that day I was on the phone to Luxembourg. "Jules, there are some TV people here in the States who want to include you and Maggy in one of their programs. Would you be interested?"

Jules replied that he and Maggy didn't want to be on TV.

I was a little disappointed, but an idea came to mind. "What would you think about me representing your materials on TV here in the States?"

Jules seemed a bit irritated with his reply, but he said that would be fine, as he and Maggy had authorized me to represent their work by publishing, editing, and commenting on it by any means I felt were necessary.

"I understand," I said. "I'll tell Lisa that I can represent your materials, but you and Maggy aren't interested in being interviewed. I know she'll be disappointed. She really wants to talk to you two."

There was a pause, then Jules said that an American TV crew would be allowed to attend their annual meeting. Every autumn the couple invited their readers and supporters to meet with them and, if possible, to experience a live contact. A few months earlier, the spirit colleagues of Timestream were able to deliver a radio contact before a group of thirty people. Jules told me I could let American TV people know about the next meeting, which would be held in September 1994.

I told Jules that would be great. I'd look forward to attending that meeting with an unobtrusive TV crew. It was nearly a year away, and a lot could change in that period of time, but it was good to know that we in the States had something to aim for, in terms of positive publicity.

The TV producer was disappointed. As I would learn from other experiences with TV people, they usually wanted to go straight to where the action is, and they wanted to go now, not a year from now. After some discussion with Lisa, I agreed to contact the Harsch-Fischbachs again. This time Jules agreed, a bit grudgingly, to work with Lisa Lew by telephone.

Lisa said that wouldn't be satisfactory for the program. By now it was mid-January, and the program was moving into other subjects. An "Extraordinary" program on ITC never materialized.

MY GUARDIAN ANGEL, JULIET IN THE EAST, NOVEMBER 1993

Meanwhile, I was spreading the word on a smaller and more controlled scale—giving dozens of ITC presentations and workshops around the country, fascinating thousands of interested individuals with the miraculous voices and images that researchers from various countries were receiving.

I completed a book manuscript I had been coauthoring with George Meek and went off to New York City on my birthday—November 15—to talk to a literary agent who had arranged to escort me around to several major publishers. While most of the editors we talked to seemed to be fascinated by the ITC information I shared with them, the general consensus was that ITC was "too leading-edge" for the mass market. The idea that spirits were in contact with us by phone and radio would boggle too many minds to allow the book to be a success at that time. It would have to wait a few years.

The trip to New York was certainly not a waste of time, however. A month earlier I had received a nice letter from a woman in Greenwich, Connecticut, which is a short train ride from Manhattan. She wrote that she had been a strong supporter of George Meek's work and she regarded the man highly for his persistence and dedication to an important cause. This Connecticut woman's name was Juliet Hollister, and she said if I were ever in the area to please visit her.

I wrote back and said, by coincidence, I would be in New York City the following week and would be happy to pay her a visit, and I hoped she could be flexible as to the day and time. She said absolutely; she had no plans the following week and would wait for my call.

When I arrived in New York, my schedule for Thursday opened up, so I called Mrs. Hollister in the morning.

"I'm free the rest of the day. Is this a good time to visit?" I asked.

"Oh, absolutely," she replied in a voice that seemed to reflect both whimsy and wisdom. "Just call me from Grand Central, Dear, and let me know what time you'll be arriving."

Following her instructions, I called her from the New York train station to report my arrival time, climbed aboard the train, and off I went to Greenwich. I was expecting to meet a kindly old woman who had high regard for George Meek's work, but that didn't begin to describe the colorful, warm, and enchanting Juliet Hollister. When I saw her for the first time at the station, I felt as if I were seeing an old friend. We quickly became good friends, and we packed a lifetime of memories into our afternoon together. I went through a scrapbook of pictures and newspaper clippings reflecting her fascinating life. The following sketch of her past emerged from our dialog that day:

In 1959, while researchers were receiving their first spirit voices on tape that would launch the worldwide field of technical spirit communication and lay a foundation for modern ITC research, Juliet Hollister was an attractive housewife in her early forties. One day while enjoying peanut butter sandwiches and a conversation about religion with a friend, she was struck by an inspiration. With all the mistrust and resentment being perpetrated in the name of God, Juliet thought the world could use some sort of organization where the various religions could get to know each other and where heartfelt dialogs could unfold.

With the support of Eleanor Roosevelt in 1960, Juliet founded The Temple of Understanding for that purpose. Within weeks of her meeting with the former First Lady, Juliet embarked on a world tour to visit international and political leaders. She met Nasser of Egypt, Nehru in India, Pope John XXIII, and others in all parts of the world. Over the years she got to befriend and collaborate with His Holiness the Dalai Lama, Anwar Sadat, Albert Schweitzer, Mother Teresa, and many other important forces for good, and the Temple of Understanding soon came to be called fondly by many people, "the spiritual UN." The Temple hosted a series of Spirit Summit Conferences involving various religious and political leaders, the first being held in India in 1968, and others in Europe and the United States.

I showed Juliet the ITC materials I had been sharing with New York's publishers that week and described the research that was under way in Europe. I popped a videocassette into her VCR. In a moment her TV screen was filled with an image of the deceased scientist Henri Sainte Claire de Ville turning his head from left to right, and Mr. de Ville's voice filled the room, telling ITC researchers it was their job to ignite the minds of people on Earth with the wondrous possibilities that lay in store through the miracles of ITC.

I paused the tape and looked at Juliet, her mouth open, eyebrows raised, and eyes fixed on the now unmoving image on the screen. She looked at me and spoke quietly, "This work you're doing is going to change the world."

I felt chills on my spine, hearing those words from a woman who had already done so much herself to change the world. "We're getting a lot of messages like that one," I said excitedly. "That seems to be our mission with this work: to jump-start the human spirit."

"A wake-up call would certainly do the world some good," she agreed.

"I like that—'a wake-up call,'" I laughed. I knew from personal experience the sad state of the sleeping spirit. When a person has severed ties with his higher self, his life is accompanied by a chronic fear of death, which boils over to become many smaller fears from one day to the next—fears of poverty, of violence, of loneliness, of loss, of heartbreak, and so on. Once he renews ties with that eternal self within—the true self—those fears begin to wash away. Then his life is accompanied by all-around joy and acceptance of life's experiences.

Juliet was charming and sophisticated, and at the same time lighthearted and playful. It was obvious from her demeanor that she was in close touch with her soul. What a delight to be sharing moments with someone like that!

We had dinner together at her favorite restaurant in Greenwich, then I had to catch a train from Greenwich back to New York to get some sleep for tomorrow's meetings with publishers.

The following week I was back at home. I sent a fax to Luxembourg asking the Harsch-Fischbachs if they could take time for a meeting with Juliet Hollister. I explained a bit of her background. They immediately received a computer contact from Timestream spirit group saying that a meeting with Mrs. Hollister could be very important. Following are excerpts from the lengthy message:

"Jesus Christ is one personality among others who belong to a higher entity. In fact one of these personalities is someone you would call an intercessor for Juliet Hollister. The union between them is due to the fact that Mrs. Hollister is working for the 'Temple of Understanding.' You know that Eleanor Roosevelt, who helped her to create it, is trying together with Bill O'Neil to build a contact bridge from our world to yours. But Mark is well informed. I don't have to tell you more. For the evolution of ITC it WOULD be important to meet the lady one day, perhaps during summer in Luxembourg."

As the message said, at that time Eleanor Roosevelt and Bill O'Neil (George Meek's colleague who developed Spiricom and who died in 1992) were working with me from the other side of the veil to establish an ITC bridge in Colorado.

Once that message arrived in Luxembourg, the Harsch-Fischbachs agreed to a meeting with Juliet, and we all decided on the first week in August 1994.

Meanwhile there was much to do here in the States—spreading the word of ITC and laying fertile soil for its future growth. Juliet was excited by the prospect and quickly became a dedicated friend and supporter of the cause.

BRIDGE OPENS TO THE STATES, JANUARY 1994

Our spirit friends must have realized that the mass media would play a big role in ITC in the States. After all, movie producer Hal Roach, director George Cukor, and other departed members of the American entertainment industry had joined Timestream spirit group and had made contact through Luxembourg in recent years. A picture had been received in April 1991 of George Cukor and Thomas Edison in some sort of high-tech lab. According to a short, accompanying letter, the image had been produced by a special scanning process developed by Timestream while Edison was in an opera house some distance from the lab. Edison and Cukor were working with Klaus Schreiber, the departed ITC pioneer from Germany, to find ways to improve picture quality.

Another picture had been received in Luxembourg in November 1992 of Hal Roach posing in a paradise landscape with Jeannette Meek and her daughter Nancy Carol, who had preceded Jeannette in death. A short letter accompanied the computer image:

"Hello, my name is Hal Roach, and I am more than a hundred years old. I am at present a member of the artistic team of Timestream and am working together with old friends like George Cukor and others in the group of Klaus Schreiber and Eli Schaefer. This picture shows you a glimpse at the fourth level as we see it. You can see Jeannette Meek and Nancy Carol coming through a dispassing place in our level.

"Well, that should be enough for you folks for today. I am eager to learn more about this new world I'm living in now.

"Hal Roach, 11-21-92.

"The best boy assembling this picture: Frank Blehle."

As mentioned earlier, Jeannette Meek was now residing at an elevated level of spirit, and she had to descend in vibration to work with Timestream on ITC projects. The folks at Timestream told us that interactions among the various levels of spirit always took place at "dispassing" points, or locations in the spirit worlds where multiple dimensions crossed or intersected.

At the time the message was received, no one in ITC was familiar with the term "best boy." I assumed it was a typographical error on the part of Timestream, and they had intended to say "boy." A few months after the contact was received, I learned that "best boy" was a title of a person on a Hollywood film crew who performed various minor tasks involved in the development of a motion picture.

A growing number of former Earth residents were joining Timestream spirit group, and they were dividing into various teams—technical, scientific, medical, artistic, and others. Newcomers to Timestream often migrated into one of the teams, depending on their interests. Apparently a number of American movie personalities were joining the artistic team of Timestream. Perhaps that was one main reason why Timestream had decided to open a bridge to the States.

* * *

On January 21, 1994, I was at home alone, working in my small office, putting the finishing touches on the English version of the current issue of Maggy's journal, *CETL INFOnews,* when the phone rang. Thinking it might be my wife Regina calling from the middle school where she worked as a counselor, I answered, simply, "Hi!"

A deep, familiar voice came through the phone with a jubilant tone, *"Good morning, Colleague Mark, this is Konstantin Raudive. We have succeeded in building a new bridge to the States. You are the first to be contacted by this means. This is the first contact you get from us. This is Konstantin Raudive!"*

Before I could say, "Thank you," a soft, almost inaudible click indicated the call was already over. I sat there waiting with my ear to the phone for a few moments before I finally lowered the receiver back to the hook. It was a historic moment—the first telephone call in the United States between an ITC experimenter and his spirit colleagues. We were on the threshold of a new era. I sat motionless for another minute as the adrenaline finally kicked into my system and the emotions began to build up like lava in a volcano about to end a long period of dormancy.

"Wow!" I shouted to the walls of the empty house as I got to my feet and began a powerful stride toward the door. *"Thank* you!" The words tumbled over my lips, intended for the invisible ears that I could sense were listening. I was surrounded by dozens of unseen, smiling faces. I could almost hear them say in unison, *"Mission accomplished."*

My gratitude and love at that moment were aimed not only at my friends across the veil, but also at friends across the Atlantic—in particular, the couple in Luxembourg—whose minds and hearts were in the right way. Our close collaboration had empowered me to make the leap from the tiny-voice phenomenon to the miracles of ITC.

Four other American researchers would receive phone calls from our spirit friend Konstantin Raudive in the near future—George Meek, Sarah Estep, Walter Uphoff, and Hans Heckmann. Sarah was president of the American Association for Electronic Voice Phenomena in Maryland, the foremost organization in the United States for the study and proliferation of short, faint spirit voices captured on tape. Walter Uphoff was president of New Frontiers Center in Wisconsin, which studied many paranormal phenomena and gave special attention to ITC. Sarah and Walter both published newsletters and dedicated a small amount of space to the progress being made by the Harsch-

Fischbachs in Luxembourg, fostering the spread of ITC information to hundreds of Americans.

George Meek left his house around 10 A.M. on January 27 to drive to the post office. The phone rang, and his office assistant Sande Tydings answered, "George Meek's residence."

A deep voice with a thick foreign accent spoke, *"This is Konstantin Raudive. I wish to convey a message to George Meek."*

"I'm sorry," replied Sande, "George is out of the office. May I have him return your call?"

"Please tell him I will call again in twenty minutes."

"Who did you say—"

Click.

When George returned home a few minutes later, Sande told him about the unusual call from a man with a foreign accent, and George felt a rush of excitement. He knew that I had received a call from Dr. Raudive a week earlier.

"Was it a man named Konstantin Raudive?" he asked.

Sande tried to remember. "Hm, it could have been."

In either case, George went to his office to await the call, and he made sure his tape recorder was ready to register. Sure enough, a few minutes later the phone rang, and he answered. "Hello, this is George Meek."

A deeply gratified voice boomed through the earpiece. *"This is Konstantin Raudive. George, my friend, at last we succeeded in contacting you. Jeannette is beside me, and she wants to give you all her love . . . I suppose that you can hear me?"*

George replied, "I can hear you very well, very plainly."

"Fine. So, this is the beginning of a new story, a new chapter, George. You are a very good friend of ours, even if we haven't met . . . Mark was contacted, and I must interrupt now. This is Konstantin Raudive."

That afternoon, Sarah Estep was sitting near the phone in her Annapolis home when it rang. She too was able to capture most of her phone dialog on tape—a good thing, as this contact proved an important point: We carry our sense of humor along with us into the next life. When Sarah picked up the receiver, a deep, familiar voice said, *"This is Konstantin Raudive."*

Delighted, Sarah pushed the Record button on the tape recorder next to the phone as she exclaimed, "Dr. Raudive, how are you?!"

"I'm as fine as a 'dead' one can be," the late researcher replied in a wry tone. Then he continued, *"Dear Sarah, thank you very much for everything you did for the propagation of the voices . . . We are very proud and honored that we could contact you. I must interrupt now. This was your first contact. This is Konstantin Raudive."*

ANOTHER MEDIA DEAD END, MARCH 1994

In March, a prominent Hollywood agent named Barry Perlman caught wind of the phone calls to the States. He called me to make an interesting proposal. He'd like to persuade a well-respected American celebrity such as Walter Cronkite to travel to Luxembourg, to be convinced of the legitimacy of the work, and to break the news to the American public in an immense way.

I thought it was a great idea. With Walter Cronkite involved, it would invariably be a respectable program. At the same time I was a little nervous. A project of that magnitude would be out of the control of ITC researchers, including me. Still, my general feeling was to proceed, so I contacted Luxembourg once again, this time by fax.

"I think this is exactly the opportunity we have been waiting for," I told Maggy. "Walter Cronkite is a retired news announcer known, loved, and respected by almost everyone in this country. If he were convinced that ITC is legitimate, Barry Perlman feels that he could approach the three major U.S. networks, and *no* network executive would turn down Walter Cronkite. The program would be very believable, very serious, very scientific . . ."

I heard nothing from Luxembourg for more than a month, and nothing ever about Perlman's proposal. Eventually the idea died. I was frustrated. I was supposed to be spreading the word about ITC in a positive, believable light, but I was beginning to feel as if my hands were tied. The media wouldn't get involved unless they could go to Luxembourg to see for themselves that the contacts were legitimate, but the Harsch-Fischbachs apparently were far too busy with more important matters to cater to every request. They were especially dubious of sensationalistic reporters and skeptical scientists, and understandably so.

BOGGLED MINDS, FEBRUARY 1994

For one thing, the couple were busy defending themselves against skeptics rather often. Many people simply couldn't believe the incredible contacts were for real. The skeptics who shook their heads and went about their business posed no problems for ITC. Some people, however, felt threatened by new information that would upset their understanding of the world. Some had invested a substantial amount of their lives and their efforts establishing and defending a worldview that was being proved incorrect or incomplete by ITC research. Some of those people went on the attack, leaving ITC researchers in general, and the Luxembourg couple in particular, to feel like zebras being stalked by hungry jackals and hyenas.

Tensions came to a head in the States in February, a month after my colleagues and I received phone calls from our spirit friends.

While there was little doubt in my mind about the legitimacy of the phone calls, some people suspected a hoax—particularly a few longtime voice experimenters who had never received such loud, clear contacts from spirit. To Bill Weisensale in particular, a California experimenter who published a technical newsletter called *Spirit Voices,* these phone calls were suspect. While listening to the tapes, breathing could be heard on the part of Dr. Raudive. Weisensale declared in his newsletter that since spirits no longer had physical bodies, they had no organs with which to breathe. Therefore, the phone calls were a hoax.

I argued that our findings indicated otherwise. "The astral body is almost an exact duplicate of the physical body at the prime of life, organ for organ, maybe even cell for cell," I wrote, explaining that not only do astral beings breathe, but they can eat foods much more succulent than anything available on Earth, they can run faster, play musical instruments better, paint pictures more beautiful, and even enjoy sex with a willing partner. Breathing is just one of many familiar patterns we carry along with us into the next life.

Despite the explanations, some people still assumed that the whole phone call scenario was a hoax, simply because they couldn't believe it was real. Their minds were boggled. Weisensale himself and others were suggesting that since Raudive and Jules Harsch both had deep voices with European accents, Jules Harsch must be faking the calls from a phone in Europe.

On February 20, German experimenter Adolf Homes presented solid evidence that the phone calls to American researchers were legitimate. He received a message on his desktop computer, which was attached to nothing but a printer and the power outlet in the wall (no attachments to any information sources, eliminating any possibility of the message coming through a public network). The message said, in part:

"This is Konstantin Raudive via the devices at Station Rivenich. Dear Colleague Adolf Homes, I herewith confirm my own contacts with Mr. Malkhoff, and with Mr. Meek and Macy in America. More contacts have been made successfully in China and Japan. Our tests are necessary because humanity is in a state of being—created by themselves—which is negative for us to the point that we cannot influence consciousness. We therefore ask you to open the psychic barriers to a greater extent. Only then is there a possibility for us to finish off contacts via radio receivers, televisions, and computers. Unfortunately messages from our side by telephone and fax do not suffice to make clear to humanity our reality as one of many realities."

So, not only did Raudive confirm his contacts of the previous month, but he revealed the primary difficulties facing the spread of ITC via computer and television: negative thoughtforms among people on Earth, and psychic abilities that have become weak through lack of use.

Still the doubts lingered, so Homes had a dedicated telephone line installed and paid the German Telecom company to monitor all incoming calls. In the course of two months he received four spirit phone calls and no other calls on that line. After the two-month experiment, a Mr. Thomas Binz reported as follows, on behalf of German Telecom:

"We have concluded the requested monitoring of your telephone line . . . During that period, no calls were made to you . . ."

It confirmed our understanding that our spirit friends had equipment on their side of the veil which was existing, from our perspective, right there in the room with our equipment, but invisible. When they contacted us through phone or radio, their messages didn't come through the public network or across the public airwaves; they came directly into our system from theirs.

I reported the results of this important, conclusive experiment in my ITC newsletter, but the doubts lingered among die-hard skeptics, who ignored the proof.

Sarah Estep mentioned the Stateside controversy to Jules Harsch in Luxembourg, expressing her concern that the intense skepticism was a problem, but by the same token, she said, there could also be a problem with some people being too gullible when it comes to ITC contacts that are truly questionable.

Jules Harsch for years had contended with accusations. He'd even been taken to court for fraud, and had won the case. Somewhere along the line he had run out of patience. On April 12 he snapped back at Sarah that two types of people were involved in ITC—the gullible and the closed-minded—one being dangerous, the other stupid.

He told me the same day that he and Maggy had received many phone contacts over the years and had implemented enough controls to be thoroughly convinced that the calls were originating from beyond the Earth. For example, they had commissioned the Luxembourg telephone company to monitor their telephone some years earlier, as Homes had done this year, and the results had been the same: several spirit calls were received, but none were detected by the phone company.

Also, their spirit friends sometimes gave them information which was known only by one person alive on Earth. That person would happen to be visiting the couple at the time of the spirit phone call, and the invisible colleague at the other end of the line would be a departed friend or loved one conveying the bit of information that only the two of them knew. Such was the case of Hilde Schickerath when she received the call from Scott Joplin on behalf of her late husband Otto.

Jules added that, after all his years of involvement in ITC research, he had no doubt about the legitimacy of the spirit phone calls. For him to be wrong, he said, would make him either a fool or a victim of a complex hoax, and he assured me he was neither.

Another possibility, according to skeptics, was that the Harsch couple were elaborate con artists. My experience, and the experience of just about everyone who got to know the couple, indicated otherwise. Regardless of any rough edges the couple might have had, they were obviously honest, sincere, and wholeheartedly dedicated to a moral, ethical approach to ITC research.

I contacted physicist Ernst Senkowski to get his reaction to all this. Knowing there was no love lost between him and the Harsch-Fischbach couple, and that Ernst adhered strictly to facts as he saw them, I knew I could get an objective view from the real expert in ITC.

Ernst said, "I'm sorry to see that Bill Weisensale is spreading the opinion that the Harsch-Fischbachs are hoaxers. There are more than enough examples of cross-contacts between the Harsch-Fischbachs and Adolf Homes which cannot—by any normal understanding—be manipulated by the Harsch-Fischbach couple."

I started looking for a pattern in the question of who did and did not receive enhanced ITC contacts. The two most vocal critics of enhanced ITC were Bill Weisensale in the States, and Fidelio Koeberle in Germany. Both of them published journals with interesting and informative articles, and both were dedicated to the research. Judging from the technical content of their journals, they were rational men with both feet planted firmly on the ground. Why had neither of them ever received the more miraculous forms of ITC contacts? Were they too heavily focused on the technical aspects of ITC? After all, modern researchers were uncovering what mystics and prophets had known for centuries—that miracles come to those who believe. Perhaps they had not achieved that needed balance between material and spiritual. Perhaps time would tell.

OPEN MINDS OPEN DOORS, THE SPRING OF 1994

In 1994 it became clear to me that ITC was my calling. I began receiving a series of contacts from my spirit colleagues via radio and telephone that year, and if there had been any hesitation before then about immersing myself fully in otherworldly pursuits, it quickly disappeared. Now I became firmly committed to ITC research.

It was becoming clear to me then that, during my struggle with cancer, I had been recruited into ITC. In my dreams and meditations I had been escorted to Timestream on numerous occasions to observe the equipment and processes under development on spiritside. While much of the information had been subconsciously received, it was now starting to leak into my conscious mind. I would relive scenes from my out-of-body experiences. I would feel compelled by familiar urges to locate and develop various forms of futuristic equipment—subtle energy devices that could help penetrate the veil to allow clear communication between my colleagues on Earth and our friends in spirit.

ITC needed good publicity in North America. While the research was heating up quickly in Europe, it was still virtually unheard of on this side of the Atlantic. In Europe, information was pouring across the veil through various experimenters' televisions, computers, telephones, and radios in the form of voices, images, and text. Here in the States a small network of experimenters were receiving little more than short, faint spirit voices on tape. Several of us had received a short flurry of phone calls a few months earlier, but otherwise ITC had not opened up in the States as it had in Europe.

It seemed odd to me that the initial breakthrough for ITC—the Spiricom device of George Meek and Bill O'Neil—would occur in the United States in 1980, then all the subsequent development would take place across the Atlantic. It seemed to me that something must be inhibiting progress in the States, and I eventually came to the conclusion that there was a shortage of research teams here who dedicated their full efforts to enhanced ITC experiments based on a balance between their own personal spiritual and physical qualities. There were several hundred individuals collecting voices on tape—most of them subscribers to Sarah Estep's newsletter—and there was one fellow working with video, a Massachussetts man named Erland Babcock, but as far as I knew, there were no serious team efforts by people devoted to enhanced contacts through close collaboration with spirit colleagues.

But perhaps a more crucial obstacle to the development of enhanced ITC in the States was a lack of knowledge and an apparent rejection of miracles on the part of the general public. When we humans focus our attention on spirit beings, they in turn start focusing their attention on us, but if we ignore them, they ignore us. Only if we believe in miracles and expect them can miracles come into our lives, courtesy of the angels.

It was my observation that Americans, for the most part, ignored the larger, more wondrous spirit worlds. Churches focused people's attention only on Jesus, and people losing loved ones kept those departed loved ones in their thoughts and prayers for a time, but beyond that the spirit worlds were some sort of dark mystery in most American minds—an eerie realm of ghosts and demons. Certainly a false perspective.

ITC involved heart-to-heart, long-term working relationships between researchers on Earth and positive, supportive beings in subtler worlds. In Europe they had achieved such relationships; here in the States we were still drawn to strange "anomalies" such as weeping icons and spooky "phenomena" such as hauntings. Perhaps we Americans were spiritually immature.

I was determined to spread the word. If enhanced ITC contacts were more widespread in the United States, the field would attract the attention of the American public. Then, as has always been the case throughout the history of our country, Yankee ingenuity would take over, and ITC would soon light up the world.

Most spirit-voice researchers in the United States viewed their work as a relationship between themselves and their equipment. That kept the spirit colleagues at a distance, yielding poor results in their experiments. Good communication across the veil is like good communication on Earth: it requires an opening of the heart on the part of the folks at both ends of the line—an acknowledgment of each other's being and a sincere concern for each other.

Up until recently, any Americans who made it known that they were trying to establish that sort of personal rapport with Beyond would be regarded with suspicion and humor. Fear of ridicule on the part of researchers diminished the possibility of new contacts. Before ITC could come to the States, that would have to shift.

I knew that if dozens, then hundreds, then thousands of Americans could become excited about the prospects of enhanced communications with positive, vibrant residents of the worlds of spirit, the field would grow strong, and ITC contacts would flourish. That knowledge gnawed at me, driving me to spread the word. Besides publishing a journal on ITC, I started coauthoring a book, gave a series of presentations and workshops from coast to coast and up into Canada, granted many radio interviews, and worked with TV producers, as best I could under the tight constraints from Luxembourg, to include ITC research in their programs. I worked at a dizzying pace.

I was starting to realize that I'd have to be careful presenting our work to the mass media in general, and TV in particular. ITC required a serious approach to publicity, but it was all too easy for editors, producers, and reporters to sensationalize such subjects, because the public liked sensational stories, and the media thrived on popularity.

In fact, there was a rather troubling trend under way in the American media: They had found that they could stir people up and attract them to their information much more effectively by appealing to people's fears and stimulating their hormones, than by appealing to their hearts or their intellects. And most networks and programs and producers and editors and writers were competing with each other to see how well they could stir up the viewers' hormones with programs and movies and books centered around violence and promiscuity.

That fact did not bode well for ITC. If we plowed ahead with ITC research under a shroud of fear, uncertainty, and other destabilizing human emotions, then we would draw into our work the types of spirit beings who enjoy stimulating our fears and uncertainties and destabilizing our lives. Serious spirit researchers had long known that they drew beings of similar attitude into their work and into their lives. It was absolutely vital, then, for my sake, for my family's sake, and ultimately for the sake of the world, that ITC develop under an umbrella of love and spiritual understanding, not of fear and uncertainty. On that point I could not compromise, so I proceeded discerningly with the media.

MORE UPS AND DOWNS IN THE MEDIA, MAY 1994

On May 18 I got a call from Michele Marsh, a newsanchor for WCBS-TV in New York City who had a reputation for digging into controversial topics in a fair and intelligent way. She said she had enjoyed lunch with Juliet Hollister, who had told Michele about the research I was involved in. She said she was fascinated.

Ms. Marsh asked me to fill in any details that Juliet might have left out, and the more I talked about ITC, the more excited she seemed to become. By the end of our conversation, she was determined to produce a serious, in-depth report on the miracles.

The idea captured my interest. Here was a young, vibrant TV personality, obviously very bright, and respected by millions. If word of ITC were spread widely in a positive fashion by someone like Michele Marsh, the contact field would be strengthened immeasurably by people's good feelings about the work, and ITC contacts would flourish in various parts of the world, especially here in the States. Juliet Hollister apparently liked Michele Marsh, and I trusted Juliet's tastes, so I viewed this as an excellent opportunity for ITC.

"I'll do what I can to help you," I said.

Ms. Marsh said she would love to visit the Harsch-Fischbach couple in Luxembourg and asked if I could arrange that.

I thought of the annual meeting in Luxembourg that was coming up in the fall. Jules Harsch had said it was the one time when TV crews could observe the work. "Yes," I said, "you'll be able to meet them in September, at their annual meeting. That's about the only time each year they talk to TV people."

That would turn out to be my first broken promise to Michele Marsh.

Meanwhile, in Germany, physicist Ernst Senkowski and experimenter Adolf Homes were getting ready to be on a live TV show the following day. The feature magazine program on SAT1 television network had set aside two blocks of time totaling thirty-three minutes, during which Homes would try to make a live contact with the dead before seven to eight million viewers.

The next day, the program started off badly. The live ITC experiments were sandwiched in time slots between filmed reports on rape and other subjects that attract negative spiritual influences. My later research would lead me to conclude that trying to make positive contacts in a negative field of thoughts and emotions as established by that program would be virtually impossible. As the cameras zoomed in on Adolf Homes, he went through his typical routine of summoning his spirit colleagues in an otherwise silent studio. The moderator, a vivacious young woman, apparently found the process rather odd and started to laugh. She excused herself and struggled to maintain a serious demeanor, but a somewhat comical air had already been set for the ITC experiment, further damaging the contact field for the experiment.

No contacts were made, and most of the viewing audience probably felt a little bit let down. The more skeptical viewers might even have shrugged Homes off as a nut, which was certainly not fair to the serious experimenter from Rivenich. Nor was it a good sentiment to equate with the young field of ITC. Such attitudes might disrupt the broader contact field that was developing among researchers in various countries.

The Luxembourg couple, Maggy and Jules Harsch-Fischbach, seemed appalled by the outcome. Maggy claimed that the researchers had damaged ITC badly by participating in a sensationalistic event such as that program.

Ernst Senkowski and Adolf Homes disagreed. Ernst argued that it wasn't so bad, considering the general nature of TV anyway. He felt the program probably made a lot of people think about the possibility of ITC, even though the on-air contact attempt had failed.

Interesting to mention, within days Adolf Homes and Maggy Harsch-Fischbach received messages from their spirit colleagues which were also of divided opinion. Konstantin Raudive delivered one opinion to Maggy:

ITC can only work when the minds of those involved are resonant and ethically pure. Public ITC experiments in a sensationalistic environment will not only fail, but can damage the contact field as well.

Meanwhile, another spirit colleague, Professor Bender, gave an opposing view to Adolf Homes, saying that no irreparable harm had been done and, in fact, many people's minds had been opened up a bit to ITC.

Some researchers were a little puzzled by the two opposing messages. We all knew there were numerous spirit realms beyond the physical universe, each representing different realities, but the more we received conflicting opinions from beyond, the more difficult it was to give complete trust to the information we received. It was, in the final analysis, largely a matter of opinion, and it would be up to us ITC researchers to decide whose opinions we should accept. For most of my colleagues, the Timestream spirit group had proven themselves highly reliable over time, and I took on a personal motto: When in doubt, listen to Timestream.

MIRACLES IN NEW YORK, THE SUMMER OF 1994

In June, Juliet Hollister arranged two speeches for me in New York. One would take place at the Wainwright House in Rye. The other would be held at the New York Genealogical Society at 124 East 58th Street in Manhattan, sponsored by the Friends of the Institute of Noetic Sciences, a circle of strong supporters of Willis Harman's work.

To stir up interest in the events, Juliet contacted Michele Marsh, the news anchor at WCBS-TV. Michele had made it clear that she was excited by the prospect that a group of scientists and researchers were in communication with the other side of the veil using computers, faxes, telephones, and television imaging. Both women agreed: If it were true, it would change the world in a dramatic way. They were interviewed together on a popular New York radio talk show a few days before Regina and I arrived, and several hundred remaining tickets sold out quickly for both of my presentations.

From the onset of the trip, miracles began to unfold, and it became apparent to Regina and me that higher forces were at work. Regina picked up a book, *Angels of Mercy,* at an airport bookshop a few minutes before we boarded our plane in Denver.

An hour later I was meditating to the steady drone of the jet engines that were pushing us toward New York when I was startled by Regina's hand on my leg, shaking it with some vigor.

My eyes bolted open and blinked quickly a few times as I turned to my wife in the center seat. "What is it?" I asked. "What's the matter?"

"Read this," she said, handing me her new book, which she had just opened and begun to read. The author, Rosemary Ellen Guiley, had devoted the first chapter to Juliet Hollister! According to Ms. Guiley's book, Juliet had experienced a miraculous and life-changing event one chilly autumn day in 1984. It had happened like this:

On behalf of her Temple of Understanding, Juliet was making final preparations for a world conference which would be held at Saint John the Divine Cathedral in New York City, and would involve His Holiness the Dalai Lama, Assistant UN Secretary-General Robert Muller, and many other spiritual and secular leaders whom Juliet had befriended over the years.

Juliet was lying down for a rest before the event when a being of Light appeared in the room. The being was aware that Juliet would deliver the closing speech at the conference, and he asked her to remind the thousands of people in the audience that angels are real, that they love us humans, and that they want to help us. Before they can help us, however, we have to acknowledge their presence and invite them into our lives, said the being, who thanked Juliet on behalf of the angelic kingdom for her good service over the years, and who then identified himself as Archangel Michael.

Overwhelmed by the encounter, Juliet complied with the request and told thousands of people in the audience that evening that angels are poised and ready to help our world; we only need to ask. To thunderous applause, she smiled to the crowd, and in the coming weeks she received a flood of corre-spondence—testimonials from people who had also experienced angel en-counters, or who believed firmly in their positive presence, behind the scenes, in our world. They were thankful that Juliet had gone public with the message.

"Wow," I muttered to Regina. "Archangel Michael. I had no idea." A chill ran down my spine. Nor did I have any idea that Michael and some of his ethereal friends apparently would be accompanying us through the week, raising our lives to a higher level from which the world would seem lighter, almost surreal. As Regina would say later, "Once we left home, we were in a higher vibration. I'd never felt anything like it, and haven't to this day. The two presentations, the dinners with supporters . . . it felt as though every-thing were unfolding miraculously, guided by ethereal puppet strings."

On the first night we stayed in a small guest house behind Juliet's cottage, a few short steps from the shores of Long Island Sound. Moonlight poured through the windows, creating mystical shadows on the walls, as the warm breeze stirred the curtains, carrying refreshing moisture into the room. De-spite the fact that I'd be giving a major presentation the following evening before a capacity crowd, as well as a TV interview with Michele Marsh, I slept like a rock. So did Regina.

We enjoyed a delightful next day relaxing with Juliet, who said we'd be spending that night as guests of our mutual friend, Sandy Houghton. "Sandy has a small place a couple of blocks from where you'll be speaking. I think there's a spare room with a fold-out sofa you can use," Juliet said.

Regina and I expected modest accommodations and were absolutely over-whelmed when we arrived at Sandy's "small place"—a penthouse condo-minium atop a high-rise building on West 57th Street. Through a window that took up an entire wall, we overlooked Central Park off to the left, and the Upper East Side of Manhattan off to the right. As I stared out over the world, it occurred to me that the scene out there represented, in a magical and beautiful way, the three dimensions of classical geometry: breadth (look-ing outward), width (looking left and right), and height (looking up and down). I wished at that moment that I could see into the many other dimen-sions of reality that were teeming with life all around me. I could sense the close presence of higher spiritual beings there with Regina and me as we stood before this awesome scene. If only the window were a portal to other worlds. If only I could step through that portal to behold the majesty of the angels, as Juliet had seen Michael—as so many people had seen angels manifest in their lives at special times. I thought it would be like a glimpse of Heaven.

That evening Regina and I walked two blocks to the Genealogical Society, arriving an hour early so that I could talk to TV reporter Michele Marsh before delivering my presentation.

I spent a half hour in front of the camera discussing the miracles of ITC with Ms. Marsh, then gave my talk. TV viewers throughout the larger New York metropolitan area were deprived of her presence on the 6 o'clock news that evening, as she sat through my talk. She told me afterward, "I really enjoyed the presentation. Fascinating!"

A DARK CLOUD, JULY 8, 1994

The following month there came a shift in my relationship with the Luxembourg couple that had the effect of a bombshell on my plans to introduce ITC to the American public. The couple were starting to withdraw from media exposure, stirred apparently by fear from the Homes-Senkowski TV appearance—which the Harsch-Fischbachs viewed as a disaster. They contacted me on July 8, suggesting I forget about their annual meeting in September. Jules had told me I could bring an American TV crew, but now he said the meeting would be a waste of my time. The TV crew would be disappointed and bitter.

I was confused. "I was under the impression that you had a live contact every year at these meetings, regardless of the mixed audience, and that I would be allowed to bring a small TV crew with me to visit."

Maggy clarified the situation somewhat indignantly, stating that she and Jules had made a decision about TV crews and had already discussed it with me in detail. She asked why I was bothering them with matters that had already been settled.

In fact, I'd sensed a reluctance on their part, a growing shyness of cameras, but no firm decisions had ever been made or discussed between us. So I became a bit frustrated.

Maggy explained that a Luxembourg TV team led by Rainer Holbe had visited the meeting in 1992, had taken some film footage, and had chatted with Maggy briefly in private, all handled very carefully so as not to intrude on the meeting. A live contact occurred during that meeting. The following year, however, a French TV team were allowed to cover the event, and they had no consideration for the meeting. Maggy and Jules had been disturbed by the bright lights and cables to the point that no contact attempts had been possible.

I thanked Maggy for giving me this clearer understanding of their uneasiness with TV coverage. Still, I was optimistic about Michele Marsh. I said, "Juliet Hollister is the person who introduced her to ITC and to me. Michele assures me that she knows how to attend a meeting or lecture without intruding. She can fade into the background and have one camera person at the scene moving around very quietly to take pictures. She's also excited about ITC and wants very much to help introduce it to the American public in a good way."

By the end of our conversation it was apparent that chances were slim for an American TV crew to attend the annual meeting in Luxembourg in September.

The following week I contacted Michele Marsh to break the bad news. "If you and CBS need to have a live interview with Maggy and Jules in order to include their material in the program, well, that interview looks doubtful now," I said, explaining the situation.

Ms. Marsh expressed disappointment, but she was already exploring other options. She was aware that Ernst Senkowski had a large archive of videotape and documentation from most of the major experimenters in Europe. I promised to help her get an interview with Ernst. She said that before pursuing the project further, she would need assurance that I would work exclusively with her. Since her program was planned to air in the autumn—just two or three months away—I gave her that promise as well. That would be my second broken promise.

DISTANT THUNDER, JULY 15–17, 1994

The following month I was scheduled to speak at a major conference on the survival of human consciousness after death. It was sponsored by the Institute of Noetic Sciences (IONS) and would be held in Chicago. These annual IONS conferences were major events attended by thousands of members and supporters of Willis Harman and the pioneering work of his colleagues and friends in the frontier sciences.

In order to get a good seat I entered the main ballroom about a half hour before the opening addresses were to begin. Already the place was starting to fill up. As I laid my conference packet on one of the chairs, I spotted Willis Harman in the front of the room near the stage, and I worked my way over to him. I tapped him on the shoulder and introduced myself. "Hello, Willis, I'm Mark Macy," I said, extending my hand.

"Mark!" he exclaimed with a broad smile, grasping my hand with both of his. "It's good to finally meet you."

I told him how delighted I was to be there, but I didn't want to take up too much of his time, as he was obviously busy checking the final details in preparation for the opening ceremonies. "I'm going to go find my seat now, but I hope we get a chance to talk more later on."

He said that we should both make an effort to do that, and as I was leaving, he remembered something. "Oh, Mark, there's someone here I'd like you to meet," he said, glancing across to a serious-looking older gentleman in a gray suit, who was seated nearby in the front row. "Dale!" he said, raising his voice to be heard above the buzz of the crowd, as he started leading me over toward the man. "This is Mark Macy, the fellow I told you about. Mark, this is Dale Palmer."

We shook hands, and as Willis Harman went back to work, Dale Palmer and I spent a few minutes getting to know each other. He described himself as a lawyer from Indiana who had been a member of IONS since the late 1970s, and he hoped to do something in a related field of research once he retired in a couple of years. He mentioned a book he'd written titled *True Esoteric Traditions* and how he had spent years exploring the ancient spiritual roots of modern civilization. He said he had grown up an orphan, and it was obvious from his stature that he had successfully overcome many of the disadvantages that situation might have dealt him.

I told him about my own research, and he interjected, "Willis told me a little about your work. If what you and your friends in Europe claim to be doing is true, it could change the world."

"After all I've experienced, there's no doubt in my mind about its legitimacy," I replied.

Palmer said that if I could authenticate that work scientifically, it would have more impact on the world than the transatlantic voyage of Columbus. Tears welled up in his eyes.

The emotions surprised me. They seemed out of character for this man who appeared to me to be very tightly controlled. He must feel really strongly about scientific authentication of life after death, I thought.

Dale Palmer said that if I was ever in the Indianapolis area, I should feel welcome to stay with him and his wife, Kay. As a matter of fact, I had been planning a trip to the Midwest the following summer to give a series of workshops and presentations, and so I told him I probably would contact him in the coming weeks to accept some of his generosity.

"Certainly!" he said emphatically.

Both of my ITC presentations went well. A few people seemed skeptical, but most were hungry for the information we were receiving from our spirit friends. They were particularly moved by the actual phone conversations captured on tape. Several people made it a point to attend both of my presentations—a major commitment, considering that there were a half-dozen sessions going on at the same time every hour from which to choose.

One of those people moved by ITC was Willis Harman's wife, Charlene. She told me later that she and Willis discussed the work quite a lot. They both were fascinated by ITC research and excited by its potential benefits to the world. Indeed, the competent staff of invisibles in the Timestream spirit group were opening new vistas for mankind, and the Harmans were fully aware of the profound implications.

Producers for a popular daytime TV show, "The Other Side," drew me aside after one of the workshops to ask if I'd be interested in sharing ITC information on their program. I thought of my promise to Michele Marsh. "As long as it's after October there shouldn't be any problem," I said. I was wrong.

THE PROFESSOR AND I,
JULY 23–24, 1994

During that time, the noted German physicist Ernst Senkowski was scheduled to give a series of ITC presentations at the International Institute for Integral Human Studies (IIIHS) in Minnesota. Willis Harman called me to suggest we take advantage of the opportunity to invite Dr. Senkowski to speak in Colorado and California as well.

I called IIIHS and Ernst Senkowsi, and I made arrangements for him to fly into San Francisco, then on to Denver, before his Minnesota engagement.

Speaking to a gathering of two hundred IONS members in San Francisco, the German physicist received a standing ovation.

In Colorado, Ernst Senkowski and I gave two copresentations, one before a small gathering of the Denver chapter of IONS, the other before a larger public gathering at a church in Boulder. I shared many of the miracles that were under way in Europe and the States. Ernst discussed the challenges involved in analyzing ITC from a scientific perspective, then we responded together to comments and questions.

One man confessed that he was having a hard time believing much of our information. "How can a spirit call a person on the phone? Where's he calling from? How does he make the phone ring?" he asked, shaking his head and looking around for support or agreement. The woman next to him glanced at him with an empathetic look and shrugged.

I answered, "We've learned that the phone calls don't seem to be coming through the public network. As I mentioned earlier, the spirit worlds are right here in the room with us at all times. Apparently our spirit friends assemble their equipment right over our telephone. They make our phone ring, we pick it up, and they talk to us. We don't know much more than that at the present time. But we *do* know that their world is a lot different from ours, and they use energies that are much different from the electromagnetic energies we use on Earth. Is that a fair assessment, Ernst?"

I handed the microphone to Dr. Senkowski.

"I agree to an extent," said Ernst, "but it is an open question whether our 'spirit friends' use equipment comparable to ours. Some of them tell us they do, but that does not make it so. Also, I have an objection with the term 'energy.' To a scientist, energy has a very narrow meaning. Such terms as 'subtle energies,' 'healing energies,' and 'psychokinetic energies' don't really fit into the scientific model."

Another man, perhaps a scientist, certainly a skeptic, interrupted, stating pointedly, "I don't know how you can fit *any* of this stuff into the scientific model."

Ernst paused, then addressed the audience at large, "The scientific model that has been in use for the past centuries is undergoing a change. An upheaval, really. Matter and energy are not basic components of reality, as we are taught. They only exist in our minds, or call it spirit or consciousness. The modern term would be 'information.' Matter, energy, and everything else are special forms of 'information.'"

A young woman stood up. "You mean reality is all in our head?" she asked to get a laugh. She succeeded. It had been apparent from the expressions on the faces that not everyone had been able to follow Professor Senkowski's line of reasoning, but everyone at least smiled at the young woman's comment, amid chuckles and laughter. Even the skeptic smiled and noticeably relaxed.

"Obviously the world is not in our head," replied Ernst. "It is part of our nonlocal mind. On the other hand, if we learned to 'play' with our minds, we could be wizards, creating and changing the things around us.

"There *are* no natural laws or physical laws really. They are just mental constructs formed by the way we have forced ourselves to observe and interpret reality during a few centuries of history."

The room was quiet for a few moments. Everyone could at least sense the importance of Senkowski's words if not fully grasp their meaning, and it would take a while for everyone, myself included, to absorb the new information.

PLANTING SEEDS FOR INTERNATIONAL COLLABORATION, AUGUST 1994

There are certain people in the world for whom doors open and around whom miracles unfold. Juliet Hollister was one of them. Juliet, her good friend Alison van Dyk, and I flew to Luxembourg in late summer as planned, and met with Maggy and Jules Harsch-Fischbach in their home.

Jules informed us that a few days earlier, the Timestream spirit group had told Maggy that this meeting with Juliet, Alison, and me was a very important one. My impression was that much would be determined that day about the fate or direction of ITC. As you might guess, that was surprising news to us, and also a little bit awesome. Was something expected of us that none of us knew about?

We were sitting around the couple's dining room table getting to know each other. A configuration of radios tuned between stations stood on a table a few feet away on the other side of the sofa, emitting a soft blanket of white noise that filled the room with a gentle sound of static.

Suddenly a tiny, high-pitched voice pierced the noise.

"Contact!"

Maggy walked quickly to the radios.

"Hallo? Hallo?" she said, adjusting the dials.

In a moment, the radio sounds faded away, and the voice of spirit colleague Konstantin Raudive faded in:

"It can only work when the vibrations of those present are in complete harmony, and when their aims and intentions are pure," the spirit voice stated with some enthusiasm. This introductory comment, which presented a basic principle of ITC contacts, was followed by very personal messages for Juliet and Alison. Then:

"Last but not least, Mark Macy. You know by experience, Mark, how dangerous drugs of all kinds can be."

Indeed, having grown up in the sixties, I had been exposed to heavy drug use in college among fellow students and friends. While I never developed any habits or addictions for illegal drugs, I did wrestle for a number of years with the more socially acceptable substances—alcohol, nicotine, and caffeine. After my cancer, I had some troubles with addictive prescription painkillers. I had indeed seen the destructive results of all sorts of drugs.

Konstantin Raudive continued, *"Try to warn humanity that they not only alter their present lives on your side, but also influence in a negative way their future lives."*

He was telling me that drug addiction is carried over into the next world with harmful consequences. It supported what I had read elsewhere: When alcoholics and drug addicts die, they sometimes carry with them into the spirit worlds an intense craving, and since drugs and alcohol work on the physical nervous system, the craving cannot be satisfied without a physical body. So the person in spirit can either suffer through a painful period of withdrawal before getting settled into the next life, or remain in very low levels of spirit near the Earth, moving into the physical bodies of alcoholics and drug users to feel the effects to which he or she had grown accustomed.

This condition is one example of what is often called spirit possession, or spirit attachment, a situation in which one or more astral spirits share a person's physical body in a parasitic relationship over a period of time. It is actually quite easy and natural for spirit beings to move in and out of our bodies, and it happens quite a lot throughout our lives. Departed friends and loved ones, supportive helpers, spirit guides, and others often "drop in" for a visit. We often receive vague impressions from these visiting invisibles, but beyond that, their presence is almost unnoticed. When troubled spirits decide to settle in for a period of time, then problems can develop. That situation can usually be prevented or remedied by positive inner work—prayer, meditation, breathwork, etc.

Dr. Raudive continued, *"Go on with your experiences, and you will see that the bridge to the States will soon be strengthened."*

I was already seeing evidence of this. As I experienced the miracles of ITC through my contacts with my spirit friends, and as I spread the word through my writing and presentations, it was becoming evident that these situations fueled each other. The more Americans who saw the positive side of ITC and joined my subscription list, the better my contacts seemed to become. By the same token, as my contacts improved, I was able to spread the word about ITC research more effectively and more positively from personal experience.

"Regina, as your twin soul, can help you a lot," Konstantin Raudive continued. *"Listen to her inner voice, and you will be in the right way."*

My marriage was like many others I had encountered. Male hormones and goal-oriented thinking gave husbands like me momentum to move ahead in the world, but it was our wives' intuition and sense of relationship that kept us males moving in the right direction without stepping on too many toes. Konstantin Raudive's words were prophetic. In the coming years I would begin to rely more and more on Regina's intuition. We discussed the research in detail, she read all my important letters and articles before they were finalized, polishing up the jagged edges of the male ego, and together we charted a course through an unknown sea of miracles called ITC and through the rugged terrain of interpersonal relationships.

* * *

The next day, Juliet, Alison, and I were still digesting the miracles of the previous day. Over lunch at a nice Italian restaurant along the plaza in Luxembourg City, sitting outside, enjoying the sunny, warm autumn day, the three of us decided to do what we could to bring to life the dream of an international ITC association. Juliet knew someone who had expressed tremendous interest in ITC and would almost certainly supply the necessary funding to get an association on its feet. We broke the good news to Maggy and Jules Harsch-Fischbach a few days later, and they were delighted. Once again they would get an opportunity to try to bring to bear their dream, as well as fulfilling the wishes of The Seven higher beings.

TV EXPOSURE AT LAST, NOVEMBER 26, 1994

In the fall of 1994, Juliet Hollister and I agreed to appear on a popular hour-long, daytime TV talk show called "The Other Side," to discuss ITC and our recent experiences in Luxembourg. I wanted to be careful with my efforts to open up ITC results to network television, so the show's producers talked to me after my workshops in Chicago and Los Angeles, convincing me that they would do a serious job of presenting our work. While it was popular, entertaining, and dedicated primarily to life beyond death, the program was not overly sensationalistic.

I sent the producers a short video sequence of inventor Bill O'Neil talking to the spirit of Dr. George Jeffries Mueller through the Spiricom device; the sequence of nineteenth-century chemist Henri Sainte Clair de Ville in his spirit body, turning his head slowly from left to right; and an audiocassette containing Konstantin Raudive's recent phone dialogs with George Meek and Sarah Estep.

Finally the day came. I was eager to experience the final result; I had shared so much good, positive information with the producers of "The Other Side" that it would have to be a purely positive look at ITC. Or so I thought. After Juliet and I got seated on the stage before the live audience, the director gave the signal to begin, and a deep, intimidating voice boomed into the room, delivering a frightening message. It was Konstantin Raudive! The producers had dissected his dialog with Sarah Estep, and the portion they played to open the show said, simply, *"I'm as fine as a 'dead' one can be."* The cameras panned the audience, and in the monitor I could see the facial expressions being transformed quickly from anticipation to trepidation, from "oh-boy!" to "uh-oh."

If anyone listening to the show had been afraid of death before that, their fears were now locked in a bit more tightly. Just the effect I'd been hoping to avoid. One main purpose of ITC was to remove the fear of death from humanity, not to stir it up! Fortunately the show was live, and I had the opportunity to explain to the audience that the line had originally been intended as a humorous, warmhearted reply to Sarah Estep's greeting, "How are you, Dr. Raudive?" That seemed to ease the tensions in the audience a little bit.

The rest of the program went well. Juliet used her eloquent, flamboyant style with lavish arm gestures to describe the miraculous contact we had experienced in Luxembourg three months earlier. The audience was captivated by the wise woman's words. Film footage of Bill O'Neil talking through the Spiricom device to an invisible colleague ran on the monitor as I talked about the historical background of ITC. Then the image of spirit friend Henri Sainte Claire de Ville turning his head was played as I discussed the miracles under way in Luxembourg.

Later I told the producer it had been an excellent show, except for the deceptive use of that opening line.

"Ah, well," he shrugged, "we had to make it a little 'sexy' to stir up the audience." In Hollywood, apparently the term "sexy" had come to represent anything that stimulated the hormones instead of the mind.

Argh, I thought. ITC publicity might continue to be an uphill struggle.

TWO WOMEN SCORNED, END OF 1994

Near the end of every year, TV stations in the United States start revamping their calendars, scheduling the top shows for early the next year in order to compete in a ratings war. As a result of that battle, called "The Sweeps," the ITC report by Michele Marsh was postponed from October 1994 to February 1995. When she learned in October of my upcoming appearance on "The Other Side" in November—three months before her show was scheduled to air—she called me on the phone and blasted me for the betrayal. I had promised to help her be the first American TV person to air a program on ITC, and now I had appeared on another program.

I could have argued with her, claiming that the postponement of her program by her network had caused the troubles, but the fact remained: I had broken my promise. Thanks to the wisdom of my wife, Regina, I learned a crucial lesson from my experience with Michele Marsh: From that moment on I would make every effort to promise little and deliver big. Making careless promises calms the waters for the moment while planting seeds for future storms.

When Maggy Harsch-Fischbach learned of my appearance on "The Other Side," she blasted me too. She questioned my judgment for appearing on a "poor quality" program and said that if other researchers wanted to compromise their morals for a little glory, that was their business. I should have known better. Then she said my only role was to publish the results of their work in English and to present them before groups of people who already were spiritually aware.

So, I thought, the criteria had changed once again. Initially, in October 1992 Maggy had asked my help in dispersing all of her research results to the public through articles, books, and conferences. A year later Jules authorized me to publish, edit, and comment on their results at my own discretion. Now I felt like a dog in a choke collar as Maggy said my only role was to publish the English version of their journal and to speak before small groups of well-versed individuals.

Family members and close friends asked me why I was putting up with all this antagonism from various directions, and my answer was simple: The incredible contacts being received in Luxembourg, in my view, were unprecedented in human history. The miracle of ITC was the most important event unfolding in the closing years of the twentieth century. Employed wisely, it could usher in a new era of peace and spiritual understanding to a very troubled world. So I would do whatever I could to nurture its growth. That meant not only supporting Maggy however I could, but also spreading her miracles far and wide in a positive light. If that involved getting stuck in the middle once in a while between strong egos, self-centered motivations, and irrational demands (my own as well as other people's), then so be it. After all, what is life on Earth, if not a perpetual dance between the light and dark elements of our inner natures? The point of the dance is to learn the steps and keep moving toward the Light.

Chapter 4

~~~~~~

GETTING ON THE SAME WAVELENGTH

TROUBLED SPIRITS, JANUARY 1995

John J. was twenty years old and lived in São Paulo, Brazil. One morning, as he entered the post office where he worked, a voice startled him, *"Be careful! No! No! No!"*

He spun around to see who was in danger, but there was no one there. He shook his head and walked toward the mailroom. Other voices started taunting him. Again, John whirled around. Again, no one there. Throughout the day he heard the troubling voices, and from time to time he asked his coworkers if they heard them too. They shook their heads and began to look at John suspiciously as the day wore on.

As days turned into weeks, and weeks into months, the voices didn't go away. Like most other Catholics, John assumed that voices in his head were a symptom of a sick mind. He was gripped by growing fear, which seemed to get the voices more excited, so he underwent six months of psychiatric treatment. He was diagnosed as schizophrenic.

The voices became more frequent and more emotional until John was forced to quit his job at the post office. For a short while he took a job as a clerk in a restaurant, but the voices intensified, and he left that job too.

After that, working a regular job was impossible. John was afraid to leave home and became completely dependent on his parents.

At age twenty-five he decided to move to the United States and live with relatives. He hoped that the voices would stay behind in Brazil. After all, the personalities behind the voices seemed to be Brazilian in character. Sure enough, John quickly got settled into a new life in the United States, free of the voices that slowly had been driving him mad. He was deeply relieved and, for the first time in years, began to get a good night's sleep. He took a job, and although he felt out of place in the States, he decided he'd stay away from Brazil—and those voices—for the rest of his life.

Then, a few weeks after settling in with his relatives, suddenly he started hearing rapping and knocking, as though someone were beating on the wall or the door. Frequently he would answer the door, only to find an empty porch. Now, gripped once again by fear, he decided not to tell his relatives of the rapping. Voices returned to haunt him, but now they seemed more American in character. Still, they were troubling voices. Life became so hopeless for John that he quit bathing, never left the house, and smoked three packs of cigarettes a day. After six months, he returned to Brazil.

He went straight to the hospital, where a doctor gave him an injection that he promised would remove the voices. The next day John returned home, and the voices came back. His parents accepted the doctor's diagnosis that their son was mentally ill. Again, being Catholic, they could think of no other explanation for his behavior.

One night, as the voices wailed and mocked him relentlessly, John fell to his knees, crying and begging, "Please, *why* are you doing this to me?! What did I do? What must I do to make you stop?!" The laughter picked up, and a voice shouted in his head, *"You're mad!"*

At that instant, John had an idea. He would prove that the voices were for real. The next day he would buy a cassette recorder and capture the voices on tape. He was unaware that thousands of people around the world were involved in the field of research called EVP, or electronic voice phenomenon, in which experimenters would capture short, faint spirit voices on tape. He assumed he'd be the first person in the world to record these inaudible voices on tape.

John bought the tape recorder and returned straight to his bedroom. He prepared the equipment while the voices taunted, *"It's not recording."*

"Mad, mad, mad, mad, mad . . ."

John pressed the Record button and went to take a shower. When he returned twenty minutes later, he played back the tape, and he was stunned. Several loud, clear voices were registered on tape! *"Mad, mad, mad."* There were rapping sounds followed by loud, indistinguishable whispers, then a shout: *"HE IS MAD!"* Then another voice shouted, *"He's taking a shower!"*

John was ecstatic. At last he was certain he wasn't crazy. As soon as he got dressed and combed his hair, he rushed the tape to his psychiatrist, still overjoyed. The bubble was burst when he played the tape for the doctor, who became angry and told John with an accusatory voice, "This isn't real. You faked it. Recording voices of spirits? You don't expect me to believe such nonsense, do you?"

As John made his situation known to friends and family, he was soon led to the office of Dr. Hernani Guimaraes Andrade, an aging physicist and a pioneer of ITC research. Dr. Andrade referred John to experimenter Sonia Rinaldi in São Paulo, who coordinated a network of several hundred tapers throughout Brazil. Sonia invited John into her office and played some of the spirit voices that she and her colleagues had received in recent years— friendly, helpful voices. John shared the voices he had been receiving on tape, and Sonia was impressed by the clarity of the voices but concerned by the disturbing nature of the messages.

She offered some insights on spiritual matters, explaining that spirits were here among us, but they existed in finer dimensions, beyond the range of most people's eyes and ears. Sonia said that some people were sensitive and could hear the spirits. The voices themselves were not a sickness, she emphasized, but negative spiritual influences could certainly make us sick.

Like a man lost in the desert without the water of spirtual understanding, John drank down Sonia's words. With remnants of desperation still in his voice, he asked what he could do to get away from the bad spirits.

Sonia said she had a friend who hosted spiritual sessions at her home. She recommended John attend one of those sessions, and she calmed his concerns by explaining that understanding the situation was the first step toward alleviating his fears. As the fears diminished, the negative spirits would have less power over him. More positive spiritual influences could then move into his life. Sonia told John that he needed to believe that the voices would go away.

As John left her office, Sonia hoped that the man was on the road to healing. Somehow—perhaps through fear and spiritual misunderstandings—he had achieved resonance with negative spirits. If John could somehow overcome his fears and learn spiritual truths, perhaps he could free himself of the negative influences. Sonia thought wistfully that the poor man might have avoided fifteen years of mental agony if only medical doctors, psychologists, and religious leaders had knowledge of spiritual research. Lack of spiritual understanding throughout much of today's world was adding to the suffering of many tormented individuals such as John.

Over the years, ITC researchers would develop various techniques to help keep themselves cleared of troubled and troubling voices. One thing that helps is simply to understand one's place in a complex omniverse of many dimensions all jumbled together in the same space. It's important to realize that many types of invisible beings, from ghosts to angels, move in and out of our lives often from day to day. Those which have the most profound effect on us are those who can resonate to our thoughts, feelings, and attitudes. So, if we really wish to be happy, our intention is to elevate our mind in order to attract positive beings into our life.

For many, it requires a concerted effort to make appropriate choices throughout the day that will help strengthen our character. We are told that our spirit friends see us much differently than we see ourselves. While we think of ourselves as being composed of blood, bones, and tissues, our spirit friends see us as a composite of things we consider to be abstract—time, willpower, honesty, confidence, integrity, and so on. If we have strong character, they see a firm body full of vitality. If we have weak character, our body seems to them to be rather gelatinous and marked by dark spots. Apparently they are viewing our spirit body as it is superimposed over our physical body, and it is our spirit body which attracts appropriate spirit beings into our lives over a period of time. So, as it becomes a habit to try to make the right choices from day to day about the things we eat, the things we do, the things we watch on TV, and so on, our spirit body becomes firm and vital, and we draw more positive spiritual influences into our lives.

There are many exercises that can help us stay anchored to higher spiritual influences. Three that I especially like are breathwork, heart meditation, and creative visualizations. Breathwork (lying down and breathing quickly) can stir up buried feelings, and if we feel caught up in negative spiritual influences, breathwork can very often shake us free of those influences. Once we are free of negativity, heart meditation (moving our awareness from the head to the heart) allows positive spiritual energies to flow into our body, mind, and spirit, filling us with peace and joy.

Creative visualizations can be used to rebuild our mental picture of the world as an effective tool for getting through life. I sometimes imagine myself standing with both feet planted firmly on the Earth and being influenced by all sorts of spiritual energies and entities, depending on my moods and choices. I think of my body from the waist up being influenced by God, angels, my spirit guides, playful nature spirits, and departed friends and relatives who have my sincere best interests at heart, while the lower half of my body is subject to lower or darker or denser spirits (poltergeists, lost souls, and negative spirit groups).

As I look around me, there is beauty everywhere. When I revel in the glory of life, I can hear the birds in the trees singing their happy songs. The sunshine warms the lush, green vegetation. The rushing of a nearby stream soothes my soul. These wonders of life are made possible by my self-restraint and good decisions. They represent the Light, love, and wisdom of higher spirit, and when I remain steeped in the beauty of nature, I feel strengthened by the positive spiritual influences in my life. My movements are smooth, as though guided by supernatural forces. Ahead, in the distance, is a mountaintop bathed in glorious sunlight. That's my destination, my soul purpose in this lifetime.

At my feet there are loose stones on the path, thorny bushes, and snakes, rats, and other vermin hiding in the shrubs. They represent negative spirit energies that can trip me up and cause pain. It's the frailties of my basic human nature (compulsions toward addictive substances, promiscuity, vengeance, and other harmful temptations) that make me vulnerable to all these obstacles of the lower world.

While I need to be wary of the obstacles, I don't allow myself to be preoccupied by them. I keep my main focus on the beauty around me and on my destination, or soul purpose. Remaining focused on the higher reality gives me the confidence and strength to reflect on my inner nature, to discern between my weaknesses and genuine strengths, and to make decisions each day that guide me toward long-term happiness rather than fleeting pleasures that might weaken or destabilize my body, mind, and spirit. As I remain immersed in the beauty of my surroundings, I find myself moving to higher ground. The rocks and thorns make way for a carpet of luxuriant grass under my feet. The vermin are replaced by butterflies with large wings of incredible beauty.

Being human, there are times when I find myself giving way to temptations and making inappropriate decisions. When my thoughts, words, and actions begin to stray, I find myself moving once again to lower ground where the terrain becomes more difficult and the dark creatures begin to make their presence known.

TO TAKE THE LIGHTED PATH,
THE SPRING OF 1995

Around 1995, I was learning from experience what many other researchers already knew—that there were people in the spirit worlds representing all human moods and attitudes. Whenever someone held on to a certain mood—bliss or enthusiasm or empathy on one hand, or depression or resentment or envy on the other hand—appropriate spirit beings would come into the person's life to heighten that mood. People immersed in love attracted into their lives higher beings and helpful spirits who warmed the heart. People steeped in fear would attract negative spirits who stirred terror in the gut.

By 1995 Sonia Rinaldi and I were part of a growing circle of ITC researchers from various countries who recognized this situation and were focusing our efforts on positive interactions with each other and with our spirit colleagues. Our intention was to draw into our lives and into our work only beings who were positive and supportive in their attitudes, and who were competent and creative in their ability to communicate with us. All of us were aware of the miraculous contacts through phones, televisions, computers, and other devices that had been enjoyed by a few researchers over the past decade, and we were all eager to foster the spread of those miracles. It was our ultimate aim to bypass the troubled realms of spirit near the Earth, and to tap into the loving, supportive levels of spirit of finer vibration.

These desires spanned national boundaries and dimensional barriers and became the impetus for a meeting that would be held in the autumn of 1995. Hopefully an international association of researchers would emerge from the meeting to set world ITC on a positive course. The meeting would be built around the work of Maggy Harsch-Fischbach, whose life was filled with unprecedented ITC miracles. That had been decided the previous year when I had accompanied Juliet Hollister and Alison van Dyk to Luxembourg. The three of us had experienced miracles firsthand in the presence of Maggy and her husband Jules, and the two American women had committed to help them. With their combined experience with the Temple of Understanding and other worldly projects, Alison and Juliet had gotten to know many influential people. Now they became powerful allies to the cause of world ITC.

Juliet had written a note to the couple a few weeks after our get-together in Luxembourg. The note reflected Juliet's disarming style and grace:

"We are all very enthusiastic about this conference, and September 1–4 sounds perfect to us! Quiet, small-ish and run really by you both—with assistance from Alison, Mark and myself. YOUR job is to let US know how we can be helpful and NOT drive you crazy!"

The Luxembourg couple each had two full-time jobs—their regular jobs and their ITC research—leaving little spare time to get absorbed in the details of an upcoming meeting, so it fell upon me to coordinate the event. I pushed all my other responsibilities to the back burner and made this my top priority of 1995.

Despite my best efforts, there were problems. In particular, there was great debate around whom to invite and how to get everyone to the same place at the same time. Through journals and conferences, ITC researchers were developing many friendships and professional relationships that spanned national borders and cultural backgrounds, and if everyone in that growing network were invited, the meeting would quickly become diverse, unwieldy, and far too expensive.

Planning a meeting of this type was unfamiliar terrain for me, so I sought help. I knew one person with a lot of experience organizing and running international meetings: Willis Harman. I contacted him at IONS to announce the good news about the upcoming meeting, and he was excited. He envisioned a symposium involving bright, scientific minds.

Willis said, "It's important to have really solid people to present and discuss the evidence, and well-established, friendly scientists and philosophers to explore implications of the research. It's important at this stage not to popularize it too much, but to present it in a well-based, historical, and cultural context."

I was a little concerned. "ITC isn't very widespread yet," I warned. "There aren't many scientists who really know about it, and most of those who do, find it hard to believe that we're actually getting contacts from deceased colleagues."

"Well, your evidence is pretty compelling," said Harman, referring especially to long, clear radio contacts and to the images and text files received directly from spirit via stand-alone computers. "They don't all have to agree with the meaning of the evidence, but you certainly don't need any total skeptics, even for the sake of 'balancing' the program."

I absorbed the picture that Willis was painting and gradually became excited about an ITC symposium, especially when he said his institute would most likely be able to support it in some way. Having the support of a highly regarded organization such as IONS would help plant world ITC on a solid foundation. I started to compile a mental list of the leading ITC researchers, such as Senkowski in Germany, Andrade in Brazil, and Meek in the States. Such experts, meeting with the Harsch-Fischbach couple, would provide the knowledge and experience needed to let world ITC take root. There would also be top parapsychologists who were close colleagues of Willis Harman—Charlie Tart, Ian Stevenson, and others of their ilk. Participation by these experts would plant the unfamiliar field of ITC research firmly into the frontiers of modern science.

I contacted the Harsch-Fischbachs in Luxembourg with the good news of a symposium, but they were cool to the idea. Jules Harsch said the notion of an ITC symposium might be well intended, but it had been tried before, in 1989, with poor results. He said it would only produce endless debate, and there would be little chance of an ITC association emerging from the event. He and Maggy were fed up with fruitless repetitions, he said.

He had a point. The main purpose of the meeting was to get world ITC headed in the right direction. For that, perhaps we didn't need scientists and philosophers at this point so much as we needed serious ITC researchers who knew from personal experience the reality of spirit communication—its tremendous potentials and its hidden dangers. Only those of us steeped in the field of technical spirit communication would be able to discern the best path toward a healthy future while avoiding the paths that would be strewn with obstacles. As long as we received guidance from our invisible colleagues in higher spiritual realms, we would probably stay on track.

I contacted Willis Harman to discuss the new focus of the meeting. "We may be looking at a very small meeting of researchers who are closely aligned to the Luxembourg group—folks who have been interested in the formation of an international ITC organization since the mid-1980s."

"That narrows the field significantly," he said, obviously disappointed. He indicated that IONS probably would not be able to play a big supportive role in a closed meeting of that type, but Willis Harman made it clear that he personally would always support our work.

I was disappointed too, but said, "The organization that comes out of the meeting will be the first step in providing the protection and direction that some of us feel global ITC desperately needs."

After some discussion, I felt IONS, a potentially powerful ally of world ITC, slip quietly into the background as an interested observer of our future progress rather than as active participants, but I was reassured that Willis Harman's underlying personal support of ITC research was unwavering.

Occasionally The Seven higher beings would share a view of our situation from their perspective, in an effort to enlighten our path. In January they warned us through Station Luxembourg of a growing problem of "falsely understood esoteric" thinking:

It will present problems in regards to the September meeting, as you will see. It involves a misbegotten love that wants to embrace everyone and everything. Such feelings will be like a brick wall; they will block the good efforts that we try to apply from our side.

The higher beings were suggesting to us all that trying to include too many people in the meeting would strain or break the resonant bonds that made ITC contacts possible, by introducing dissonant attitudes into the field. They emphasized the need to maintain the harmony among a small, inner circle of researchers involved in the miracles.

As coordinator of the meeting, I had mixed emotions about this principle. I felt that it rubbed against the American way. I had grown up in a society of ethnic, cultural, and religious diversity in which the driving aim of government, schools, and society in general was to embrace everyone, forcing all people to learn how to deal with the inevitable conflicts that come from incompatibilities. I had always seen this as the way of the future if there were ever any hope for peace on Earth. And I subconsciously saw it as the way of the future of world ITC. Now I was being told by the experts—the higher beings—that everything I had grown to believe about democracy might be helpful in terrestrial society, but it was an obstacle to peace in higher spiritual pursuits. For the sake of harmony, we would have to exclude dissonant researchers from our meeting.

This was by far the most difficult mental shift I would have to make. As the meeting approached, I would find myself slipping in and out of my old mind-set, stirring up friction in the fragile field of ITC. Part of me would be compelled to open the meeting to all leading ITC experts, while the other part struggled to keep the gathering exclusive.

On January 29, with advice from Luxembourg, I assembled a list of people to invite to the meeting. It read like a partial *Who's Who* of world ITC: Dr. Claudius Kern of Austria; Dr. Hernani Andrade and Ms. Sonia Rinaldi of Brazil; Ms. Irma Weisen of Finland; Fr. François Brune, Jean-Michel Grandsire, and Dr. Remy Chauvin of France; Dr. Ralf Determeyer, Dr. Guenter Emde, and Friedrich Malkhoff of Germany; Dr. Franco Tellarini of Italy; Maggy and Jules Harsch-Fischbach of Luxembourg; Dr. Sinesio Darnell of Spain; Dr. Nils Jacobson of Sweden; Dr. Theo Locher and Dr. Hans Luethi of Switzerland; Mr. Jon Marten from the UK; and Dr. George Meek, Mrs. Juliet Hollister, Alison van Dyk, and myself from the United States.

Through letters, I invited these ITC researchers from a dozen countries to attend the meeting, saying, "The organization will provide ITC with protection, spiritual integrity, access to information, and a forum to deal with conflicts and differences of opinion."

From Luxembourg, Jules Harsch added that attorneys and right-thinking individuals could defend our group's research against attack. He said there were plenty of fools and bigots in the world who would invariably attack us.

Several of the members were more than seventy years old, and a few of them had to decline our invitation due to physical incapacity. They included two of the most highly respected pioneers in ITC research—Dr. Andrade and Dr. Meek.

THE ISSUE OF MONEY,
THE SPRING OF 1995

Funding for the meeting fell smoothly into place. Money had never been a problem nor an issue for me. My wealth had never been excessive, but neither had I ever found myself without money. When I needed money, it was always there. As I took on the responsibility of coordinating the upcoming meeting, the same principle came to bear—money seemed always to be there when we needed it.

At one point in March we seemed to be short of funds to pay all looming expenses, and I suggested to the Luxembourg couple that we ask people to pay some of their own expenses if they could afford to do so.

Jules Harsch said no way. Most of the invitees gave of themselves to be involved in ITC research. Paying trip expenses would be an excessive burden on them. To get an acceptable turnout we'd have to pay all expenses for every researcher, and if we couldn't do that, Harsch suggested postponing until a future date.

I continued with the meeting plans, assuming that all the details would fall into place, and sure enough, within a month I received a generous grant that would pay for everyone's travel and lodging, with enough left over to cover extra expenses. A small foundation called Lifebridge had been pointed in my direction by Willis Harman. The bright, young founders of Lifebridge—Barbara Hancock and her fiancé, Charles Overby—were admirers of Willis Harman and supporters of his work. His endorsement of my efforts encouraged the Lifebridge couple to help us out. Additionally, Barbara had studied the esoteric works of Alice Bailey, which predicted the coming of enhanced spirit communication near the close of the twentieth century. So the miracle of ITC was not a new concept to her. In fact, she recognized it as a vital project for today's world, and she became one of our principal supporters for a few years.

SPEAKING TOUR,
THE SPRING OF 1995

In April I was to give a series of presentations and workshops in the Midwest. Some months earlier I had accepted an invitation to stay with Dale and

Kay Palmer in Indianapolis. On April 23, after giving a presentation and five-hour workshop in Chicago, I drove to Indianapolis and spent three nights at the Palmer home in a setting of kind hospitality. Dale was winding up a career as a successful Indiana district attorney. He said that over the years he had tried several murder cases, and had lost only one of them.

Success as a lawyer had brought him material comforts—a nice car, a nice home, a life of travel—but it was not a case of extravagance or conspicuous consumption. Quite the contrary. The Palmers lived in a small, comfortable condominium in a manicured subdivision at the edge of a golf course in Plainfield, an upscale town near Indianapolis. He told me that he and his wife Kay often flew standby when going on trips. Also, he was an attorney for American Trans Air, the largest charter airline in the world, and that allowed the couple to fly to Europe on company planes.

Dale shuttled me to radio stations around the city for a series of live interviews. When I went into each station, he sat in his car to listen to the interview on the radio. He gave me his polite, brief impressions afterward, as we drove to the next station.

There was one particularly grueling interview by a bantering personality on a morning talk show who squeezed in a few potshots about talking to dead people, and who seemed to enjoy my struggle to retain some dignity for a field of research that I obviously took seriously. He made it clear that he didn't believe a spooky word I was saying.

Afterward, I opened the car door and slid into the seat across from Dale Palmer. "I'm glad *that's* over," I muttered, shaking my head. Of the many dozens of radio interviews I had done, this had been one of the worst.

"Oh, it wasn't that bad," Dale replied, as though to neutralize my gloom.

"Well, it didn't feel very good from where I was," I muttered as the car pulled out of the parking lot. I thought of the hundreds of men and women driving to work, listening to the humorous bantering of the radio personality mixed with serious dialog between my good friend, the late Konstantin Raudive, and me. They had heard me comparing the spirit worlds to the radio waves on which my voice was being delivered to their car radios. What were *they* thinking about ITC? Was it just one more source of a morning chuckle, or had it stirred something deep within some listeners? Would they search out more information about ITC, or would they quickly forget it and go about their mundane business? I would never know. Such was the nature of publicity through the mass media. You could do your best to prepare the seeds of information you wanted to cast to the world, but you could only hope they would fall on fertile soil.

At the university radio station a few hours later, the young talk show host admitted that he had a deep interest in spirit communication. The half-hour interview went so well that it was extended to an hour, and we discussed the research in some detail. It was one of the better interviews I had enjoyed.

In the car afterward, I exclaimed with some satisfaction, "That was better!"

"I thought you handled yourself well," said Dale Palmer calmly.

The two of us shared ideas in the car between interviews and also in the evenings, sitting in his den, where shelves brimming with books lined the walls. He seemed to have a particular fascination for volumes of esoteric information from various exclusive societies such as the Rosicrucians. Palmer struck me as a well-read man, and I thought he might fit in to our international research group. Jules Harsch had discussed with me the need for an attorney in our group—someone who could protect him and Maggy and other INIT researchers against slanderous attacks—and I decided during that visit to invite Palmer into INIT, pending approval from Europe.

Dale suggested I look into joining an esoteric society such as AMORC, the Rosicrucian order. I told him that I'd always felt a little intimidated by those groups. Knowing so little about esoteric matters, I'd probably feel like a dunce amid all the wisdom.

Dale assured me that the men and women in these esoteric societies were every bit as human as anyone else. They even had what he called their "money agendas" (being in it for the money) and their "priest agendas" (wishing to guide people's way of thinking). He said there were members in America and Europe who he felt were on money and priest agendas.

Dale Palmer had established a nonprofit organization called The Noetics Institute, which I assumed he might have named after the well-known and highly regarded Institute of Noetic Sciences (IONS) that was run by our mutual acquaintance, the famous frontier scientist Willis Harman. Having experience with establishing nonprofit organizations, he offered to help me in setting one up for ITC research. That way, grant money from supporters could be channeled directly into a fund to support our work. Most large supporters would not give money except to nonprofit groups because of the tax write-off. So in the coming months, with Dale's help, I would establish INIT-US, Inc., a 501(c)(3) corporation that could receive tax-free grants for scientific and educational purposes. Dale would be an attorney and agent for the corporation. Directors would be Hans Heckmann, Sarah Estep, Palmer, my wife, Regina, and myself.

Meanwhile, my three-hour presentation at a church in downtown Indianapolis went well, and the following morning I packed up my things. The Palmers met me at the door, each sipping a mug of coffee. I thanked them for their generosity. I gave Kay a small hug and prepared to give Dale a friendly embrace, but as I took a step toward him, he seemed to tighten up, I bumped his arm, and a splash of coffee spilled onto the carpet like a large raindrop splattering onto a dry sidewalk to announce a storm had arrived. I apologized for my clumsiness, we shook hands awkwardly, and I was on my way.

CULTURAL DIFFERENCES, AN OBSTACLE TO HARMONY

By March, the Harsch-Fischbach couple and I had narrowed down the options for a meeting place to two possibilities—the Hotel Excelsior in Geneva and a small college campus at Dartington, England—and by April we had agreed on Dartington Hall, largely because it was well known to Juliet Hollister, who felt it would provide a quiet, rural setting for our important first meeting. Also, Jules Harsch had a special affinity for England.

The French and Italian delegates declined their invitations partly because of the heavy American influence. One gentleman didn't speak English and felt he would not fit in. Another expressed an uneasiness with the fact that Americans were coordinating plans for a meeting that would be held in England rather than on mainland Europe. He was under the impression that American and English researchers had not been involved deeply enough in ITC to play a prominent role.

That surprised Maggy, who would never have gotten involved in ITC experiments were it not for the inspiration provided by the pioneering work of George Meek, and she held high regard for the in-depth research of Dr. Walter and Mary Jo Uphoff, a well-known paranormal investigative team from Wisconsin. Also Maggy told me she could not have spread ITC news as effectively without the help of Hans Heckmann and me.

So, perhaps Americans were playing a larger part in ITC than was generally known among Europeans. In all fairness, though, the mild anti-American sentiment present in Europe was understandable to some degree. For one thing, nationalistic biases had played a big role in European affairs for centuries, and they could not simply disappear for our project. Also, Americans were not known to be real compromising and open to other cultures. In a world that was struggling to be a melting pot of cultural, political, and religious diversity, Americans often appeared to want the world to adapt to the American way of thinking and behaving. Many people felt that if we Americans had any genuine concern about world peace and compatibility, we would have adopted the metric system into our culture many years ago. The English, likewise, would have started driving their cars on the right-hand side of the road many years earlier had *they* wanted to promote international compatibility, but they too were reluctant to make the sacrifice for the good of the world.

As far as I was concerned, such reluctance of individuals or groups to make changes and sacrifices for the larger good had always presented an obstacle to peace, and if some of the Europeans were concerned about that quality of human nature undermining our upcoming meeting, perhaps their concerns were justifiable. On the other hand, if we could take a close look at humanity, we would find such qualities obstructing peace and harmony in all cultures—among all groups of people on Earth. The qualities can be especially brutal when they manifest in groups involved in higher spiritual pursuits. The coming months and years would see an escalation of these small biases into intense battles between narrow interests and higher principles that would shake the young field of world ITC to its knees.

Meanwhile, I moved that complex issue of cultural and linguistic incompatibility to the back burner and went on with my plans, hoping it would resolve itself. Unfortunately it did not; there would be no French or Italian contingents at the September meeting.

EXCLUSIVITY, ANOTHER OBSTACLE

Dr. Jacobson of Sweden wrote to me. "I think this is a most important event," he said, "and I certainly look forward to it. I'm only a bit sorry that Professor Senkowski isn't invited. I thought he would be an important person for such an organization."

I reflected on the important words of our spirit colleague, Konstantin Raudive: *"It can only work when the vibrations of those present are in complete harmony and when their aims and intentions are pure."* Based on that principle, all established ITC researchers who could achieve resonance with our small group and who entered with pure intentions rather than selfish motives could be a valuable addition to our meeting. Having met the brilliant, warm, and convivial Ernst Senkowski the previous year, I too sensed that he would be an asset to the meeting. But what if my instincts were wrong? What if his individualism would prevent him from becoming a cohesive part of the group? This dual aspect of human nature—the need to unite with others versus the need to be oneself—lay at the crux of ITC, and it was an issue I would wrestle with in the coming years within myself and as a player in world ITC.

Meanwhile, Sonia Rinaldi of Brazil echoed the sentiment of Nils Jacobson. She asked me, "When Konstantin Raudive spoke to us about the need for harmony, don't you think he was referring to the disharmony among the main experimenters on Earth—Maggy Harsch-Fischbach and Adolf Homes? Perhaps as long as Adolf Homes and Ernst Senkowski don't join our group, we'll all be without contacts."

That was an important point to consider. Since receiving a flurry of phone calls from Timestream spirit group the previous year, researchers in the Americas had received no further ITC contacts—only short, faint voices through radio sounds. Some researchers were getting impatient, even though we knew that our spirit friends had obstacles of their own to contend with.

One obstacle was the complexity of multidimensional communication. We were starting to learn that our spirit friends were not simply drawn to the Earth to help humanity out of some obscure global dilemma; it didn't work that way. Rather, individual spirit beings and groups of resonant spirit beings could contact and influence individuals on Earth of compatible vibration, either telepathically or with short, faint voices on tape.

World ITC would require a giant step forward; it would depend on a group of researchers on Earth coming together and achieving resonance with one another and with their equipment, so that a capable and compatible group of spirit colleagues could interact with them. Understanding the implications of that truth and bringing it to bear on Earth would be one of the most important challenges humanity has ever faced.

Sonia continued, "Perhaps you could present Maggy with a summary of all the letters you received about this situation . . . If you show her the opinions and doubts of all the others who wrote to you, maybe she will reconsider."

I had also received messages from Ralf Determeyer of Germany and Claudius Kern of Austria, among others, indicating that Ernst Senkowski should be invited, so on April 1 I contacted Maggy to discuss the situation. I said, "There's a general sentiment that Ernst Senkowski's absence from the meeting will be felt by a lot of people . . . I think I can still rustle up enough money to include them in the September meeting. Of course, that will be entirely up to you."

I heard nothing more on the matter for three weeks, when Maggy contacted Dr. Jacobson in Sweden and Ms. Rinaldi in Brazil. She said she respected Ernst Senkowski as a knowledgeable researcher and scientist but felt he'd be unwilling and unprepared to join a group of researchers trying to achieve unified thought. Anyway, she said, it wasn't important who attended the meeting. The important consideration was that those who attended would be able to unify their attitudes and thoughts about ITC and its role in the world the way our invisible colleagues could achieve group resonance.

The Seven higher beings working with us had told us that they were not individual beings as we consider ourselves on Earth. Having no flesh as physical boundaries and no egos as emotional boundaries, higher beings fused together to live in clusters. Our spirit partners in the astral planes told us they sometimes had the opportunity to meet with the higher beings, and it was truly an awesome experience. They compared the clusters of brilliant beings to banks of supercomputers exchanging oceans of information at lightning speed.

Naturally it would be impossible for people on Earth—constrained by our limited brains, our troublesome egos, and our physical bodies—to act as brilliantly and as selflessly as higher beings, but moving in that direction seemed to be a requirement for enhanced ITC contacts. We had to achieve a semblance of harmony and unified thought among us in order to attract their help. That would help bring the needed resonance. I wondered at the time whether the closeness experienced between identical twins might be something like the closeness among higher beings. Perhaps identical twins are among the few people on Earth who have established a deep-seated resonance.

It was the experience in Luxembourg that when people's love, enthusiasm, and mutual intentions were fostered within a group, a strong contact field developed. That group harmony provided the necessary vibrations or energies to establish an ongoing relationship of mutual influence between the physical world and the positive spirit worlds. The worldwide development of ITC would have to begin with a small, resonant group—no easy matter for dwellers on this planet.

Maggy reiterated that a sound ITC association need not—and *should* not—try to include all researchers. It should include only those researchers who could acknowledge, accept, and commit to a higher path. Hidden agendas, desires for fame or fortune, and a determination to place personal aims at a higher priority than the aims of the group were qualities of human nature that produced dissonance in the contact field. Minimizing the disruptive effects of those qualities would be easiest among a small, select group.

I digested that information, and in May contacted Ralf Determeyer in Germany. I told Ralf, "It would be nice if all of our personality conflicts, incompatibilities, and ego problems would disappear while a calmer, saner era unfolds on Earth, but unfortunately I don't see any of that happening very quickly. And I think the meeting cannot wait. It is my hope that between now and September, our friends Ernst Senkowski and Adolf Homes will take serious steps toward our other friends, Maggy and Jules Harsch-Fischbach, and they will do likewise. But I'm not holding my breath."

I was learning that grudges that might be quickly forgotten in America could last for years in Europe, creating walls among people and groups.

"I believe that intellectual harmony, purity of thought, and dedication to the need for international cooperation must be the cornerstones of the organization," I told Ralf, "and I am confident that we can achieve that with the people on the list. It is my intent that the organization, once formed, will be open to serious experimenters and ITC supporters everywhere."

Through all this dialog across the Atlantic, my instincts told me that exclusivity would eventually lead our group into troubles, but the fact that the Harsch-Fischbach couple were getting undeniably the best ITC contacts in the world convinced me to support them. They obviously had higher spiritual beings committed to their efforts, so they were apparently in the right way. That was my assumption.

Still, I continued to apply small pressure to open the meeting to individuals who I thought would bring harmony to the group. It was a rather frustrating time for me, torn between my in-bred tendencies toward open forums and this need for exclusivity and resonance.

STRAINED RELATIONS, THE SPRING OF 1995

With the publication of my first ITC book, *Conversations Beyond the Light,* I got pressure from my coauthor, Dr. Pat Kubis, and our small California publisher to help spread the word about ITC through television. It seemed to me that the Harsch-Fischbachs had developed a fear of TV coverage of ITC because of bad experiences in Europe, but I hoped to alleviate their fears with good publicity that I knew I could get here in the States. There were a number of popular programs that handled spiritual subjects rather well, including "The Other Side," "Sightings," and "The Oprah Winfrey Show." To pursue TV coverage here in the United States, either I'd have to proceed without notifying my friends in Luxembourg, or else I'd have to persuade them that TV coverage could be a good thing. Aware that hidden agendas and secrets disrupted the ITC contact field, I decided on May 10 to approach Maggy and Jules carefully by fax.

"At the present time there's great interest among the American people for all spiritual information, from ghosts to angels," I wrote. "I have an important opportunity to spread a good message to the public here in the States." I asked the couple if they would trust me to represent the work in a good light on American television. After all, Jules had told me in the fall of 1993 that I was entrusted to represent their work in any way that I deemed appropriate. The following year Maggy had told me, on the contrary, that my rights and responsibilities were very limited. If my responsibilities were to continue ebbing and flowing like the tide, I was hoping that the tide was currently in.

No such luck. Jules had run out of patience. He blasted me in a letter, saying he and Maggy were sick and tired of having to address the same subject over and over as though addressing "a stubborn boy."

Not only was the tide out for TV coverage, but it appeared there would be spines and sharp coral edges hiding in the sand on the way to the water. It became apparent at that moment that unless something shifted, my collaboration with the Harsch-Fischbachs might not last. Meanwhile, I was in a difficult position. My main role in world ITC was to help spread the miracles around the world in a positive light—of that I had no doubt. If I found myself in a position to ignore the broadcast media, effectively tying my hands behind my back, then I'd either have to free my hands or do the job of spreading the word from this weakened position.

The easiest thing to do in the face of insults would be simply to sever ties with Luxembourg, but again, that would be turning my back on the most important miracles to come to our world in a long time. I think the higher beings not only recognized this dilemma, but maybe even planned it this way. There are so many rough edges to human nature that it's a miracle at all that we on Earth can ever find any level of harmony among us. The beings hadn't chosen a group of mediators or meditators or mystics to usher the miracles of ITC to Earth in a peaceful setting; they'd chosen typical people with typical inconsistencies and imbalances of personality—the Harsch-Fischbachs, myself, and the small circle of researchers who would be meeting in September.

Turning my back on Maggy and Jules was out of the question. We were like cats and dogs tossed into a boat, and we had to figure out not only how to navigate the unfamiliar waters, but how to maintain some level of rapport and coordination as we did it. I decided to try to calm the situation for now.

I sent a fax to the couple. "Despite the occasional storms we have—with you at the helm and me struggling with the sails—I still believe that the September meeting will be exciting and very successful in its mission. Maybe these are storms that we have to go through to find the calm sea necessary for the meeting."

AN UP-AND-COMING PSYCHIC, THE SUMMER OF 1995

Among the many presentations and workshops I was giving, two were in association with a talented, young California psychic named James van Praagh, who at that time was starting to attract a rather large following. James would tune in to various people in spirit, receive psychic impressions from them, often in convincing detail, and convey the information to their grieving loved ones who were sitting with him.

As was the case with all skilled psychics, James had a team of spirit guides who worked closely with him. When he would sit with, say, a woman who had lost her husband, the spirit team would assist the husband in getting his message through to his wife on Earth.

As his popularity increased, the demand for readings became unmanageable for James, so he began to sit with groups ranging in size from a few clients in someone's living room, to packed auditoriums of hundreds. These situations kept his spirit team especially busy, he told me. Sometimes there would be hundreds of spirits trying to get through to their loved ones on Earth, and the spirit team had to keep order. They would essentially keep the invisibles in line, waiting their turn, so that only one communicator could come through at a time. Otherwise James would have been flooded with impressions and messages.

On one occasion I was visiting van Praagh to give a presentation that he and our friend Marilyn Jensen had organized. The three of us met with a small group of sitters the day before my presentation, and James tuned in to Konstantin Raudive, who talked of the importance of ITC.

"Let it proceed at its own pace," Konstantin told me through James. "It will come about when *we* are ready. Continue with your efforts to spread the word in a good light. That helps a lot. And be sure to bring only elevated people into the inner circle of the project."

That last piece of advice would be crucial, but I would learn later that it was not always easy to discern people's spiritual level or motivations from the external view that we on Earth have of each other. Our spirit friends were able to see "into our souls" much more easily than we.

A gifted psychic could be especially helpful in the early stages of developing an ITC receiving station, as the spirit team typically would have much important advice to share with experimenters in getting the system set up. The trouble was, psychics varied widely in the accuracy of the messages they brought through, depending on how extensively their own minds filtered the incoming information. Psychics such as James could minimize the filtering process to let information come through with a high degree of purity. Timestream no doubt appreciated his skills.

James, likewise, was extremely excited about ITC research that was just starting to unfold on Earth. Several good psychics told me they could actually see the buildup of forces beyond the veil as the growing team of spirit-side engineers developed technical connections with ITC experimenters and their equipment, all ramping up for a future day when the communication network between worlds would light up like a Christmas tree.

James expressed an interest in attending the autumn meeting of ITC researchers. I thought he would be a good addition to the project, so I contacted Maggy in Luxembourg to suggest that James might fit nicely into the upcoming meeting, which was now less than two months away.

"If he comes to England," I said, "you'll see that he is a very good medium. He is quickly gaining a reputation in this country—also in England and Brazil—as well as among our spirit friends."

Maggy made it clear that she liked to keep a sharp division between technical communication (through equipment) and mediumistic communication (through the mind). Apparently ITC was more than just a communication project; it was an effort to heal the world, and that required special qualities, such as bright minds. The intent of ITC was for intelligent, capable men and women to solve problems in our world with help and support from Beyond. When mediums got involved, people sometimes started depending too much on guidance from Beyond while their own wills became dormant.

Also, messages coming through a medium are usually filtered or colored by the mind of the medium, so the information via mediums was not always reliable. In the early days of Maggy's ITC research, mediums were included in the experiments. They would receive advice from the spirit team for configuring equipment, but once the spirit team could speak through the equipment, they would sometimes tell Maggy that the mediums' messages were incorrect.

So Maggy now was opposed to inviting a psychic to the September meeting, saying that the "medium" in our case would be the spirit and harmony of our group. The miracles that would unfold in the coming years for our group would be made possible by all the members working in harmony.

James and I were disappointed, but we both had important work to do, so we struck out on our separate paths.

THE LAST STRAW, THE SUMMER OF 1995

Through the summer, pressure was applied to the Harsch-Fischbach couple by several people to open the meeting to Ernst Senkowski and others. Eventually the pressure became too much, and the couple delivered some shattering news: They had decided to cancel their participation in the September meeting.

"Why?" I was flabbergasted.

Maggy said it would be a waste of their time getting together with a group of dissonant individuals. They had been warned by The Seven higher beings:

There are men and women among you, in your own circle, who resist our efforts or try to upset things. They are not necessarily bad people, but they are subject to negative influences because of their lack of experience.

I found myself again in a difficult position—caught between the desires of those who would like to open the meeting up, and the need to keep the ranks closed for the time being.

But if I was in a difficult position, Maggy was apparently exasperated. She seemed strongly guided by spirit to include only the right people, and whenever she insisted on adhering to the list, some people bristled, accusing her of being bossy. Other people accused her of fearing an enemy camp.

Nothing could have been further from the truth, she said, insisting that those whom she refused to include in the meeting were not enemies of hers; they had simply chosen to go their own way. Many people sensed enmity between her and former colleagues such as Koenig, Koeberle, Senkowski, and Homes, so it was important that she clarified her position.

In the coming weeks I wrote careful letters to Maggy and to other ITC researchers, suggesting that we all be totally open and sincere in our desires and work hard toward reaching an agreement. Other researchers wrote to Maggy, imploring her to reconsider. After all, what would a meeting about miracles be without the presence of the main recipient of those miracles?

Within a few weeks' time, Maggy announced that in the light of letter exchanges and new perceptions, she and Jules would definitely attend the meeting. Timestream spirit group had suggested they attend, telling Maggy they welcomed a suggestion I had made "to put all cards on the table." Again, Konstantin Raudive's words came back to me:

"It can only work when the vibrations of those present are in complete harmony, and when their aims and intentions are pure."

If we could convince enough people of that principle, our spirit friends could work their miracles.

As I considered the situation carefully, I began to see my mission in all this. I would do what I could to help apply this higher spiritual principle of sincerity and resonance to our troubled planet, whose history has been marred consistently by dissonance and conflict. I would have to search for ways to spread the resonance as far as possible out into the field of world ITC and beyond. I would have to try to stress the importance of these higher spiritual principles. It was the only way to ensure that the fruits of ITC would shower humanity with love and spiritual understanding. Indeed, I was beginning to believe that achieving a degree of resonance throughout humanity would be the only hope of getting us out of our current dilemmas.

Without unity among researchers, dissonance, misconceptions, and fear would open the doors to negative spiritual influences, as they had done throughout history. Removing as many of those influences as possible from world ITC would have tremendous benefits to our work, but it would take the cooperation of many. In the meantime, for the sake of the approaching meeting, it would be necessary to include only a small circle of close supporters.

I wrote a fax back to Maggy saying I would need time to digest the information in her lengthy letter. I was fully committed to supporting a small, closed circle of researchers for the meeting, but in the larger picture I still wanted to give all researchers a chance to see the value of resonance with higher principles.

A few days later, Maggy wrote back to me, saying she was fed up, and if it weren't for Timestream spirit group, she would end our friendship then and there. After my indecision over the issue of whether to open the September meeting up or to keep it exclusive, and after my recent comment that I needed time to digest her information, she and Jules were now ready to sever ties with me.

Our spirit friends had changed the couple's mind. They had told Maggy by telephone:

"Mark is going through one of his most difficult phases of perception (realization). He is really working hard to realize, which is very difficult for him, but he will be successful. It is Mark's ego. He recognizes only step by step that it is the ego which hinders his capacity to realize. He will stand the test. He will stand the test. Mark has a lot of good friends here on our side among the humans. Most of them know him well. He is also protected by higher beings. He has friends among higher beings who are observing his work. He will totally leave this time of difficulties. You will keep him as a good friend, and you will get proof.

"Mark is that fellow who is really qualified for ITC."

Maggy was surprised by the message, and she asked if she should share it with me.

"Of course," Timestream replied. *"Mark is that fellow who is really qualified for ITC. Juliet is Mark's guardian angel."*

If Maggy was surprised by the message, I was overwhelmed by it. It opened so many questions. What would I have to do to "realize"? How would I know I'd achieved self-realization? In what way was I *that* person who was *really* qualified for ITC? What exactly were those qualifications? And most important, was my ego really a primary cause of the current troubles between Maggy and me? If so, what could I do to heal the situation?

If the message had been delivered by other spirit beings, I'd suspect they were toying with my ego—putting my self-esteem on a roller-coaster ride, as lower-vibration spirits sometimes do—but our friends at Timestream had proven themselves to be highly reliable, supportive, and honest over the years. I felt I could trust the message, even though I didn't yet grasp its full implications.

Many times in the coming months I requested explanations through ITC systems, with no results. I prayed and meditated for clarification, but again, received no definite explanations. Even as I write this book, I'm not certain of the full meaning of the message.

Be that as it may, my relationship with the Harsch-Fischbach couple had become strained to the breaking point by the late summer of 1995, and it was our spirit friends who kept it from blowing up.

I contacted Willis Harman a few days before the meeting to report the situation. "I was stubborn," I admitted, "trying to open the meeting to as many ITC researchers as possible so that we could all lay our cards on the table, start carving some order in the field of ITC, and develop a general plan for the future."

I explained that the idea made perfect sense to me, as it was based on a framework of democracy—the backbone of American society—but I described how it had led to a blowup between the Harsch-Fischbachs and myself which nearly destroyed our friendship.

I said, "I assumed it was largely their hurt pride and their ego which compelled them to exclude Ernst Senkowski and Adolf Homes—the men who had both turned their backs on the couple at crucial times in their research—but now I realize there's more to it."

I explained that now, a few days before I was to leave for England, an understanding had been reached. I didn't mention the message about me which the spirit team had faxed to Maggy. I was too uncertain of its meaning. Instead, I spoke of resonance.

"Willis," I said, "I think it is that ethic, more so even than democracy, that will lead humanity into the next century. Timestream has made it clear to us that ITC can spread only when there is harmony and unity among researchers. Everyone involved must be sincere and open—no hidden agendas to disturb the field. This is the way higher beings operate during a meeting of the minds. They see into each other's souls; they're totally open, transparent. People who are political and manipulative can't seem to fit into ITC. When those human qualities enter the system, the system falters."

Willis Harman seemed interested in the idea that ITC might have such a built-in safeguard against the lower aspects of human nature. "Mark, I trust that your meeting will be completely successful and help move this important research to another level of effectiveness," he said.

A BROKEN CONNECTION

The next day I received an important phone call from Konstantin Raudive. The message was delivered first in English, then in German. It lasted about twenty-five seconds, but I was not able to record it because there was no tape recorder attached to that particular phone at the time. We had four phones in the house, only three had tape recorders attached, and I had answered the wrong phone!

As the message came through, I was too busy fretting to focus on the content. Should I bolt to the kitchen phone and switch on the tape recorder, or should I tell my son Aaron, who was standing nearby, to run to the kitchen? Before I could decide anything, the contact ended, and I had only a general idea of the content of the message.

It conveyed moral support and good thoughts for the bold researchers who had survived the storm leading up to the meeting. I was supposed to share the message at the meeting that weekend. It included the phrase: *"There are blue skies on the horizon for world ITC."*

Since I would not be able to play back the message for the group, as our spirit friends expected, I would have to paraphrase as best I could based on what I remembered, and I didn't remember much. After that disappointing incident I made certain all phones in our home had functioning tape recorders attached at all times, and at the meeting I would encourage all the other researchers to do the same. There were even recording systems available that would automatically record *all* calls coming in the home, regardless of which phone extension was picked up. I decided that would be a good setup for our home. Only later would I learn that using such a system could be illegal in the United States, since some states require that both parties of a phone call must be aware that the call is being recorded. Otherwise it is an illegal phone tap.

At times like that I certainly wished that the plethora of laws and statutes spread wildly throughout the fifty United States could be standardized and simplified. They seemed to benefit few people other than lawyers. It seemed to me that the sheer complexity of the legal system bred dissonance, conflict, and uncertainty—the very things we would have to start scrubbing out of world society if there were any hope for a bright future.

HOMES RECEIVES A CONTRARY CONTACT

Tensions were mounting among those who were being excluded from the meeting. German researcher Adolf Homes contacted me a month before the September 1 meeting to say the getting together of ITC researchers, in his view, was not a good idea at that time.

"There should be greater representation," he said. "If you hope to have an umbrella organization for international ITC research, the meeting you are planning is too exclusive."

Indeed, Homes had received a contact from his spirit colleagues Hans Bender (a recently departed German researcher) and Doc Mueller (the same departed NASA scientist who had provided spiritside expertise in the development of the Spiricom equipment of George Meek and Bill O'Neil). Bender and Mueller had sent a computer text to Homes that said, *"It is still too early to create a stable field and then maintain it, because of differences in vibration still among you."*

Homes reiterated to me, "There will not be a wide enough representation to create a strong contact field. I think you should wait."

"I'm sorry," I told Homes, "but the plans for the meeting are too far along now to cancel. Besides, I've committed myself to it. Many people are depending on it."

When Maggy Harsch-Fischbach learned about the contact to Adolf Homes, she made it clear that Bender and Mueller were not part of Timestream spirit group, and Timestream thought that a meeting was necessary. Again, the key was not the number of experimenters who would be involved in the group but the degree of harmony among those involved. The contact field between Timestream and the Luxembourg couple had existed for a decade, and it was now expanding to include other bridges as well, especially to Sonia Rinaldi in Brazil, to Fritz Malkhoff in Germany, and to me in the States. Maggy's contacts were by far the most positive and miraculous of those being received anywhere.

There were forces on both sides of the veil trying to disrupt the miracles for various reasons, and we would have to work together in a unified way in order to prevail.

Chapter 5

FORGING AN ASSOCIATION,
BEING SHOWERED BY MIRACLES

Amid the misty, rolling hills of England, a team of scientists and researchers from various countries met in Dartington Hall to discuss the miracle of ITC. It was in the early autumn of 1995, and the air outside was crisp and chilly, in contrast to the smoldering sense of expectation and heated dialog within. There were sixteen men and women present from different walks of life, from eight different countries, and with diverse opinions on a wide variety of topics. One thing everyone had in common was a fascination with ITC as it was unfolding in the lives of Maggy and Jules Harsch-Fischbach of Luxembourg.

I had organized the meeting and arranged adequate funding to cover the expenses of all the attendees, thanks to the advice, assistance, and connections of my Connecticut friends, Juliet Hollister and Alison van Dyk.

Dr. Hans Luethi, a retired Swiss microbiologist, summed up the tone of the meeting. "This is the greatest breakthrough of the twentieth century!" he exclaimed. "The information we're receiving from our transpartners furnishes the first hard, objective evidence of continued life after death. What has been a belief in immortality for thousands of years, has finally become consolidated knowledge." Heads were nodding and excited whispers could be heard among the gathering. Later on we would elect Dr. Luethi as our group's first coordinator.

The miracle of ITC had been unfolding on Earth during the past decade, and these experts had come together to decide how best to understand it, perpetuate it, and foster its growth in the best interests of the planet.

Dozens of questions had to be answered during that extended weekend meeting in England. Where exactly is this information coming from? How should it be presented to humanity? Is the world ready for the information, much of which is highly esoteric and, well, alien? Would the media be willing and able to handle the research responsibly, or would they portray it in a sensationalistic framework of fear and skepticism? Would the information stand up to the test of conventional science, or would mainstream scientists reject it outright? As the more orthodox religions learned that people on Earth are in contact with beings from Beyond, would they react with open minds, or would they accuse the researchers of collaborating with demons? What, if anything, could be done to make ITC more palatable to the more traditional factions of science and religion?

And most important, how could the delicate contact bridge between worlds that had been built painstakingly over the preceding decade be preserved and strengthened? That was the most difficult question to answer. After all, many of the principles and energies involved in the research were being supplied by otherworldly sources and apparently were beyond the scope and understanding of modern science. So little was known about the deeper realities of life which made such miracles as ITC possible that it would be easy for the miracle simply to fall between the cracks, and the almost unimaginable benefits to the world would be lost until a more knowledgeable humanity emerged on Earth.

It was the first time a challenge of this nature and magnitude had ever faced humanity. Miracles certainly were not new to the planet, but with six billion people in a modern world integrated by elaborate networks of communication and transportation, the impact of miracles such as ITC could be far more earthshaking than ever before. So we had much to discuss.

When Maggy Harsch-Fischbach spoke, the room fell silent. She and her husband, Jules, had been waiting for this meeting for a long time. The couple had been receiving by far the most exciting contacts reported by any ITC researcher anywhere in the world. In the presence of scientists, journalists, and others, Maggy and Jules had been receiving all sorts of information from their transpartners—phone calls from departed colleagues and loved ones, moving television pictures of faces and landscapes from the spirit worlds, long orations through specially configured radios, and lately, even large files planted on the hard disk of their computer—files containing long letters or detailed images.

Just about everyone in the room had sat in on the Luxembourg experiments at one time or another and had walked away believing—no, *knowing*—that the elaborate contacts being received at the Luxembourg lab (contacts that most people would find unbelievable) were for real.

Maggy spoke in a quiet, steady voice, her eyes mirroring the expectant gaze of the group members. She spoke of four forces shaping world ITC, the first being the intervention of angels such as The Seven.

Indeed, everyone in the group had become familiar with The Seven ethereal beings who were opening the gateway between our world and the world of our ancestors. For centuries beings in spirit had been in touch with people on Earth through telepathy, or channeling, and that was a pretty easy feat to accomplish; all it took was a psychically sensitive person on Earth as a receiver. Making the leap from psychic channeling to enhanced ITC was an impossible task for our departed friends and colleagues to achieve without celestial intervention.

So, as Maggy Harsch-Fischbach told her colleagues at Dartington Hall, for the first time in history people on Earth—the men and women in that room—were receiving objective, unfiltered reports of the lives and surroundings of "the Dead," and it was the involvement of The Seven ethereal beings that made it all possible.

Maggy said that it was a commitment to ethics among researchers on Earth that attracted the higher beings to our work. So ethics, she said, was the second force shaping world ITC.

Again, there were nods of agreement. Everyone in the room knew that the interaction between Heaven and Earth was a constant, ongoing reality—that the thoughts and attitudes generated in one world spill over into other worlds, affecting and shaping some of the reality in those worlds. It was common knowledge throughout the room that people on Earth draw into their lives spirit beings of like attitude. Love and empathy expressed by people on Earth are fueled by the support of loving and empathetic spirit beings. And conversely, resentment and fear felt by hateful individuals on Earth are fueled by the eager support of negative spirits.

These interplays between worlds have affected everyone on Earth to a greater or lesser degree, for better or for worse, from time immemorial, but their effects are most strongly felt by people involved in spirit work, such as ITC researchers. If the people meeting at Dartington Hall wanted to enjoy the miraculous fruits of enhanced ITC, they knew they would have to nurture the relationship with higher beings through positive, ethical thoughts, attitudes, and service.

Dr. Claudius Kern, an educational scientist from Austria, drew an important conclusion. "The comment, 'Ignorance does not protect against damage,' is as true for contacts with the Beyond as it is for contacts with high voltage," he warned. "The lack of spirit discernment can be harmful to the health."

Then Maggy continued, her voice still soft and steady. The third force was intention, she said. There had to be a common commitment to foster the spread of ITC in a positive light.

Everyone in the room was well aware of ITC's potential benefits to humanity. Imagine the relief of grieving relatives if a recently departed loved one could call his family on Earth to share his new adventure. Imagine the benefits if the greatest medical minds throughout history could share vital breakthroughs with doctors and nurses on Earth. Imagine the beauty that would unfold around the globe like a rose if the Michelangelos and Monets of all eras could send artistic masterpieces across our televisions, or if the Bachs and Debussys could deliver ethereal compositions to ITC researchers' computers equipped with music sequencing programs and MIDI interfaces. Imagine the crimes that could be prevented if all potential criminals realized that their actions were observed by invisible eyes and could be reported immediately to authorities. Imagine especially if a murder victim could name the murderer.

Most of the researchers at Dartington were eager to see the rapid spread of ITC, but a few serious minds advocated discretion. "ITC information ought to be dealt out widely, but also wisely," warned Irma Weisen, a Finnish journalist. "We must be careful with the media. For a journalist it is easier to be cynical and destructive than constructive, especially when it involves phenomenal information such as ours." There was a general sense of agreement in the ensuing discussion. ITC researchers would not be able simply to trust newspaper reporters, TV producers, radio talk show hosts, and others to treat their information appropriately. They would have to employ discretion in future publicity efforts.

Perhaps the only people the researchers could trust in their work at the present time were their fellow researchers. And even that trust would have its limitations, especially in the future. One of the participants was Dr. Guenter Emde, president of the spiritually oriented association Via Mundi and founder of the Ethics Protection Initiative, an international organization that assisted individuals such as whistle-blowers, whose consciences and right decisions had made them victims of organizations. So far, said Dr. Emde, there was every reason to feel confident that everyone in the room was totally sincere and honest in their research, but that might not always be the case. We are, after all, human. "On the one hand, we must search for ways to detect false contact phenomena, but on the other hand, we have to protect true contacts from aggressive skepticism and other disturbing influences," Dr. Emde stressed.

After some discussion on that point, Maggy disclosed what she regarded as the fourth factor in the healthy spread of world ITC: scientific involvement. Science would have to take the reins of ITC research before it could flourish to its full potential. Only scientists would have the in-depth knowledge to understand the complex forces at work in ITC contacts.

Nils Jacobson, M.D., argued, "We must be careful with science." Dr. Jacobson was a Swedish psychiatric specialist and parapsycholgist, and he had had extensive experience grappling with the problem of trying to validate spiritual and paranormal events scientifically. Just a year earlier he had received two phone calls from spirit colleague Konstantin Raudive, and now he seemed to be in the difficult position of having to reconcile those very personal, subjective spirit contacts with his highly intelligent, analytical, and objective nature.

"If I tell my colleagues that some people in Luxembourg and Germany claim to have two-way contacts with the spirit world by phone and radio, and that I believe this to be true, I would lose my scientific credibility."

If the good doctor were to tell his colleagues that he himself had talked to a spirit friend on the telephone, I wondered whether they might even laugh at him.

Nils continued, "Scientists are only interested in what can be proved or disproved in the conventional scientific way, and this work we are involved in is virtually impossible to prove in the conventional way."

"That's right!" exclaimed Dr. Ralf Determeyer, a German scientist and ITC researcher. At six-foot-three, with a tautness in his posture and an earnest intensity in his voice, Ralf almost barked his approval of his Swedish friend's comments.

"There is *plenty* of solid evidence that our spirit contacts are real," he said, "but conventional science is unwilling or unable to accept any of it."

Someone asked, "Are you referring to cross-contacts?"

"Yes," Ralf Determeyer replied. "Also telephone monitoring. As we all know, Adolf Homes received four paranormal calls while his phone was monitored by Deutsch Telekom, but the phone company detected none of them. *Not one!* He registered those calls with Senkowski's Association for Psychobiophysics."

I detected a bit of tension in the room as Ralf mentioned the names "Homes" and "Senkowski," two highly regarded researchers who were conspicuously absent from the meeting.

"Several experimenters in other locations also had their phone lines monitored, including our friends from Luxembourg," Determeyer continued, "and always the same results: *No paranormal calls* were detected, although several such calls were received."

I exclaimed, "That kind of evidence is almost rock solid! And still science ignores it."

"Yes," Ralf Determeyer stated flatly. Nils Jacobson nodded.

Yes, scientific authentication of ITC would present a difficult challenge in the coming years.

Another unavoidable challenge would be skepticism stirred up by opponents of our intended aims. German researcher Fritz Malkhoff mentioned the well-known experimenter Fidelio Koeberle in particular. As one of the leading authorities on electronic voice phenomena, the study of short, faint spirit voices captured on audiotape, Koeberle circulated a technical EVP newsletter to several thousand German-speaking researchers. He had expressed excitement about video images and loud, clear voices when they first started occurring for Klaus Schreiber and Hans Otto Koenig in the mid-1980s, but as time passed he began to question the legitimacy of the enhanced contacts. Others were claiming miracles while he continued to get only tiny voices on tape. Something was wrong. Lately some people were saying that he had been accusing the Harsch-Fischbach couple of outright fraud.

"In my opinion, people in this situation can become very bitter," said Fritz. "If they have been working with EVP longer than most people, they might think they deserve to receive such contacts themselves."

I said, "Fritz, we have the same trouble in the States, with a man named Bill Weisensale. He's been involved with EVP since the early eighties. He publishes a technical newsletter—a good journal—just like Koeberle's, and lately he's been accusing our friends Maggy and Jules of fraud. He says there's no proof that our phone calls are for real."

"Of course they are for real!" Fritz exclaimed. "Most of us have plenty of proof." He mentioned various cases of cross-contacts—the same information sent to several different researchers at the same time by radio, computer, and telephone—and he acknowledged the phone-monitoring experiments mentioned by Determeyer. He also cited an incident that happened to him on May 17, 1994:

"A German journalist and former EVP experimenter named Mr. Wilbertz visited me," Fritz said. "Mr. Wilbertz mentioned that he had known Konstantin Raudive personally during his lifetime, and had had some discussions with him at his home. At 3:45 P.M. Raudive phoned me. He asked to speak to Mr. Wilbertz, so I handed him the phone. Raudive then said, *Colleague Wilbertz, pass on the word to the world: It can only support what we talked about a decade ago.*' In other words, Raudive confirmed what Wilbertz had told me a few minutes earlier. That, to me, is incontrovertible proof that the phone call was from spirit. No one on Earth knew Mr. Wilbertz was visiting me."

Fritz mentioned several other, similar incidents that had proved to him that the contacts did indeed come from spirit.

Dr. Ralf Determeyer of Germany had observed ITC in Europe for more than ten years. He made it clear once again that there was no question in his mind about the legitimacy of the phone contacts. He recalled six days of miracles in his own home, beginning in June 1987.

"The ethereal being called 'Technician' rang my phone to announce the founding of an international ITC organization. The 'contact field' remained stable for six days to allow contacts from other entities. As witnesses have confirmed, our piano, which is close to the telephone, started to play by itself."

There was a moment of silence in the room as we all digested the significance of that miracle. I smiled when I imagined an invisible friend sitting at Ralf's piano, banging out a ragtime melody or performing a classical sonata. What sort of spiritside intervention must have occurred to make that possible?

Sonia Rinaldi of Brazil broke the silence. She said that she too had received evidence recently that the contacts were legitimate. A year earlier she had received a call from both Konstantin Raudive and a departed Brazilian researcher, Carlos de Almeida, who spoke in Brazilian Portuguese.

"I remember it clearly," said Sonia. "It was April 14 [1994]. The phone rang, and I knew it was them. I knew it was Timestream." Ms. Rinaldi was a tireless and dedicated ITC researcher, coordinating a network of more than a hundred active experimenters in Brazil and publishing a monthly newsletter. From a young age she had been a "sensitive"—a person who receives mental impressions from spirit friends frequently and quite naturally.

"When I answered the phone, I was not too surprised, then, to hear the deep familiar voice of Dr. Raudive. He said, *'Good morning, Sonia Rinaldi,'* I talked for a while with Konstantin Raudive in English, then he said, *'I'll give the microphone to Carlos.'*"

Some of us listening to Sonia recounting her experience found it particularly interesting that Konstantin Raudive was turning over a "microphone" to Carlos. We were all aware that our spirit friends employed various forms of spirit-world apparatuses to make these enhanced ITC contacts possible. We had been told that they often used something resembling a telephone receiver. Now we were learning that they could also use a sound system with a microphone with which to contact us by telephone.

Sonia Rinaldi shared the long message from her Brazilian colleague-in-spirit, Carlos de Almeida:

"Greetings! An embrace to all our friends in Brazil. Dear friend, Sonia Rinaldi, this is the second contact we send to your country from Timestream. We thank you for your efforts. We can hear but cannot answer.

"Time is not a line but a circle. Horizons far from you do not finish in the world but enter a sacred universe. Certain details are visible but the most important are not. The world as you see it is an extension of what we have here, and altogether [help make up] the universe.

"A special embrace to Dr. Hernani Andrade, who knows all this, and Dr.

Marlene Nobre, who understands the importance of all religions . . . All these are a help to life, together with ITC.

"Timestream, Carlos de Almeida, and Father Landell Moure send an embrace to all of you.

"Good luck, Sonia, in your speech! You will be helped."

Skeptics had accused ITC researchers of being gullible victims of a hoax, pointing out that the voice of Konstantin Raudive was deep and reminiscent of the voice of Jules Harsch. They had suggested that it was Jules Harsch, not the spirit of Konstantin Raudive, who had been making all those phone calls to researchers around the world.

In this phone call to Sonia Rinaldi, Raudive had turned "the microphone" over to Carlos de Almeida, who spoke in fluent Brazilian Portuguese, a language totally unfamiliar to Jules Harsch. So, for that call to be a hoax would have required Jules Harsch to have acquired an accomplice, someone fluent in Brazilian Portuguese. Now the accusations by the skeptics were having to become rather gyrated in order for the attacks to continue. But continue they would, causing more troubles for serious ITC researchers.

As the meeting continued, it became crystal clear that ITC researchers had received ample proof that technical spirit communication was under way. Science would simply have to adjust its narrow worldview to accept the possibility. Until that happened, there might be little chance of finding common ground between science and spirit.

The researchers at Dartington Hall agreed that skeptics would have to be excluded from the work in order to maintain a cohesive contact field, but somehow, despite our best efforts, skeptics with hidden agendas would leak into the group in the coming months, causing immeasurable damage. Even a few members present at this first meeting would eventually wrestle with doubts in the coming years.

Meanwhile, the question arose during the meeting of the reliability not only of our colleagues on Earth, but also of our spirit partners. While Timestream had proven itself to be a team of competent, positive beings, other spirit groups had proven themselves to be quite the opposite—unpredictable, troublesome, even dangerous at times. How could our group ensure that we were working with positive beings?

Dr. Emde suggested that the most effective way to "test the spirits" is the same as the normal way to determine the reliability of fellow humans.

"When someone speaks to us in a reasonable, intelligent manner over a period of time, we gradually develop a trust in that person," Dr. Emde said slowly, choosing his English words carefully. "The same is true with our transpartners. If those who work with us today have communicated with us in a reasonable fashion for many months, then a trust has developed." Nevertheless, he concluded, in the future we must continue to assess our transpartners. This is done by carefully considering the information they deliver to us and by intuitively experiencing their honesty and moral quality.

The most awe-inspiring of the otherworldly beings were The Seven and others who claimed to be residing in light, ethereal realms of existence where love and wisdom reign supreme, where fear and darkness are absent. These angels had told experimenters that they had never lived in physical bodies in a physical world, yet they knew humans inside and out, especially the experimenters, being aware of their moods, their attitudes, their strengths and weaknesses, even their past lives.

Among the oldest, wisest, and perhaps most patient of the researchers were Dr. Theo Locher and Dr. Hans Luethi, both from Switzerland and both in their eighties. Both men realized that they might leave the Earth before global ITC arrives, but they would most likely be here to observe and assist in one way or another, from one side of the veil or the other, if our small group of researchers were successful in forging an alliance at this meeting and maintaining it in the coming years, most likely in the face of adversity.

Dr. Locher, a trim man of medium height, impeccably dressed in a black, three-piece suit, had founded the prestigious Swiss Parapsychological Association. The serious expression etched on his face reflected the no-nonsense reputation he had earned as a world-renowned parapsychologist. The world was intrigued by such mysteries as UFOs, OBEs, NDEs, apports, mediumship, and bilocation, and parapsychologists such as Dr. Locher were trying to unravel those mysteries, but he admitted that nothing seemed more important or of more profound implication than the coming of ITC to this planet in the final years of the twentieth century.

But was ITC really new to the planet? His good friend Dr. Luethi, appearing relaxed in a sport coat and comfortable slacks, and exuding a warm, gentle humility, didn't think so. He was a retired microbiologist with a lifelong appetite for spiritual information, and the appetite had grown bigger since his retirement. He shared some research which suggested that ITC was not as new as everyone else in the room might think. He quoted a passage from his Swiss Christian Bible, Mose 7/89:

When Moses entered the tent of revelation, he heard the voices speaking to him from the cover plate on the Ark of the Covenant, exactly from the space between the two cherubs, and he thus spoke with them.

Dr. Luethi suggested that this passage from the Old Testament provided an interesting possibility that ITC was on Earth more than 2,000 years ago.

On the last day of the meeting we agreed on the name "INIT" (International Network for Instrumental Transcommunication) for our group and we completed a statement of intent, emphasizing that INIT members would take an ethical, moral approach to ITC research. One by one we signed it.

The long discussions that weekend planted much deeper seeds of collaboration among us. We all agreed that the underlying goal of our joint work would be to understand the nature of multidimensional communication, to protect the energy field that made it possible, and to foster its spread around the world under a moral umbrella of love and friendship.

Near the close of the meeting, Maggy Harsch-Fischbach shared a message from the higher beings which had arrived days earlier, and which stirred great excitement within the group: Seven new receiving stations on Earth were being planned by our spirit friends. In the coming months and years, seven new experimenters or experimental groups scattered around the world would begin to receive enhanced ITC contacts, such as those being enjoyed in Luxembourg. The message had the effects one might expect—tremendous excitement and inspiration among all members, coupled perhaps with a tiny seed of uncertainty among each individual member, who would begin to wonder in the coming weeks, "Who will be chosen? Will I be among them?"

Meanwhile, we all had some soul-searching to do in the light of this vital new association we had forged. What changes, not only in Earthside technology but far more importantly within each of us individually, would have to be undertaken to allow enhanced world ITC to come to fruition?

Not all was upbeat and positive at the meeting. Being human, some of us harbored quiet doubts about the miracles and their implications for humanity. Should they be shared openly with the world? Was humanity ready for

ITC, or would the miracles be buried under the violence, pornography, and other debris of the times?

More important, some of us harbored doubts about the implications of such a powerful new technology that was beyond the understanding not only of modern science, but also of those of us who were receiving the contacts. Even we didn't understand how these miracles were possible. Sonia Rinaldi brought into the open the doubts that were hiding quietly within most of us.

"It is difficult to talk about the future of ITC when I have so many doubts in the present," she said. "First of all, realizing that we on Earth are responsible for less than five percent of the work, and the contacts depend more than ninety-five percent on the spirits, I wonder if *we* can decide the future of ITC development. At best *we* are at *their* disposal to help *them* to implement *their* plans."

All of us in the room realized that the miracle of ITC was a puzzle. Our friends on the other side possessed the secrets, while we on Earth held only a few puzzle pieces. A part of us sometimes wondered why they didn't simply send us blueprints for an ITC system that would open the doors to their world. That would certainly make things simple. Instead, we were being given hints—an occasional morsel here and there—that kept us moving in the right direction.

Another part of us realized that things were not so simple. We were learning that ITC is fueled by a complex soup of life forces, electromagnetic energies, human attitudes, intentions, and collaborative efforts that would be impossible to portray in any Earthly document. It was the sheer complexity of our research that stirred doubts within many of us.

Sonia also said she felt poorly informed about the progress of contacts in Luxembourg. A valid complaint. I was the person who received the bulk of the reports from the Harsch-Fischbachs, and my highest priority was to organize the information for publication. I was also obliged to share the information with Sonia, who published the results in Brazil. I did not always share information quickly, so she had good reason to be anxious.

I gathered contacts as they streamed into Luxembourg via computers, telephones, TVs, and radios and were shared with me. My good friend Hans Heckmann translated them from German to English. I edited, assembled, and published them as quickly as possible, then sent the result to Sonia and others in a form that I felt would require little effort on their part to use in their own publications. I assumed that a finished product in English would be more useful to them than raw materials in various languages, mostly German. It was certainly easier for me to send out one complete package than to mail and fax dozens of one- or two-page reports from Luxembourg. Still, if I were in Sonia's position under those conditions, I too would feel uneasy.

Finally, Sonia was in charge of coordinating 140 Brazilian researchers with a newsletter and frequent correspondences. The contacts were primarily short, faint voices on tape. Some of the Brazilian researchers were clamoring for direction toward enhanced ITC contacts as published in our ITC journals, and Sonia was not getting suggestions to pass along to them. The key to getting miraculous contacts was unknown to all of us at that time.

Many of us at the meeting had quiet concerns like Sonia's, but in the enthusiasm and camaraderie of the moment they got swept under the rug. From there they would begin to fester like a thorn broken off under the skin, causing pain and eventual eruptions within our group in the coming years.

LEFT OUT IN THE COLD

In the weeks after the meeting, friction began to develop between our new INIT group and others who had not been included. On September 4, the final day of our meeting, German experimenter Adolf Homes was at home in bed, recovering from the removal of a kidney. Judging from letters I had received from him in recent weeks, I suspected that the thought of our meeting in England, without his presence, was not a source of comfort for him. He received a contact that day from his spirit colleague Doc Mueller, who tried to calm his concerns:

"The disagreement over 'the good' between people in your time prevents the building up of instrumental contacts among the acoustic researchers. None is better or worse than the other. Wanting to position oneself at the top makes no sense. People with an enlightened consciousness are in time able to make everything possible. Therefore a little while will pass until seven more ITC stations will be established at intervals on your planet. Until then, please continue to exercise patience and love."

Our spirit friends were telling Homes not to worry; the various ITC researchers all had their own ideas about what was best for ITC and what was best for the world. While the Harsch-Fischbachs were getting the best contacts, their view of the situation, like everyone else's, came through the limitations of human eyes and human brains. The development of seven new receiving stations would not come to bear until some agreement could be reached among researchers.

BY THE WARMTH OF
CELESTIAL FIRES

Meanwhile, progress in our small group came rather quickly. On September 7, three days after the meeting in England, spirit colleague Konstantin Raudive made contact with Fritz Malkhoff in Germany to announce that the meeting had charged up the energy bridge between spirit and Earth.

"I must tell you, Friend Malkhoff," said Dr. Raudive, *"that the spiritual has to rule the world. Material wealth must not be the criteria for everything. After all, man does not live by bread alone but needs spiritual values and the freedom for personal development. When this is missing on your side, there is no actual assurance of human ascension. Those who deal with ITC on Earth need our help urgently in the form of psychological, ethical, or religious knowledge and perception. Only then can the experimenters and researchers be led out of the blind alleys in which they are momentarily stuck, and a truly just and peaceful cooperation can be established. Dear Friend Malkhoff, seven stations are to be built. You, of course, are not included since you already operate a station."*

Fritz was excited by the confirmation that seven new stations were being planned. "Can you tell me more about these seven stations?" he asked.

"No," replied our invisible friend, *"it is something that will be played out on your side, and I cannot say much about it at this moment."*

"If I understand you correctly, it will depend on the experimenters?"

"Yes, you understand the situation exactly, Friend Malkhoff."

"It is very nice to hear about this," Malkhoff exclaimed.

"It may be that the message about the seven stations already has come to Adolf Homes at Station Rivenich," Raudive said.

"Well, I have had little contact with Colleague Homes lately."

"Yes, that is exactly what I was going to talk to you about. You have to get organized on your side. It would be beneficial if a certain cooperation would develop. Do not misunderstand me, Friend Malkhoff. You need not initiate

anything; you have done enough. It is now up to the other gentlemen and ladies to approach you."

"Yes, I understand . . ."

So, our spirit friends at Timestream apparently were encouraging greater cooperation among experimenters on Earth, implying that a renewal of friendship between Adolf Homes and Maggy Harsch-Fischbach was not out of the question. Sadly, that broken friendship would never be healed. Bruised egos are sensitive and stubborn matters.

HELLO FROM HEAVEN, 1995–96

Miracles began to pour into our group through the lives of the Harsch-Fischbach couple, made possible by the united thoughts and energies of the INIT members. It was exciting to see the tangible products of a living organization that was coming to life.

We received a series of contacts from The Seven higher beings in the coming months which shed much light on our path. Following are paraphrased excerpts from those contacts, with my explanations and comments:

Since God is everything, it doesn't matter which religion you follow. The one and only universal truth is found along the path of decency. Committing to eternal principles opens the doors to freedom.

The Seven were telling us that kindness, empathy, and love in our dealings with other people are more important in the larger, spiritual picture than are our religious beliefs.

Your present level of science cannot measure or even identify the many dimensions beyond the physical. Still, you place such trust in that limited area of human endeavor that many among you—even some who believe in the continuance of life beyond death—sometimes are skeptical of messages which you receive from these dimensions. As you share the information you receive, they say you do so out of blind hope, wishful thinking, and fear. Your task is not an easy one.

We were being warned that we would face enormous challenges in the coming years as we would spread the news of ITC to a well-grounded, skeptical public.

We have heard your concerns that the information we give you is not new to you. While that may be true in some cases, we have already said that you should first spread more widely the information already received before new information can be given.

Many contacts deserved analysis and elaboration, but often we were given so much information that it was difficult to do anything more than just re-produce the contacts in the journal as they poured in. Occasionally our spirit friends stopped sending new material to us, giving us time to consolidate what we'd already received, and to find ways to spread the word more widely. Some of us let our fears and insecurities get the best of us, worrying that the slowdown was a sign that the contacts were drying up. Others were driven to shun the media completely for fear of bad results. An appropriate spread of ITC information would take time and patience.

We notice your frustration when a long "time" passes between contacts. We remind ourselves often that, being of the Earth, your lives revolve around time. As we have told you, constellations must be favorable to allow contacts, so there is only so much we can do. Also, from our perspective it is sometimes better if the voices across the veil are silent.

We were reminded often that our invisible friends lived in a world that was not guided by clocks. From their perspective, things on Earth did not unfold from hour to hour, day to day, and year to year. They observed life on Earth as a complex web of interacting thoughts, feelings, intentions, and actions among us humans. They didn't count the weeks and months as they waited for INIT members to find the cohesion and understanding necessary to facil-itate miraculous contacts; rather, they observed our inner desires and compul-sions to see how well our group was functioning as a single, living organism.

As long as we were all enthusiastic about the purpose of INIT and the promise of ITC to the world, the communication channels could open up and miracles could flourish. If there were selfish interests and hidden agendas among us, the growth of ITC would be stunted. To our spirit friends, achiev-ing resonance among a group of humans was all-important; whether it re-quired a day, a year, or several centuries was not so important to them.

The deep spiritual connections among INIT members are felt among some of you. There is growing confidence in your path. Many of our messages to you seem fragmented, but you are starting to detect an underlying goal and purpose in them. This is the path we can walk together as you derive a deep sense of returning to your spiritual roots. Or you might find your path with another group instead, or maybe not at all this time on Earth. You are free to decide whether or not to walk this path alongside us.

The Seven made it clear on many occasions that they would never command us, but would sometimes give us suggestions and invitations, such as this one, to reveal choices that would be in the better interest of world ITC. They also spoke of the importance of spiritual connection with each other while we live our lives on Earth.

Many of you look for technical proof of ITC's legitimacy, but most of the tests available in your present world are unsuitable. We appreciate the phone taps you arrange with the telecommunications companies, but they provide only a partial picture of what is really happening during phone contacts from us. The bottom line is honesty and sincerity on the part of ITC researchers. Without honesty, there can be no legitimate ITC.

Some people, perhaps out of fear, were reluctant to accept any information coming through ITC without solid proof that it did indeed come from our spirit colleagues. The higher beings told us that no testing methods available to us on Earth were able to take into account all the complex variables involved in a spirit contact. Those variables were not even fully understood by humans.

Skeptics could certainly use this situation to their advantage, "disproving" something not because it is false, but because science is ineffective. In the larger picture, of course, it would be silly to discount everything. The most important element to ensure validity in ITC research, as in all human endeavors, would be honesty. It made sense to me that if a researcher wanted to enjoy miracles, he or she would have to establish a resonance with ethereal beings based upon honesty and sincerity. If the researcher suddenly became dishonest, then the miracles would fade away. The most important elements in ITC, therefore, would always be honesty on the part of a researcher and trust on the part of his or her colleagues.

A true ITC researcher tries to get contacts through various apparatuses, but successful results are no more important to us than spiritual growth experienced by you along the way. We view your world and your efforts through spiritual eyes.

We were finding that the individuals who received enhanced contacts were not necessarily those who experimented diligently with improved equipment and new processes. Those who made conscientious efforts to struggle onto a more spiritually elevated path also drew the attention of our spirit friends. They could actually see that spiritual growth occurring in our bodies in the way that doctors might monitor the development of bones, teeth, and organs in a growing child.

Some of you believe an eternal spark—a piece of God—resides within everyone, and through this flame all people on Earth could achieve oneness in their relationships and rapports. This is not entirely true. Being in a physical body in a physical world, you are subject to the shortcomings and daily struggles that your rugged life entails. As you know, when you pick up a rock, you can sometimes find worms, bugs, and other things that are repulsive to you. Likewise, when you find yourself under the weight of negative feelings such as fear, insecurity, doubt, and envy, repulsive things emerge in the form of hatred and compulsions toward vengeance and destruction. Such negative forces in your world cannot easily be swept aside. You can't make those around you see the "Light" simply by trying to appeal to that divine inner core.

The Seven delivered this message to our group as we wrestled with the question of whom to invite to join. Should INIT be open to all ITC researchers or should we be selective? This message urged discretion on our part. We were learning that in the worlds of spirit, people migrate naturally into resonant groups; after we die, we tend to find ourselves in the presence of other people in spirit whose attitudes and desires are compatible with our own. In this world, on the other hand, we are all jumbled together with other people of diverse attitudes, incompatible desires, and selfish interests, so a great deal more care is needed as we forge alliances in our lives—especially when we are involved in important projects such as world ITC. In addition, we all have our own private struggles to contend with here on Earth—addictions, insecurities, illnesses, temptations, and so on.

The contact below was delivered by the higher being Technician to the phone answering machine of Maggy Harsch-Fischbach in the fall of 1996, a few days before our second annual meeting in Tarrytown, New York. It was delivered in English in a lovely, lilting voice that could not easily be determined as male or female. It was not human, but could best be described as ethereal in nature. The message was placed on tape by the higher being with no human intervention whatsoever. I reproduce the contact in its entirety, without paraphrasing, and include only a few remarks in parentheses. The message was intended as a gift from our ethereal colleagues to our INIT group. On behalf of the INIT members, I share it now with you, and I let you, the reader, study the contact and derive meaning from its important message.

"In the course of bygone decades, of thousands of earthly years, beings interested in the human species met to decide on the continuation of the project. You must not imagine that only The Seven implicated in the actual development of INIT are there. No, it is a coming together of all entities interested in mankind.

"The interests are various.

"We, The Seven of the Rainbow People, have decided to help and support the way chosen by you, in INIT. It is the way of morals, which means to understand, to acknowledge, to devise, and to act. It is not to be mixed up with religion, which means to believe. However, the two can be complementary. But they are independent one from the other.

"You already know that also Pharisees, ghouls, swindlers, thieves—yes, even murderers—have their interested supporters here among the dead. And the term "higher being"—notice that we never gave us this name ourselves—does not stand, as it is often misinterpreted by falsely religious people, for purified [here, a section of Technician's message seems to be lost in the transmission as often happens during paranormal voice contacts by phone] . . . *rid of all sin, whatever the word 'sin' means for them. There are also entities here interested in* that *situation.*

"This is The Seventh time that we accompany and guide you on your progress toward a free, wealthy, and sane future in which humanity would have stripped off the chains of intolerance and cruelty—a future in which it will be able to establish a fruitful, endurable relationship with the Light, ethereal realms of existence.

"Our and your opponents tried to prevent this by all meanings. Your meeting in Tarrytown is a decisive one—men and women of [here, the message became scrambled, but I think it was intended to say something like, "goodwill working things out"] *together to make true the dream of a strong international association based on morals and on ethics, not only by giving it a fundamental*

constitution and sheltering it this way from the wind, the rain, and the storms of pernicious attacks, but also by strengthening love and friendship true, the best qualities of mankind.

"*The first step was made in Dartington.* [In recent] *weeks, some of your best were cruelly hit by illnesses, diseases, and personal problems in order to keep them away from their valuable work. Be assured, even if we cannot avoid the plague, we can control the gravity. Whatever has happened, do not lose courage. We are there. You are in the right way. You are a small number, but much depends on you and your decisions on those days. We trust in you.*"

OUR EXTRATERRESTRIAL HERITAGE

To me, the most fascinating information we received from The Seven had to do with man's distant past. Following is the story that has been coming together like an elaborate puzzle in recent years through a series of ITC contacts. Italicized passages in the story were adapted from ITC contacts. Nonitalicized information is included to make the story more complete. The information not derived from ITC contacts comes from various sources, including books by Zecharia Sitchin, Erich von Däniken, and Philip José Farmer.

A physical planet called Marduk once shared our solar system, located in a regular orbit between the orbits of Mars and Jupiter. It was a lush planet, thriving with riverine communities, *home to a human civilization far beyond modern Earth in scientific and technological achievement. Immense powers were attained* by such means as large-scale manipulation of subtle energies with crystals. Stone blocks the size of a small house could be moved and situated with great precision by this means in order to construct elaborate buildings. An intimate knowledge of these subtle energies, or life energies, allowed the people of Marduk to be in touch with intelligent minds in other worlds, as well as with each other in silent, direct, mind-to-mind communication.

The sciences and industries of Marduk had followed a different course of evolution from humanity on Earth, and they far surpassed us in depth and complexity. *Genetic engineering, energy production, and other paths of technology brought great wonders to the people of Marduk, but they also presented prob-*

lems. Simple mistakes by genetic engineers could produce bizarre mutations, and mistakes by energy researchers could cause powerful explosions. *After a certain point, scientific technology on Marduk took on a life of its own, and there seemed to be no stopping it, even if the people had wanted to.* The rewards of scientific achievement were absolutely wonderful, dwarfing the occasional accidents and potential dangers, or so the people thought.

The reality of life after death was a simple truth to everyone on Marduk. They were fully aware of their spiritual makeup and knew that many physical ailments have their origin in the subtle bodies. The healing arts took that into account. They were also aware that not just people, but all living things have subtle bodies. And not just *living* things, but all physical things animate or inanimate have subtle bodies that coexist with the physical body and continue to exist after the physical body disintegrates. Rocks, mountains, and entire planets have subtle bodies.

The people realized that their very own planet Marduk had spiritual counterparts—parallel worlds existing in subtler dimensions. *One branch of science on Marduk involved a space-time doorway through which people could travel between dimensions.* They could enter the portal on the physical planet Marduk and emerge in astral worlds. *The natural laws and the physics of the two realities were quite different from each other. For example, in the astral worlds there were no gravity, no time, and no space as there were in the physical world.* Scientists studied these differences as part of the natural sciences of multidimensional living.

One small branch of *the complex Marduk scientific establishment involved itself with space travel.* It was not travel by propulsion as we know it today. Rather, the travelers would leave the physical world to enter the subtler realms of spacelessness and timelessness, then simply reenter the physical realm in a new location. *Like Marduk, the Earth was flourishing with life, but life on Earth was very primitive by comparison.* Mars supported life at that time as well. Teams of scientists on Marduk—the equivalent of our geologists, climatologists, biologists, chemists, and physicists—would take exploratory journeys to Earth and Mars from time to time to gather data and monitor the development of life on these very primitive planets. *There were species of primates living on Earth at that time,* and the scientists of Marduk familiarized themselves with their characteristics and behavior.

Colonies of people from Marduk eventually settled on the surface of the primitive planet Earth and, like pioneer families in the American West, worked intensively to carve a sense of order in the wild environment.

The home planet Marduk had evolved into a paradise much like the legendary Eden, in which people lived for hundreds of years in physical bodies that showed little signs of aging. There was no need to eat other living things for nourishment, nor even to procreate. It was a perfect, idyllic life for most residents of Marduk, but not for everyone. The rugged way of life on Earth tugged like a magnet at some of the heartier souls and pioneering spirits of Marduk.

As people became increasingly concerned about the dangerous trends of science and technology on Marduk, colonies on Earth began to expand. People brought seeds of their civilization to the new world, and those seeds quickly took root.

Suddenly it happened. *Unbridled science led to the destruction of the physical planet Marduk. The planet exploded, and the colonies that had taken root on Earth were now marooned here.* All life on Mars was destroyed in the explosion as a thick rain of rocks, boulders, and planetary debris showered the red planet. Fortunately the castaways who survived on Earth had brought along enough science and technology from their home planet to build an advanced civilization on Earth over a period of several thousand years. *It was called Atlantis, among other names.*

Centralized at a location on the Earth where the north Atlantic Ocean is today, the civilization of Atlantis made tremendous strides over a period of several thousand years, and the people achieved scientific and technological prowess nearly equal to their ancient ancestors of Marduk. Genetic engineering developed quickly, altering the genes of ferocious tigers to produce the cute, lovable house cat, for example. *They also produced monstrous beasts that future generations would have to battle for their lives. Some of these beasts became the subject of ancient legends which are still told today. Modern archaeologists shouldn't be too surprised if one day they come across dragon bones.*

The people of Atlantis did not learn from the mistakes of their ancestors, and *about 25,000 years ago they destroyed their civilization in a similar way that Marduk was destroyed,* only this time it was just a continent, not an entire planet that was annihilated.

Gradually, through crossbreeding with the primitive human population of Earth, the people evolved to become more compatible with life in their new world. It was a violent world in which animals consumed plants and other animals in order to subsist—a world of short life spans and intense competition for mating rights. Sex was an integral part of life here. All these qualities which the people of Marduk had considered barbaric slowly became a way of life in the new world.

This was the true fall of Man, as documented later in religious texts, and Atlantis would become interpreted as the Garden of Eden. The serpent and the apple would come to represent the circumstances surrounding humanity's fall from Grace not only after the destruction of Marduk, but also after the rise and fall of Atlantis. Because Atlantis did indeed fall in a similar, cataclysmic fashion. The godlike beings of Marduk, stranded on Earth, had "fallen from grace" when they began to crossbreed with the primitive hominids of Earth and thus became part of the terrestrial food chain.

ON THE THRESHOLD OF
SPIRITUAL SCIENCE

Willis Harman was becoming ever more excited by the progress we were enjoying, and he invited me to write a second article for the IONS journal, the *Noetic Sciences Review.* I gladly obliged, and in turn I invited Willis to be the keynote speaker at a one-day conference that would be part of the next INIT meeting in the fall of 1996. He gladly obliged, and a few weeks later he sent me a paper that he would present to ITC researchers and supporters from around the world.

THE DOOR SLAMS SHUT

Then, in the late summer, a few weeks before the meeting, Willis Harman called me with horrible news. He had been diagnosed with a brain tumor. There was little chance of treating it successfully, and so it was just a matter of time before he would die. Day-to-day activities were becoming harder for him; while talking to people he was forgetting his words.

"Under the circumstances," he said, "I think I would not be able to do the job that your conference deserves, and it would be difficult for me to give the presentation we planned. I'm very sorry to do this, but I would like to cancel my participation. I know this puts you in a terrible bind, and so if you really need me to be there, I will be."

I was choked up, unable to speak for a moment. During my brief immersion in spiritual matters in recent years I had seen more and more a sort of magic in the scheme of things as life unfolded on the planet. People would think of a loved one or run into an old friend on the street at the most synchronistic of times. Perhaps they had been talking about that person a few hours earlier, or maybe the person had been on their minds. There seemed to be a wondrous plan to our lives on Earth.

How, I was wondering at that moment, could something so horrible be part of that plan? We were living at a time of bridge building between science and spirit, and Willis Harman, perhaps the most important bridge builder of our time, was dying of brain cancer. How was that possible?

I pushed my shock aside and said, "My God, Willis, I'm *so* sorry. Of course I'll find someone to fill in for you at the conference. Your only concerns now should be happiness and healing."

We talked for a while, and after I hung up the phone, I felt an emptiness and aching inside. Willis Harman had been the main U.S. lifeline between science and enhanced ITC, and from that tragic day in 1996 until the time I write this book in the early spring of 2000, that would not be replaced. The second article I wrote for the *Noetic Sciences Review* would never get published in that journal.

The following day I called Juliet Hollister, who had already heard the news. She suggested, and I agreed, that it would be better to ask someone to present Willis's paper than to find someone suitable at this late date to prepare a presentation. After considering a number of people, we decided to invite Barbara Hancock Overby, the bright young philanthropist from the Lifebridge Foundation, a former actress who was now steeped in esoteric and spiritual matters.

Chapter 6

THE GATES TO HEAVEN AND HELL

On the morning of April 5, 1996, seven months after the meeting at Dartington, I was eating breakfast when the phone rang. I answered, and a bizarre voice said, "This is Konstantin Raudive."

The short message was repeated three times in three distinct voices, none of them being the deep, friendly, and familiar voice of our spirit colleague, Konstantin Raudive. The first voice could best be described as mechanical, the second as spiteful, and the third as demonic. Fortunately I captured the disturbing message on audiotape. After studying it, I considered some possibilities: Perhaps it was a prank by someone on Earth or a prank by someone in spirit, or perhaps it was a genuine attempt by our spirit colleagues to contact me through an energy field that was strained, causing the message to break up and sound surreal.

So which was it? I posed the question to our spirit friends at Timestream, and the answer came back to me the same day (via Station Luxembourg):

"It was of course not K.R. who phoned Mark, but a negative entity from here (on the mid-astral plane) known as ———. We cannot do anything against this as long as people like Weisensale and Koeberle are not stopped on your side. Unite your efforts and you will be strong. Avoid contact with those on your side who do not know where they belong.

"1996 April 5, 16:22."

It was becoming clear that the battle lines were being drawn on both sides of the veil. As long as a circle of ITC researchers remained united in trust, love, friendship, and common purpose, miracles would flourish. If envy, doubt, resentment, bitterness, fear, and hidden agendas were allowed to leak in and disturb the work, negative entities would take the opportunity to move in close, break through the weakened protective barriers set up by our ethereal colleagues, and disrupt our lives.

Scathing commentaries on the Luxembourg couple published by Bill Weisensale and Fidelio Koeberle apparently produced troubled vibrations that attracted negative beings like flies to a rotting carcass. Simply stated, positive attitudes among ITC researchers were opening doorways to Heaven, while negative attitudes were opening the gates to Hell.

Around the same time that I received my phone call from the negative being, several other INIT members received similar contacts. Dr. Ralf Determeyer in Germany got a call from the same negative being telling him he would soon die. Ralf reported later that the contact stirred up a lot of unrest in his family.

To help us deal with the problem, Jules Harsch in Luxembourg asked our spirit friends at Timestream to come up with a code word that would be known only to them and to INIT members. The word would be stated by our spirit friends during voice contacts to assure us that we were talking to them, not to unknown spirits. In response, Timestream came up with a rather strange and enchanting twelve-letter word of four or five syllables that was not easy to pronounce, nor could it be found in Webster's Dictionary. The word was "silmarillion." (I feel safe sharing it now because it has not been used for a couple of years, and if a code word is needed in the future, a new one probably will be devised.)

I wondered if the plan would work. I assumed that since spirits at Timestream knew the word, and since spirits could read one another's minds, perhaps the word would spread quickly throughout the spirit worlds, so that *all* spirits—negative and positive—could contact us with this celestial password.

As months passed, I was surprised and pleased to discover that I was wrong. I learned that symbols such as alphabetic characters, words, and phrases are hard to convey telepathically because they are unreal representations, sometimes of real things. If our research group had chosen a code word such as "radio" or "zebra," which instantly creates a mental image, I believe the code would have been easier to break, and other spirits outside our circle would have been able to pick up the word rather easily. But the long, meaningless word created by our spirit friends summoned up no mental images whatsoever, breaking the subtle communication links among minds.

I developed an ever-growing respect and admiration for the good folks at Timestream, who could have been off somewhere in the spirit worlds enjoying splendors beyond our wildest imaginings, but instead were staying close to our world, working hard to remain in Earthlike patterns of thought and behavior for the sole purpose of opening up and protecting communication channels with the troubled home they'd left behind. Our invisible friends at Timestream spirit group were like the poor boy who worked his way out of the ghetto, put himself through medical school, then returned to the ghetto to open a doctor's office to help the poor. I have to believe there is some wonderful reward awaiting those good souls.

POSITIVE SPIRIT VOICES ON TAPE

Over the years I captured hundreds of small voices on tape—mostly positive and helpful in nature. On one occasion, early in my experiments, I asked what I could do to improve contacts, and the deep, unmistakable voice of Konstantin Raudive whispered through the radio sounds, *"Your mind's too much in turmoil."* I focused for several months in meditation to learn to clear my mind of random thoughts. That was an immense challenge for my busy mind, but it led to improved contacts.

On October 7, 1995, the Timestream spirit group sent a fascinating letter, via computer in Luxembourg, containing very detailed information which I was asked to research:

"Dear Mrs. Harsch-Fischbach,

"This letter is addressed to you as I know you are the main communicator on your side for messages like this. My name is Arthur Beckwith. I suppose you don't know me, although I know you very well.

"I am in charge over here at Timestream station doing analyses of your newsletter, also the comments resulting which are published in different countries (for example, my home colleague Mark Macy).

> *"With this I intend to give my fellow researchers in the States . . . some details allowing them to make serious and complementary research on 'deceased persons' such as I.*
>
> *"I was born in Houghton-le-Spring Sunderland (UK). I was in Jamaica in 1857 where I met my beloved wife Susan. And I was employed at the* Sun, *the* Brooklyn Daily Eagle, *the* Citizen.
>
> *"I am here now, Group Timestream, together with Scott Joplin, Marjorie Hamilton, Bill O'Neil, Jeannette D. (Meek), and my friend Bill H. Lynch, who was (as he told me) in his terrestrial days rector of St. John's Roman Catholic Church in Lambertville, N.J. (he seems to have had some difficulties in offering to perform marriages during 1912 without cost), and Francis H. Glazebrook of Morristown (a medical doctor)."*

Many of the obscure facts in the letter were confirmed through phone calls and letters to England and Brooklyn, many hours of scouring old newspapers at the Brooklyn Public Library, and a trip to Lambertville, New Jersey. I did much of the research myself, with Regina's support. A large quantity of verifying information was dug up by Betsy M., a subscriber to my journal. This interested reader spent hours digging through the national census records in Washington, D.C., and uncovered a lot of family and household information about Arthur Beckwith in Brooklyn.

At that time my two principal spirit colleagues were Arthur Beckwith and Bill O'Neil. O'Neil was the man who had developed the Spiricom device in Pennsylvania in 1980 and had developed another, perhaps similar device in the spirit worlds after his death. He was now using that device to contact me by radio in Colorado. We had struggled through the early stages in which Bill had been able to enunciate the vowel sounds, A-E-I-O-U.

On October 17, 1996, I was working on a speech on the computer in my office. The radios in the lab in the next room were emitting a steady drone of white noise, when all of a sudden a voice boomed out, *"Time just passes here."* It was my first "direct voice"—that is, a voice that can be heard loudly and clearly at the time it's created. Most spirit voices planted on tape are inaudible by the normal human ear until playback.

The following day we received, through computer at Station Luxembourg, a short message from our spirit friends at Timestream about my direct voice contact:

"Tell Mark it was the voice of Arthur Beckwith."

In the coming months, either Arthur Beckwith or Bill O'Neil, or both of them, were present at all my experiments. Following are a few of the more interesting direct-voice messages they sent through the radio sounds in the coming weeks:

"The face on Mars must be looking up at a spacecraft."

This was apparently in regards to a controversial subject of recent years. Several large, geologic formations were discovered on Mars that seemed to be man-made, including one that resembled a monkey face. We were learning through our ITC contacts that a planet Marduk had once occupied an orbit next to Mars, and debris from the explosion of that planet might have destroyed existing civilizations on its closest neighbor: Mars.

"Can you hear from Timestream?"

Timestream, of course, was the principal spirit team involved in enhanced ITC contacts with experimenters such as myself. Its invisible members were responsible for most of the miraculous contacts that had been arriving in Europe since the mid-1980s, and starting in 1996 they were busy developing methods of penetrating the veil to reach my equipment, as I heard the name "Timestream" during many of my experiments.

"Time still passes here."

That no doubt referred to Arthur Beckwith's earlier message that time just seems to pass by from his perspective in a rather Earthlike realm of the spirit worlds.

"That was Bill Harman."

That message was apparently referring to the presence of Willis Harman during one particular experiment several months after his death from a brain tumor in January, 1997.

"Konrad the cat is Arthur's pet."

Our cat Konrad had been a proud, territorial, and much-loved family member until one autumn evening he died a quick, violent death in our backyard at the hands of a marauding raccoon. On various occasions after that I would hear the name "Konrad" and sometimes a faint "meow" come through the radio sounds during my experiments.

WHO'S CALLING WHOM?

A strange incident occurred in Greenwich, Connecticut, in the early spring of 1996. Juliet Hollister was in her car, and Alison van Dyk was at home in the kitchen. Juliet had used her car phone only once or twice since it was installed, and it had never rung. On that day it rang for the first time, and she answered, quite surprised. "Hello?"

"Hello? Juliet? Is that you?" came a familiar voice.

"Yes!" Juliet said, surprised. "Alison, is that you?"

"Yes," Alison replied. There was a pause, then she asked, "Juliet, did you call me?"

"Why no, didn't you call me?"

"No," replied Alison. Both women sat in silence for a moment trying to figure out what had just happened. Neither of them had called the other. Their phones had rung at the same time, and each had picked up to hear the voice of the other say, "Hello," almost in unison. So here they were on the phone with each other. Juliet was in her car. Alison was sitting in her kitchen as she exclaimed, "This is weird!"

"I think it's our dear friend Konstantin," Juliet said with a delightful laugh, and they hung up the phones.

A PHONE CALL FOR THE RECORD

On May 3, 1996, about 9:15 A.M., my phone rang, and I answered, "Continuing Life Research."

"This is Konstantin Raudive. How are you, Mark?" said the deep, familiar voice that seemed more relaxed than I had ever noticed.

I replied, "I'm very well, my friend, and how are you?"

"As I told Sarah already, I'm as well as a 'dead one' can be."

"That's great," I laughed.

"You can register, Mark."

"Okay, I have the recorder turned on."

"Thank you. You certainly have some questions to ask me. This is the first call I have to you when I am able to respond. It may be that the contact will break down in a few seconds, but we'll try to keep it open."

I closed my eyes to focus and relax. "It's just wonderful to talk to you. Can you tell me anything about Bill O'Neil's efforts with my ITC work?"

"About Bill O'Neil." Konstantin Raudive paused for a moment. I had the feeling he was quickly establishing a mental link to Bill O'Neil to get a progress report on his efforts. Then he continued, *"Well, he's going on a steady line. Together with Jeannette he continues his work, and we think that by the fall of this year you will have results."*

"That's fantastic; that's wonderful!" I exclaimed. I had been in contact with the spirit of Mr. O'Neil for several months through a system of radios. He had been creating noises from the speakers with increasing effectiveness, to the point where the words and phrases were generally comprehensible.

"You have already noticed the beginnings."

"I see. Yes, things are happening very well every morning during our experiments. Bill O'Neil is dedicated and tenacious."

"I understand."

"Can you tell me about the meeting?" I asked. "Is that coming together nicely?"

"You are speaking of the INIT meeting."

"Yes," I replied. I was in the process of planning our second meeting, this time to be held in Tarrytown, New York.

"It will turn out very fine, very much in harmony, which is a very important thing to do. It's prepared just as it should be prepared."

"I see. We are working very hard on this side to make things go smoothly," I said.

"We know about that, and we appreciate it very much. We know that there are many, many obstacles and difficulties. But we know that you are doing a very good job on this, and that's why this contact is being realized at the moment here."

"Ah, thank you very much."

"Well, see, Mark, you are only, let us say, points on an image. You and other INIT members are all on coordination points, so to speak, and our aim is to join these coordination points. Do you understand?"

"Yes, I think I understand," I replied. He was trying to explain to me how they monitored our work here on Earth from their otherworldly perspective. I imagined a large computer screen which portrayed our world not as a globe with lines of latitude and longitude, but as a large number of dots scattered about. The dots represented INIT members and supporters, subscribers to the newsletter, and readers of our books—everyone who had an interest in the work. The dots were of varying sizes, depending upon how deeply involved the individuals were in the work at the moment, and they were connected by lines representing the feelings, mutual awareness, collaboration, and communication among us on Earth. I asked, "These coordination points, I suppose they're working pretty well right now with all the people in INIT?"

"At this moment the best things have been done to now, from our point of view."

"As far as ITC progress here in Colorado, how soon do you think we'll be able to branch into TV contacts and computer contacts, or are we going to stick with voice for quite a while?"

"Well, as we see it, the first good voices will come through in the fall of this year, and it will develop on that."

"I see," I said, encouraged. Progress had seemed to be slow and difficult in our experiments in Colorado. "And the voices I think will probably be coming through the Spiricom system that Bill O'Neil is working on on the other side? On your side?"

"The essential problem will be to have this equipment built on frequency reception, and you'll get details from Bill O'Neil and us."

"Good. I'm thinking about incorporating subtle energy technology into this system on my side," I said. It had been my feeling for several years that the key to penetrating other dimensions would have to center around the so-called "subtle energies," such forces as Holy Spirit, chi, shakti, and orgone, which lie outside the electromagnetic spectrum and beyond the view of modern science. Our spirit friends had mentioned "rest energies" on several occasions, which are related to higher beings. They had told us that when images are sent to Earth from their worlds, it is the light from higher beings—presumably these rest energies—that provide the light source for the pictures. Perhaps the miraculous results of energy healings, hands-on, and spiritual healings also could be attributed in part to rest energies of higher beings. I hoped that I and other researchers would learn more about those and other forms of subtle energies, and would employ them in our ITC systems. "Does that sound like a good idea?"

"Why sure, a very good thought, but we suggest you wait for things that our group can tell you." Obviously such information cannot be acquired from ter-

restrial sources; it would require the commitment of higher beings directly to our work. I would have to be patient.

"Okay, can you tell me about equipment that you use to produce such a perfect, almost perfect voice here on Earth? That must take a lot of work on your side," I said. I already knew that they used equipment, but I wanted to know, if possible, how it was created, how it worked, and how it interacted with our equipment. Many people were unable to equate the spirit world with apparatuses and energy-driven devices, so I was reaching for information that would allow me to explain the situation clearly to a curious public. As far as I knew, there were no spirit-world factories; almost everything was conjured up by focused intentions, probably unconscious, on the part of our spirit friends. I wanted some verification on that and other preconceived notions on the part of my ITC colleagues and myself.

"Well, it depends on your reception, mainly on your psychic reception. Because you are much more psychic than others who claim to be."

"That surprises me," I said. Konstantin was trying to stress the fact that the minds of the communicators on both sides of the veil are far more important to ITC contacts than are the apparatuses on either side. But his comment about my psychic abilities caught me off guard and took the conversation off course for a moment. Up to that point in my life I had never regarded myself as a psychically gifted individual. I often felt inspired while writing, but I was never consciously aware of any specific personalities coming through my mind.

"Well, it's really not surprising."

I paused for a moment. Konstantin Raudive hadn't given me the answer I wanted—an explanation of how they used etheric spirit-world equipment to interact with our equipment—so I asked more directly, "Do you have actual equipment on your side, as well as the thoughts and the psyche?"

"Yes, you know that we use equipment," he replied. I could tell from his tone of voice that he was a bit uncomfortable with the fact that I had asked a question for which I already knew the answer. Still, I wanted solid evidence to share with the world; I wanted a direct voice from spirit stating that they use equipment and, hopefully, how that equipment interacted with ours. I was being rather stubborn.

Apparently in an effort to put the subject to rest, Konstantin continued, *"We intend to give plans of our equipment, to send them through Hans. We also want to give a sort of map of our world, and drop it into your world. It will be done in the coming weeks and months."*

"That's tremendous," I exclaimed. "That's wonderful. Do you have any messages that I can pass along to Hans Heckmann or George Meek or Sarah?"

"Well, yes, we wanted to contact them all, but we decided to contact you because you are for the moment the main experimenter, and you are the—I don't like the word 'leading person'—but you are the manager, so to speak. But please give our esteem to Sarah, to Hans, to George, and all of them. And we will contact them in time when it's useful, but for the moment you are the person we want to address. We also wanted to contact Alison and Juliet, but this is not the time to do so. We prefer to contact you because this is the bridge that has been strengthened to your location."

"Thank you very much," I said. Then I remembered the recent incident involving my friends Juliet Hollister and Alison van Dyk, and I wondered if Timestream had been responsible, as Juliet had suspected. "Juliet and Alison have had some very unusual things happening on their telephones. Like Juliet's car phone and Alison's home phone. Is that your doing?" I asked.

"As I told you," he replied, acknowledging the incident, *"we wanted to contact them, but now we prefer to focus our energies on your home and on your phone to give information because you are acting as some kind of manager for the moment."*

"Meeting coordinator or something. Yes."

"Yes. We have forty seconds left," he warned. The contact would actually last another two minutes and forty-five seconds, illustrating the difficulty our spirit friends have to contend with while interacting with our time-based reality on Earth.

"Okay," I acknowledged. "I too have tried to avoid the words 'leading' and 'managing.' It's not easy on Earth to develop social systems that are based on nonheirarchical . . ." I grasped for a word as thoughts rushed through my head. For some years I had been intrigued with political and social systems—the means by which people on Earth try to maintain peace and order while living together in large, diversified groups. My research had suggested that there were a few basic principles that were woven through all levels of physical life as we on Earth knew it, bringing order to cells and tissues within the human body, and those principles could do the same for society if we allowed them to extend outward into the family, and into communities, and farther outward into nations and religions.

Throughout my adult life I had been uncomfortable with the typical human social system of leaders and followers, owners and slaves, bosses and workers. To me it seemed demeaning to most people, and there had to be a better way. In the years before my cancer and my immersion in ITC, I had been looking for some kind of principles that could elevate human groups to a more gratifying state of existence. Much of my research and writing had been geared to a search for a new way that would displace the old hierarchical system that made some individuals superior over others.

"Don't try to avoid it, Friend Mark," Konstantin Raudive broke in, *"because these are systems implanted in your world and you will have to deal with them. It's very important you assume the role and then it will be done because it's only for the concourse."*

Later I had to look up this unfamiliar use of the word in Webster's Dictionary. "Concourse: An act or process of coming together and merging, a meeting produced by voluntary or spontaneous coming together." It was a perfect description of INIT!

"Okay," I said. "What we're trying to establish with INIT, I think, is more of a network on Earth as opposed to a hierarchical or bureaucratic type of organization. A network without a formal structure. I think that can be done with the Internet."

"That is a fact because you are one of the main points of this network. You are one big dot on it, do you understand? And from big dots like that there are departures for other dots. Smaller dots. And it's only from this big dot that ramifications may be made."

Again to the dictionary. "Ramification: An arrangement of branches." So, our invisible friends were monitoring INIT members as an actual web or network of interactions.

Konstantin Raudive continued, *"As you know, in our way we are working together on one thing, and that's what's important. We, our group, we were very honored to be able to contact you now, and we will continue in the future."*

"Okay. Wonderful!"

"This is the first contact to you that lasted more than eleven minutes."

"Time went by very quickly," I said, astonished. "I'll do everything I can to make this work."

"We know it, Mark. Without that, we wouldn't have contacted you. And don't be afraid of small, personal differences. Do you understand?"

"Yes," I replied automatically, not absorbing the full implications of his small, last-minute comment: *"Don't be afraid of small, personal differences."* Our spirit friends were aware of the human insecurities, fears, and doubts that stirred up personal differences among us. Situations that probably seemed inconsequential to them often had devastating effects on our lives for a while. I'd think about all this later, as troubles developed in INIT. To close my end of the conversation, I said, "Please convey my love to everyone at Timestream, especially Isar."

"Certainly, I certainly will do so. Good-bye, my friend."

"Good-bye, my friend."

"Good-bye."

Less than five minutes after that phone call ended, Konstantin called again to tie up some loose ends. He began by issuing the code word to help assure me of the legitimacy of the previous contact.

". . . the code word is 'silmarillion.' I repeat, the code word is 'silmarillion.'"

"I remember the word," I said.

"The word has been given already to Dr. Determeyer, Colleague Determeyer in Germany. I use it to verify the contact."

"I forgot to ask you about the word. Jules told me to expect that. So thank you very much."

"M-hm," Konstantin hummed an affirmation in a relaxed and comfortable tone, then paused. He had another message to convey. *"Well, it's awful that in Richmond, there's a six-year-old boy, and he has beaten his neighbor. His neighbor was a one-month-old boy 'Falding Matthew'(?). And this 'Felding Matthew'(?) has had brain damage because he was beaten by this neighbor of his in Richmond."*

I vaguely remembered something in the news recently about an incident in California, but I didn't recall any details. (Later I searched the Internet and found a series of articles about a one-month-old baby named Ignacio Bermudez who had been beaten by a six-year-old neighbor in Richmond, California, on April 22, 1996. I was certain this was the same case referred to by Konstantin Raudive, but why he referred to the infant as "Felding Matthew" remains a mystery to me even as this book goes to press.) I sighed at the tragic nature of the incident, and Konstantin apparently detected my sadness.

"I know," he said in an empathetic voice. *"So that's one of those things we want to prevent with ITC. The violence. Violence among our children. Because if kids are brought up with ethical, moral . . . ITC, you know?"*

Konstantin's comment simply halted at the word "moral," and then after a five-second interval continued with "ITC, you know?" I had heard similar lapses in conversation during dialogs with spirit beings. Apparently it requires a substantial effort on the part of our spirit friends to focus on the words. If their mind wanders even a little bit, the contact can break down for a moment.

"Yes, I understand completely," I assured my invisible friend. "The boy in Richmond who had brain damage: Is he now deceased and being healed on your side?"

"Well, the important thing is that we want to prevent such things as violence affecting kids."

I wasn't sure what to say, so I simply replied, "I will work very hard toward that."

"We know that, Mark. Swejen told me to recontact you . . ." [the next phrase faded quickly to a whisper and disappeared:] *"The energy level is going down at the moment."*

"I can tell."

[Disconnect.]

It was evident not only that Timestream wanted to convey that important message to the world about violence affecting our children, but they also wanted me to experience a contact in which their spiritside equipment ran out of energy. It seemed strange to hear a voice simply run out of steam that way.

SUBTLE ENERGIES ARE NOT SO SUBTLE

As years passed, it became apparent to me that the future of ITC would involve moving farther and farther beyond the borders of modern science and technology, into the realm of subtle energies which—as my friend, the frontier physicist Bill Tiller, points out—are not really very subtle.

Bill liked to paraphrase Einstein. "'Subtle is the Lord!' is not to say the

Lord is weak," he would say. Over dinner one evening in the fall of 1997 during a conference in Colorado hosted by the International Association of New Sciences, Bill told me that the effects of subtle energy seemed weak when we tried to measure them with modern scientific devices, but that was only because science had not yet really learned how to measure them. For modern science, measuring subtle energies was like measuring the heat of a gas furnace when only the pilot light is lit.

Or as Bill said, "I suspect that our future technology in this area will reveal latent energy content and utilizaton of such subtle fields that are many orders of magnitude larger than that due to any of our presently known physical fields."

In the closing years of the twentieth century, it was obvious that most of the phenomenal ITC contacts were the results of subtle energy manipulations on the part of our spirit colleagues.

To the question of what type of energy was used in ITC contacts, Timestream had once told the Harsch-Fischbach couple in Luxembourg that they used "orgon" and something called "rest energies," which they described as "pure, positive energies free of human influence." I suspected that these "rest energies" were a form of higher consciousness—the product of ethereal beings such as Technician. We had been told that ITC would not be possible today were it not for the enhanced abilities and energies of the higher beings.

We were being told that the evolution of ITC on Earth was approaching a third phase. New systems would be developed only if there first developed a unity among the various ITC researchers in various countries.

The first phase had been the establishment of an ITC test site, or what research and development companies in America called a "beta site." In high-tech industries, newly designed and developed products are thoroughly tested in a company lab, and then they are sometimes shipped to a factory or office somewhere else to be assembled and operated under normal working conditions. This location is called a "beta site." Apparently, starting in the mid-1980s our spirit friends had been busy developing ITC systems on their side of the veil and had selected the home of the Luxembourg couple as a "beta site" for the first fully functioning ITC receiving station. With guidance from Timestream spirit group, the Harsch-Fischbachs had developed crude but incredibly effective systems of TVs, radios, telephones, and computers for receiving information directly from their spirit friends.

The second phase of ITC development began in 1995 when we met in England and established an international association for ITC research. Improved contacts began to work their way across the veil after that.

We were now entering Phase Three—achieving the necessary unity of mind—and miracles were indeed under way. Fantastic contacts were pouring into our group because of the resonance we had developed among us. It was becoming apparent to me that the subtle energies employed by ITC were intertwined with our attitudes, beliefs, thoughts, and feelings. These vibrations generated by the human body-mind-spirit were some of the subtle energies that would shape our technologies in the new millennium. If INIT could remain stable in the future, it would mean that researchers had learned how to unite their activities and attitudes under the higher energies, and we would one day soon see miracles unfold on Planet Earth as never before in history.

The key would be to move the ego to the back and put the human spirit in the driver's seat.

SPIRIT COLLEAGUES ATTEND OUR SECOND MEETING

Throughout 1996 I was busy making plans for our second INIT meeting, this time to be held in Tarrytown, New York, the site that had inspired Washington Irving to write *The Legend of Sleepy Hollow.*

Shortly before the meeting was to begin, our spirit friends gave us some fascinating insights into their methods of interacting with us. They reported that they would be traveling in parallel in their world to a location similar to Tarrytown. It was not unusual for them to stay close to us during our trips, they said, consuming similar food and drink, and traveling in conveyances similar to the planes, trains, and automobiles in which we were traveling. They had to stay close and in sync with us to avoid losing us in time and space. As Timestream told Maggy Harsch-Fischbach:

We shed our astral body which, although very subtle from your perspective, is dense from our view. As we leave that dense body, we can merge with the environment, producing a most wonderful sensation. We float freely in a sense of oneness with nature and the air around us while maintaining our individual personality. We are neither happy nor sad. When we move to this state, it is diffi-

cult to return into the denser dimensions where humans reside. If you need us for something, we can detect that need which will have an effect similar to shaking us awake. Otherwise we become lost in time and space in a most wonderful way. Years of your time may pass by in a flash. We rarely allow ourselves to travel in this ethereal way since we have committed ourselves to work closely with you on this ITC project. Instead, we resort to transportation means which resemble your Earthlike conveyances.

Our meeting at Tarrytown went smoothly during the first full day. The primary purpose of these annual meetings, from the viewpoint of our spirit friends, was to achieve unity and resonance. The Dartington meeting had been a complete success. This year at Tarrytown I felt the same enthusiasm in the air. The fact that we were meeting again, sharing good feelings, discussing statutes for our new group, and reporting on ITC progress and projects under way in our various countries was a catalyst for miracles. If the good feelings prevailed through the weekend, they would make the contact field clear, and so our spirit colleagues would be able to move more effectively in and out of our lives in the coming months to assist in our projects.

As we adjourned the meeting, everyone left for home with a warm glow. None of us knew then that some of the greatest miracles of all would be unfolding in our small, scattered group in the coming months. Nor did we know of three tragedies that would offset the miracles. Nor did we know that all our members would start to polarize into separate, incompatible factions, causing a buildup of friction that would soon erupt.

First, the tragedies: Our coordinator Hans Luethi would develop a severe case of phlebitis and would have to relinquish his role in our group (and we would vote in Dale Palmer as his replacement). Then, our good friend and quiet supporter, Willis Harman, would die from a brain tumor in January 1997. Independent experimenter Adolf Homes would die of lung cancer in October.

Following are some of the miracles that flowed into our lives in the coming months:

- Spirit colleague Richard Francis Burton, nineteenth-century author and explorer, delivered a letter to the computer of Maggy Harsch-Fischbach reporting on his visit to a Native American medicine man named Red

Jacket in his spirit world house next to his medicine wigwam. That forged closer bonds between my research team in Colorado and a Native American spirit group, who accepted an invitation from Burton to move closer to the Timestream station. From that position the Native American group would play a valuable role in maintaining the integrity of our contact bridge in the coming years (November 28, 1996).

- Maggy Harsch-Fischbach received her first color picture through computer. It showed the face of one of The Seven higher beings. Accompanying the picture was a letter from the being which told us that doubt can be justified, resulting in enlightenment, or it can be a poisoning force that creates dissonance in a group. It can lead to a life of adventure or a life of confusion (February 26, 1997).

- Again through Luxembourg we received a report from a young man named Arthur Moos describing his violent death in 1945 when a bomb exploded just ahead of the farmer's carriage in which he was riding. In spirit he instantly entered a silent darkness where he remained for fifty years, which seemed to blend together and pass by in no time at all. Then he heard lovely music, saw a violet vortex, and moved toward the light. Floating into the light he saw a lush valley and majestic mountains come into focus, and he wept like a child at the sheer beauty. He then joined Timestream spirit group (July 7, 1997).

- During a phone dialog with Timestream, Maggy Harsch-Fischbach was told of parallel worlds existing in the same physical space with the Earth, but at different vibration. Locating Earth among the many other flourishing worlds was sometimes difficult for our spirit colleagues when they wanted to get in touch with us (July 1997).

- Willis Harman, late president of IONS, became involved in ITC from beyond the veil in order to continue his direct, intentional support of our work and his efforts to help science and humanity out of their present darkness. Maggy Harsch-Fischbach received a computer letter from The Seven higher beings, who said, *"INIT is going strong . . . Famous names have joined those who already followed the path of light. Willis Harman has now completed his transition. He intends to work closely with the group who is trying to contact Mark Macy. Group Landell in Brazil is not far from a breakthrough. If all of you continue on a close collaboration, we will see that the contact field will grow clearer and contacts will improve. We, The Seven, accompany you with our thoughts"* (August 9, 1997).

- A day after Adolf Homes died, he was able to place a phone call to his friend and colleague Fritz Malkhoff. *"I just want to announce myself briefly,"* he said. *"Do you hear me, Fritz? Just want to announce myself. I have terrible pain. I arrived here together with the young fellow who was at the motorcycle rally."*

Fritz was not only stunned for the moment by the phone call from his old friend Adolf Homes so soon after his death, but also a bit puzzled by the opening message. "Which young fellow?" he asked.

"The young one who was killed at the motorcycle rally."

"Where did you say he was killed?" asked Malkhoff, still confused.

"Near the town of Fell. You know, near Fell, Osburg-Osburg. Just want to tell you briefly. I am now here in 'Ahau.' It is true, Fritz, just like we always imagined. Things go on. The fellow from Osburg is saying something. He is with me. The one who was shot, who was shot dead, is with me. I am speaking to you."

"Yes, okay."

"I am going to sleep now," said Homes, obviously exhausted.

"Yes, all right," said Malkhoff with empathy.

"Excuse me . . ." concluded Homes, the remaining words trailing off into incoherent mumbles.

TECHNICAL SUPPORT FROM BEYOND, FEBRUARY 6, 1998

I was working in the office when the phone rang in my lab in the next room. Walking to the phone and picking it up, I was delighted to hear the deep, familiar voice of spirit friend Konstantin Raudive. I told him it was great to be able to speak with him again, and I pushed the Record button on the tape recorder that I keep next to the phone.

"I can give you advice for your research," Konstantin said in his characteristic heavy, Northern European accent.

"Okay, thank you!" I exclaimed.

"You should purCHAZE the VLF receiving converter," he said, mispronouncing the word "purchase."

"The receiving converter," I said, repeating the only part of the message I had understood. "Okay."

"It's called the VLF receiving converter," he corrected me.

Still not understanding, I replied, "Oh, the LF receiving converter. Okay."

"It's a receive-radio-navigation beacon, using standard frequencies, and so on," Dr. Raudive began to explain.

"I don't fully understand," I said, "but I'm going to pass this information along to people who *will* understand."

There was a faint click on the line, indicating the connection had ended. I sighed and placed the phone on the hook. I hoped the message on the recorder would answer some of the many questions in my mind and fill in enough holes to provide some direction for my research. But I had my doubts, considering the brevity of the conversation.

Seconds later, before I even had time to replay the message, the phone rang again. The tape recorder was still recording. I knew it was Timestream, so I picked it up and said expectantly, "Yes?"

"I'll try to make it clearer this time," said Konstantin Raudive.

"Okay," I replied.

"A V-L-F receiving converter," he spoke slowly. *"It's a receive-radio-navigation beacon, and you have standard frequencies—ship-to-shore, and European 'Al-value' broadcasts. You have also a one-seventy-five-meter, license-free band. You can have a converter. You simply connect the VLF converter to your HF radio's antenna input and a suitable VLF antenna. Then you convert the entire VLF band—let's say ten kilohertz to fifty kilohertz—up to four-oh-one-oh to four-five-oh-oh kilohertz respectively."*

"Okay!" I exclaimed. "Wonderful!"

"This is technical advice from our side."

"Thank you very much, Konstantin," I said, "Um . . ." I paused, expecting him to give the code word in order to verify the contact. Also, there was a matter that had been weighing heavily on my mind in recent weeks. There were serious troubles developing among a few INIT members that had many of us concerned. Although I was not consciously thinking about these troubles, Dr. Raudive apparently dug up those feelings from my unconscious.

"I do not want to speak for the moment of the actual problems you have. I will speak on that in the future message."

"I understand. Can you give me the code word?" I asked.

"It's 'silmarillion,'" he said.

"Thank you very much," I said, as the contact ended.

At the time of that contact, there were four members of my experimental team in Colorado who met with me every week for ITC sessions. Rich Hastings was a retired senior engineer, and his wife Judy was a Reiki master teacher—Reiki being a Japanese method of energy healing. Both had been on a spiritual path for more than two decades, allowing them to fit in quickly to ITC research. Rich had maintained an analytical mind, which helped keep our group grounded. Rich and Judy lived about three miles from our home, so it was an easy five-minute commute to the meetings.

Kay Nelsen lived about twenty miles away. She was probably the most psychically attuned or sensitive member of our group, and her intuition provided a guiding light. She was an experienced taper, having collected spirit voices for several years. Kay was a medical transcriptionist when she first joined the group. Listening to doctors' recorded diagnoses on audiotape and typing them into a computer gave her excellent qualifications for voice experiments through radio. Not only did she have the right equipment for playing back tapes at various speeds, but she had developed a sensitive ear that could distinguish nuances in voices.

Quite often during our experiments, Kay would be the first to hear spirit voices coming through the radio sounds. In 1998 she phased out of medical transcriptions and opened a website called "The World's Best New Age Auction." She began taking car trips with her husband or with her son and daughter-in-law to various states to buy gems and crystals to replenish her stock of items which she made available through her website, and it quickly became a busy, lucrative, and exciting enterprise for Kay. Fortunately she kept our meetings as a high priority in her busy schedule.

Steve S. was our group's bachelor. He was a computer consultant who lived about sixty miles away in the mountains. Making it to our meetings every week was a major commitment for him, especially in the wintertime when the mountain roads were often icy and hazardous. Like the other three, Steve was excited about ITC research. With the tenacity of a postman, he often weathered storms to get to our weekly meetings. He and Rich together provided most of the technical expertise to our group.

It was natural, then, after I received the contact from Konstantin Raudive, that these two fellows would understand the message immediately and begin to track down the necessary equipment—a VLF converter, an appropriate antenna, and the necessary couplers. Steve contacted the Crane company, which publishes a small but extensive catalog of unusual electronic devices. Through the Crane company he was able to find an independent developer of electronic equipment who happened to make VLF converters exactly matching the specifications provided by Dr. Raudive. It would convert radio signals of the very-low-frequency (VLF) range of 10 to 500 KHz, into high-frequency (HF), shortwave signals of 4010 to 4500 KHz, which could come through my radios. I called the developer—Palomar Engineers in Escondido, California—and purchased one of the converters.

After some research, Rich learned that VLF radios were used extensively by submarines. Apparently along the coastlines of the United States and other countries one could find strange fields set aside for long wires of various sizes to be strung across the ground, some of them longer than a football field. These were VLF antennas, which picked up radio signals from submarines.

When I learned that, I began to get a little nervous. We live in a quiet neighborhood of houses built rather closely together. Laying a 1,300-foot piece of wire through the neighbors' yards or down the street certainly would not have made me popular.

"Maybe we can run a wire along the fence," Rich suggested at one of our meetings in the spring of 1998. There was a wooden privacy fence in our backyard, which enclosed the neighborhood. It extended about 100 feet to the west, then turned south for several blocks.

"The trouble is," he said, "the antenna has to run in one direction for about 1,300 feet."

"I guess we'll have to run it all the way west, then turn the corner south for another 1,300 feet," said Rich.

I got a little nervous again. "What do I tell the neighbors when they see us nailing the antenna onto the fence?" I asked.

After some thought, Rich smiled and suggested, "You can tell them it's for Aaron's science project." My son had called Rich a few months earlier for technical advice for one of his science projects.

We all laughed, then I said, "You know, it might work."

I thought of another possibility. The lake across the street from our house was partially surrounded by a wood-frame fence that ran almost due east for nearly a quarter mile. There was brush on either side of the fence, so there would probably be no one near enough to the fence at any time to even notice a small wire extending about three hundred feet along its length. I told Rich and Steve about that possibility.

"The trouble with that idea," I said, already having considered the pros and cons, "is getting the wire across Washington Street." The antenna lead would have to run from the lab window, across the busy street, over to the fence at the lake. If the wire were left in the street, it would be run over by hundreds of cars each day.

"We'd probably have to put a coupler at the edge of the street so we could connect the antenna for our meetings, and disconnect it afterward," Rich suggested. Things were getting complicated, and that made me uneasy.

In the coming days, Rich purchased a reel of antenna wire, Steve acquired some couplers, and I called the designers of the VLF converter at Palomar Engineers, to see if we'd forgotten anything. I said we were acquiring all the necessary equipment, but we were having a problem with the antenna.

I said, "We've read several articles on VLF, and they all say we need long horizontal antennas. I live in a neighborhood where that's not real practical. Do you have any other ideas?"

"Oh, we've found that you don't really need those long antennas the Navy uses," the engineer said.

"What?" I was delighted by his answer, but surprised.

"Right," he explained, "we've found that a twenty- or twenty-two-foot vertical antenna works just as well. In fact, it works better."

I couldn't believe it.

"Are you sure?" I asked. "Everything we've read—"

"I'm sure," he interrupted. "We've tested plenty of these converters. A twenty-foot vertical antenna works fine."

This was too good to be true. All we'd need to do was set up a twenty-foot pole with appropriate antenna wire attached to it. That went against all the documentation we'd found on VLF radios. I wondered if any other VLF radio users or designers knew about this, or had we stumbled upon the only source of this information? In any event, I was deeply relieved.

I asked him about the type of wire that would work best. His reply: basic copper wire. Insulated wire would be fine, but not coaxial cable; the metal mesh used as shielding around the wire would inhibit the wire's ability to resonate with the radio waves.

When I broke the good news to the group, everyone was relieved by the solution to our problem and eager to get started. I purchased some plastic tubing that would make an adequate pole, Rich brought his roll of antenna wire, and Steve provided the couplers.

When the system was completed, we began an experimental session with tremendous anticipation. It would have been great if the voices of our spirit friends suddenly boomed loudly and clearly into the lab.

No such luck. There was no sudden, overwhelming breakthrough as we all had hoped. In the coming weeks, though, I did notice a gradual improvement in quality of both the tiny EVP voices and the loud modulations of radio noises into voicelike sounds. Progress was being made, but it was slower than we'd hoped.

We all knew we were moving in the right direction, thanks to the advice from our spirit colleagues.

A year after assembling the VLF system specified by our spirit friends, a contact with George Meek was made on Sunday, February 14, 1999, at 2:30 A.M. He had died January 5, 1999. Occasionally I would receive responses to my questions and comments. I was taping one Sunday morning at 2:30 when a voice broke through, saying, *"Good luck, Mark."*

"It sounded like you said, 'Good luck'!" I exclaimed.

"I did," said the voice.

I muttered, half to myself, "I'll play it back in a moment while listening to the phone."

"This is George Meek," said a voice that was vaguely familiar. *"Hello!"*

I didn't understand the final words and so didn't realize it was my old friend George Meek. I waited for a few minutes for more comments through the radio-telephone system. None came through, so I said, "I'm going to close down now to play this back. Do you have any final comments in the next ten seconds?"

"No," came the reply.

Chapter 7

SCIENCE, SPIRIT, AND THE STORM

MIRACLES BEFORE THE STORM

For the first two years of INIT's existence, the contacts we received were not only miraculous, but absolutely stunning. Images of exotic, kind, wise, and playful beings from other worlds were planted on computer hard drives. A picture of a magnificent temple in the spirit worlds was also delivered in this fashion. A letter accompanied that picture, reporting that the famous French science fiction author Jules Verne had awakened in the temple after his death. After a difficult end of his life marred by rheumatism, gout, diabetes, and blindness, he suddenly found himself among aromatic fountains, solid silver furniture, and tanned dancing girls dressed in skintight, blue and orange silk clothes inquiring as to his desires. He was free of pain, and he was overwhelmed by the heavenly sensations of it all.

Ethereal beings sent a letter, again via computer, describing the death process here on Earth from their perspective:

When your lives end, and we come to lie beside you in the final moments, to comfort you, we sometimes find you in a hurry to tie up loose ends and to sweep the clutter of a lifetime under the carpet. Relax, children! We don't come to judge, only to bring you home. A single lifetime is but a moment in the day of your larger life. Your transition from Earth is a natural process. Lighten your hearts, show each other the real you, share each other's burdens, and don't make this important moment difficult for yourself or for each other. Relax.

An ancient Chinese physician named Yang Fud-se sent a self-portrait and letter. He said he had lived in the Chinese capital of Yo Lang during the reign of Shun Ti, around A.D. 150 to 200. He said that our group faced similar problems to those he had faced as a delegate of the king. He had been assigned to investigate reports of spirit communication and healing in the surrounding lands, and to distinguish fraud from genuine miracles. He warned us of obstacles in the path of our group in the form of doubt and skepticism, and he urged us to stay united in order to remain strong in the coming months and years.

An ancient Dane named Skoldung reported that he had been a Viking poet on Earth twelve hundred years ago, and since then was living happily in a small village in the "snow-land" of Marduk, which was within traveling distance of the "summerland." One day in 1986 Earth time he was surprised to find a strangely dressed man lying on the ground near his village, dripping blood into the snow from two wounds. The wounds quickly healed, the man's agony faded away, and he began to ask where he was, where was Stockholm, and where was Lisbeth. Skoldung knew nothing of Stockholm or Lisbeth, and could not answer. After the healed man calmed down, he introduced himself as Olof Palme, the world leader and Swedish prime minister who had been assassinated on February 28, 1986, in Stockholm.

An African tribesman named Bwele M'Banga sent a self-portrait and reported that his life on Earth had ended in the stomach of an African lion. Now he was a close friend of Sir Richard Francis Burton (1821–90), the English explorer. The two men led expeditions around the spirit worlds to explore new realms.

Burton himself sent several reports of his expeditions. One report came after INIT members had received a series of disturbing contacts from a negative spirit group. Burton's team scaled a mountain to a cave, where they found a holy man whose face was morphing from male to female, to small child, wise old man, young black woman, Native American, Eskimo, and a fat Chinese man. The being was all these individuals and more. The higher being told the visitors:

INIT faces troubles from people who are unable to understand the miracles. They don't want to understand the miracles because they are so full of themselves and their written ideas that there is no room inside themselves for the truth. The limits of the ego and physical brain will continue to be an obstacle to ITC, but when these narrow individuals eventually move to new lives elsewhere, they will grasp more in a moment than any truths which words on Earth could possibly convey to them at the present time. Meanwhile, their negative crusades will draw negative influences into the work. Unity among INIT members will keep INIT on a positive path.

Miracles being experienced by our members were made possible by the resonance we felt among us, and they were fueled by our positive feelings—inspiration, wonder, and delight. The contacts received between 1995 and 1997 were so incredibly good that minds were boggled—not only minds outside of our group, but also the minds of a few INIT members.

THE STORM ERUPTS, 1998–99

In the fall of 1997 we began to receive messages from The Seven higher beings about doubts, fears, and other negative feelings that were slowly developing within our group. The messages were vague, not mentioning names. Apparently our spirit friends expected the information to resonate with the appropriate individuals, who would make the necessary adjustments within themselves and among each other to keep our group strong and vital.

Unfortunately, I (and I suspect the other members as well) did not understand the messages with a high enough degree of certainty to take the appropriate steps that would heal our ailing group. As a result, destructive forces generated by doubts, insecurities, fears, envy, resentment, and other negative feelings began to fester within INIT, slowly dividing the group into factions. The factions were like tumors growing in the tissues of INIT, and with time, the sickness was allowed to grow out of control.

A number of people were hurt badly during the crisis, and there is still healing going on at the time I write this book, so I'll not mention names of people involved in the storm as it erupted internationally, involving most INIT members. If painful memories are stirred up even by this general account, I apologize to my friends, colleagues, and former colleagues.

Here is the storm as I perceived it then:

First, some members began to express doubts about various aspects of the research in their correspondence with each other. The doubts grew naturally, as they often do within us humans, but they were fed by scientists and skeptical colleagues with whom those members were in contact in their research, leading to a public questioning of the legitimacy of certain contacts received by other members.

The receivers of the contacts apparently felt as though they had been accused of fraud. They launched an aggressive counterattack with an intensity that seemed excessive to many neutral members, who backed away from the situation and observed nervously.

Psychologists have found that aggressive behavior is often the result of insecurities, which may or may not have been the case here. In any event, the resulting dissonance from the situation badly disrupted the group's contact field, and contacts slowly began to diminish.

Very often in human affairs, doubts and insecurities can become rather toxic, leading to fear, envy, resentment, and aggressive behavior that tear at the fabric of human organizations. The effects seem to be amplified when the group is pursuing spiritual quests, which seem to be more sensitive than worldly pursuits and more susceptible to damage from negativity.

As a result of this core conflict, feelings on both sides of the Atlantic were hurt very deeply, friendships as well as hearts were broken, and some members left the group. The dissonance among members and former members caused the contact field to become cloudy or opaque, according to our spirit colleagues, and they had an increasingly difficult time trying to get contacts through to our equipment.

Next, there followed a spread of misinformation by some former INIT members. Remaining members reacted in different ways to the misinformation, depending on the nature of their doubts, fears, and insecurities, but there were many volatile reactions that further weakened the group.

Realizing that the shrinking group was seriously ill, a few influential members took the reins and assumed, mistakenly, that a firm hand was needed. The majority of this leading group began to make demands, some of them irrational, of the remaining members. For instance, they demanded that INIT members not fraternize with other researchers who were not members, even if some of those researchers were old friends.

The field of enhanced ITC research in general, and INIT in particular, had attracted individual researchers who were intelligent, strong-willed, and discerning. People like that are generally ill at ease in the midst of autocracy and bullying. Several members complained, but most members just quietly turned their backs on the group—no letters of resignation, just a turning away as people began to feel intimidated.

It was a horrific time for INIT. It became impossible to maintain the needed resonance to allow ITC contacts to occur to the degree they had occurred in the past.

As the miracles faded within INIT, some former members took the opportunity to undermine the reputations and credibility of some existing members, suggesting that numerous contacts were faked—contacts which I knew to be genuine.

If there was any hope for the miracle of ITC to spread on Earth, the individual researchers who were involved with the miracle (including myself) would first have to undergo the inner work necessary to overcome the doubts, the fears, the insecurities, the envy, and the mistrust that blocked miracles and undermined our group. The Seven higher beings had told us that such negative feelings were unavoidable aspects of life in our world and, dealt with appropriately, could make life an adventure. But if allowed to fester, they would become a poison. Somehow, someday ITC researchers would have to achieve resonance among ourselves and with our ethereal friends, but the chances of that happening in the months following the conflict of 1997–99 seemed impossible.

Now we'll take a look at the storm in a bit more detail as it developed here in the States and pulled me in. Misinformation spread, stirring up negative feelings and blemishing some reputations, including mine. I hope that exposing light carefully on the facts will set things straight.

STORM IN THE STATES

It was in the spring of 1998 when I phoned Dale Palmer. Toxic doubts and insecurities had already triggered the initial eruption of INIT. Fear was now rampant in our destabilized group as many present and past members were licking their wounds. Palmer had assembled a new organization called GAIT (Global Association for Instrumental Transcommunication). He gathered up some of the former members of INIT and other people interested in ITC, apparently in order to forge ahead with a more open-door style of world

ITC and to pursue a scientific project which he envisioned. My hope was that INIT and GAIT could now proceed along our separate paths without muddying each other's way. That's what I hoped to achieve by calling Dale Palmer, but right from the start, the tone of the conversation dashed my hopes.

"I'll tell you something, Mark. You need to get some advice, and I'm talking about legal advice."

"Why do you say that?" I asked.

"I think you're terribly naive sometimes," Palmer replied. "When you get stuff like that, and you reproduce that, and you send it through the United States mail, and then you use that to raise money . . . do you know what they call that in the United States, Mark?"

I had the feeling he was accusing me of fraud then, and also a few minutes later when he reiterated, "One of the things that bothers me a great deal is that you really don't know whether this dialog that's coming out of Luxembourg is valid or not, and yet you reproduce that and send it out to hundreds of people."

I asked, "You're referring to the contacts they receive?"

"The contacts they *say* they receive," he replied.

I countered, "Of course they're valid! There's plenty of good, solid evidence. Very often the contacts they receive in Luxembourg are verified by contacts in other locations. Sometimes they receive pictures through their computer that are received at the same time through a television, say, in Germany."

Such cross-contacts were not mere coincidence; we were working with a team of highly competent spirit colleagues, most of whom had lived on Earth and were acquainted with human doubts and skepticism. So our spirit friends would meticulously plan such contacts, working hard to adjust to our sense of time, in order to provide reassuring evidence of the legitimacy of our collaborative efforts.

"Mm," he hummed what sounded like a note of skepticism.

I thought he'd known all this; I'd published it all in the INIT journal, as I reminded him. "These contacts are fully documented, and there's no doubt in my mind of their legitimacy. I've studied the contacts, I've gotten to know the researchers, I've observed the experiments firsthand, and I've talked to many people—scientists, reporters, and others—who've witnessed the contacts in Luxembourg with very discerning eyes and who attest to the legitimacy of those contacts. Before you start saying the work is false," I warned him, "you ought to talk to more experts like Senkowski."

"Mark, I'm not going to say the work is false. How could I say the work is false?"

"Well, that's what you've been implying," I said. "When you ask that question: 'Why would they resist an authentication project unless—'"

"It's a valid question, Mark," Dale broke in. He told me that he had accepted the claims of the Harsch-Fischbach couple of Luxembourg until they had refused to cooperate in Palmer's proposed authentication of their work. The resulting fury on the couple's part apparently had led Palmer to believe that they were trying to hide something. Now, although he wasn't coming out and stating directly that the Harsch-Fischbach couple were involved in a hoax, I certainly had the feeling he was implying it pretty strongly when he asked his question that way: "Now why do you suppose . . . ?"

I reminded him, "As a lawyer you're trained to frame things to lead people to certain conclusions, and when you ask people the question that way, you're leading them to the conclusion that the work is false. In legal circles, in the courtroom it may be totally ethical and right to do that, but in the real world I think you're pressuring people to draw conclusions that you know could be harmful to other people."

Palmer had made it clear since being asked to leave INIT that he held low regard for the conduct of the Harsch-Fischbach couple. He said, "I've been around people like that all my life, but I don't have to be anymore. I'm retired, and I prefer not to be around those people."

He continued, "Mark, you can talk for fifty years, and you can never justify, I don't think even to yourself, the way they have treated X—.

"X— is not the first one they've treated that way," Dale said angrily. "They treated Senkowski the same way, not once, but over and over and over again. I *am* in contact with him, by the way, and I *have* been, and he *is* involved in my project."

Well, that was news to me. Had Palmer really talked to Senkowski? If so, hadn't he asked the German physicist about the legitimacy of the couple's work? Ernst was like a growing number of researchers—he had been alienated by the couple's behavior, but he had no doubts about the legitimacy of the general results of their work, especially those experiments he had observed firsthand. Certainly Ernst Senkowski would have assured Dale that the contacts were legitimate. Somehow the pieces weren't fitting into the puzzle.

"My God," Palmer continued, "if you can't see all the hurt and deception that they have sowed. You talk about ruining INIT—if you think I'm the one that's hurting INIT, Mark, you're sadly mistaken."

"No," I countered. "No, you're definitely hurting INIT. When you call it a cult on your way out and—"

"I call it a cult because I think it is a cult," Dale interrupted. "It's run on adoration of a person or persons. Now that's a damn cult."

"There's no adoration particularly," I argued. "What ties us together is the respect for the contacts that are coming through, and the knowledge and an understanding of the high spiritual level from which these contacts are coming." Personalities and egos aside, INIT was in my estimation the most important organization in the world for the type of work it was doing. We had been receiving actual letters via computer and phone calls from departed loved ones and colleagues sharing with us in spectacular detail the absolute wonders and splendid beauty they had encountered after they had died and then awakened in the spirit worlds. We had received contacts from angels who had accompanied humanity for many thousands of years and had shared with us valuable insights into our world and our lives from their timeless perspective. Nowhere else in the world—perhaps at no other time in history—had such insightful information ever been received directly from the spirit worlds, without filtering by the human mind.

"I don't think it's that much of a cult," I continued. "If I were going to make a comparison, I guess I'd consider the founding of INIT to be kind of like the founding of the United States with its Constitution."

"Oh my God, Mark," Dale exclaimed, making it apparent to me that the comparison had the ring of blasphemy in his ears.

"That's right," I continued. "People have come together with a higher principle for a higher purpose, and they're trying to see it, amid conflict, come to life on the planet," I said. "There are some really noble ideas coming through INIT. I'm sorry you never saw that part of it."

Palmer changed the course of the dialog as he said, "You sent a copy of that tape to IONS, Mark, and that is a tape of a phone call you received, and you don't have the slightest idea in the world whether that's authentic or not. You think you do, but the fact is that you don't."

"Well, I'm reasonably certain," I argued, explaining that many phone calls from Timestream spirit group had been verified by cross-contacts via computer. For example, I reminded him that Timestream had called George Meek and me by telephone in January, and shortly after that had delivered a message to the computer of Adolf Homes in Germany, confirming those specific phone calls. "And the computer of Adolf Homes was hooked up to nothing but a printer and the power outlet in the wall," I continued, stressing the fact that Homes's computer had no connections whatsoever to the Internet nor to any other terrestrial sources of information. "Now unless Homes was involved in perpetrating a hoax, I'd say there's a pretty good chance those phone calls are legitimate."

That caused Dale Palmer to pause a moment. Then he said, "I'm intrigued by this, Mark, but I'm skeptical. You're intrigued by it, but you're not skeptical. That's the difference between us."

"I'm discerning, but I'm not skeptical," I replied. "If I was skeptical, I would never have received any phone calls."

"Mm."

"It's really as simple as that, as far as I understand it," I said. "In spirit matters, it's not a case of, 'I'll believe it when I see it,' but 'I'll see it when I believe it.' That's true in religions as well as spiritual and esoteric type pursuits. When you *believe* something to be true, and you have the *intent* for it to happen, then that opens the doors to its happening." In my experience in ITC research it had become clear to me that one of the primary laws in the spirit worlds as well as on Earth is: Our thoughts and intentions create our reality. Even quantum physics was beginning to zero in on that crucial law as a basic principle of life.

"Well, Mark, I'm a great believer that it's a subjective universe in which we live," Dale conceded. "I've put that in print for thousands of people to see." Palmer was apparently referring to his book, *True Esoteric Traditions*.

Returning to the subject of scientific authentication of spirit communication, Dale said, "Listen to me for just a moment. In Luxembourg they have a fax machine. It's about a third the size of my own fax machine. It's a very small fax machine. Lots of material comes out of that fax machine."

Indeed, Maggy Harsch-Fischbach had recently reported receiving a series of most fascinating spirit contacts by fax, including a three-page letter from the famous French science fiction writer Jules Verne. Those contacts had bog-gled some minds.

Dale Palmer continued, "That material is sent to you, and you print it in your *Contact!,* and you distribute that. Now, Mark Macy, I proposed about the first of December that . . . we put that fax machine in a Faraday cage, un-hook it from its electric supply, and battery-power it. This would be one of the simplest scientific tests that could ever be done. It doesn't take a hundred thousand dollars to do this, does it? All you have to do is put that [fax ma-chine] on a battery and put it inside of a microwave oven."

Quietly, inside myself, I believed that such a test could work under the right conditions. A microwave oven is like a Faraday cage; it has a grid of wiring around it which blocks electromagnetic radiation (for example, radio waves) from passing in or out of the oven. If an electronic receiver were put into a Faraday cage, with no inputs from terrestrial sources, and if it received information, then assumedly that information would be coming from sources beyond the Earth. But the conditions would have to be right for such an ex-periment. Mainly, there would have to be an enthusiastic and optimistic frame of mind on the part of everyone involved in the experiment—a reso-nance among them. Without resonance, a test of that type might easily fail. A conventional scientific approach most likely would not achieve the needed resonance.

"And within two weeks I am public enemy number one," Dale contin-ued, referring to the fact that the Luxembourg couple were furious with him. "Now why?" Again, he seemed to me to be implying that the couple were trying to hide something, which I knew was not the case.

"Well, for one thing," I replied, "you've kind of strayed away from the course that Maggy and Jules were trying to pursue with their work. They've been involved with scientists before who want to do this verification . . ." In-deed, a number of people had proposed some rather lavish experiments in order to verify Maggy's work, and over the years she had grown weary from the requests. Her spirit friends had provided ample proof of the legitimacy of their contacts, and they too were getting tired of spinning their wheels. Per-haps scientifically minded people should do what others were doing: simply open their eyes, broaden their worldview, and observe what's been done. At that point science would have a crucial role in ITC. Meanwhile, for modern scientists or pseudoscientists to insist on authenticating a spiritual practice such as enhanced ITC under their guidelines would be like a blind man insisting on giving the official description of a beautiful sunset. Conventional science lacked both the concepts and the instruments to explore the miraculous fruits of higher spirit.

"Mark, Mark, Mark," Dale pushed his way into the thoughts I was trying to express.

"Yeah?"

He spoke slowly now that he'd captured my attention. "Don't you understand that if what they're saying could be scientifically authenticated, it would be the greatest breakthrough in knowledge the world has ever known?"

"That's not a priority of theirs," I said simply. "They have a priority of opening the doors between a troubled Earth and a world where there's a great deal more wisdom than we have here."

"Well," he argued, "an extraordinary thing requires extraordinary proof, and the thing is, the scientific apparatus is readily available to prove whether or not it's true."

Palmer was mistaken. I said, "The facilities that make ITC possible, and the energies that make it possible, are far beyond science. Science doesn't have the capability to really judge the validity of ITC yet."

We had been told by our spirit colleagues that the contacts, while coming through electromagnetic devices on Earth, were actually made possible by a variety of so-called "subtle energies" present in their world. Such subtle energies as chi, shakti, and orgon are discussed by specialists outside the borders of modern science today, but scientists ignore such forces which cannot be perceived or manipulated by modern scientific instruments. That will most likely change in the early years of the twenty-first century, but for now there was a wide chasm between science and spirit.

When our conversation ended, neither of us having budged on our positions, I placed the receiver back on the hook and shook my head.

Serious troubles lay ahead because of a deep rift among ITC researchers. The rift was largely a reflection of the centuries-old chasm between science and spirit, between doubt and faith.

Looking back on the situation, I believe that everyone in INIT was in favor of a scientific project, but the nature of such a project was the real issue. Those who were closest to the core—that is, those who were most closely attuned to The Seven higher beings and to spirit group Timestream—favored a collaboration among scientists and ITC researchers toward the aim of opening the doorway between our world and positive spirit worlds in order to achieve greater understanding of the larger scheme of things. That core group was built around the miracles being experienced by the Harsch-Fischbach couple. I was in that group. I was not interested in an ITC authentication project, which I considered to be little more than a manifestation of doubt. I had learned from experience that harboring doubt during ITC research was like tossing a wet rag on fiery embers.

TROUBLED WATERS

Throughout 1998 and into 1999, inaccurate information spread throughout world ITC. Implications of fraud were leveled at various researchers whose work I knew to be legitimate. Again, I'll narrow the focus to events that originated in the States and affected me personally. Dale Palmer told researchers that

- people were accusing me of "charlatanism"
- he and Willis Harman had conversed in private to have Palmer "check out" my work
- he and Willis Harman both considered the paranormal phone calls "practical jokes" after I initially reported them to Willis, and
- Palmer himself was a "world authority" on paranormal phone calls.

Palmer was mistaken.

- Me, a charlatan? As an ITC researcher, I'd always had a reputation of being honest. No one, to my knowledge, had ever accused me of fraud, and I was sure that if someone had actually suggested that to Palmer, then that someone had no personal experience and knowledge of enhanced ITC. And they certainly had never gotten to know me nor my work.
- Willis Harman assigning Palmer to "check out" my work? To me, that sounded like collusion. Some of the people who had been closest to

Willis Harman informed me that he would never have asked anyone to investigate someone else. It was not his style. He was open and frank in his dealings with other people. I knew Willis Harman to be open and honest. For example, for years I would read my presentations before live audiences because I had so much information to convey. Well, reading a script almost always sounds mechanical and stripped of emotion. Thousands of people had heard me speak in this way, and only one person had ever come forward and told me directly that my presentations were lackluster: Willis Harman. He said that he had heard it from a third party, and he wanted to bring it into the open rather than let it fester behind my back. He told me of the criticism in a way that pointed me in a positive direction of livening up my presentations and bringing the inspiration to ITC that it deserves. Willis Harman was not given to furtiveness or collusion.

- Willis Harman regarding my phone contacts as practical jokes? Never. Willis and Charlene Harman both told me they were quietly excited by the ITC contacts in general, and the recent phone calls to the States in particular. In the fall of 1995 Willis sent me a letter and small grant, saying that he and the IONS board were "especially interested in the research and eager to see it supported as fully as possible." Willis Harman may not have been quick to accept the notion that all the ITC contacts were legitimate, but I felt confident that at no time did he regard my phone contacts as "practical jokes." Willis had arranged for me to present them publicly at the annual IONS conference in 1994 in Chicago, and having attended that conference, and having worked with Willis on other projects, it was clear to me that he was careful to ensure that practical jokes played no part whatsoever in his conferences nor in his work.

- Dale Palmer, a world authority? I disagree. To my knowledge, Palmer at that time had never had any firsthand experience witnessing an enhanced ITC contact, such as a phone call or an extended radio dialog with spirit friends. By suggesting the phone calls were a hoax, he was ignoring the opinions of ITC researchers such as Ernst Senkowski and Ralf Determeyer who had experienced many such contacts, and he was ignoring the solid evidence of the phone calls' legitimacy—cross-contacts and the monitoring of dedicated ITC phone lines by European telephone companies. This evidence was registered and on file with the Association for Psychobiophysics in Mainz, Germany.

I hoped Dale Palmer's comments would leave no permanent scars on world ITC. At the time they stirred the embers of fear in some of the remaining INIT members, especially in me. After all, I had invited him into the group in the first place. I had told the other members that he would be a good addition to the group. Now his letters appeared to me to be damaging INIT badly. As he left INIT at the end of February and formed his new group—GAIT—he made it clear that he wouldn't tolerate any insults cast his way. He warned all members that he would sue anyone who libeled him. There would be a trial, he said.

Then the remarks about me and my work, described above, began to spread.

In the late winter and early spring of 1998 I woke up in a panic many a night after a few hours of restless sleep. I descended the stairs to the living room couch, where I tried to meditate, but fear gripped my mind and heart. I worried about the contact field. Contacts within INIT were already diminishing. Would the higher beings get fed up with the bickering among ITC researchers and simply turn their backs on us? What a horrific loss for humanity that would be!

For the first time in my life I started worrying about the house and the little nest egg Regina and I had been saving toward retirement. What were Palmer's intentions? Did he want to wrestle these things away from me through courtroom tactics? Or darken my reputation to such a degree that I'd become a laughingstock—the man who thinks he's talking to dead people? Or subject me to some kind of modern-day Inquisition, placing me before a judge and jury en route to a jail cell as an accused "charlatan"? Or take the nonprofit funding out of INIT-US to use for projects that *he* considered important—such as scientific authentication of ITC? If I had had the vision of the higher beings, I would be able to observe people's motivations clearly, but being human, I could only wonder and worry.

During those bouts of panic, I became irrational. It was impossible to move myself to that place of peace at the center of my being. My heart was unable to find Light.

By day I was temperamental. I snapped at Regina and our son Aaron several times a week, usually for no reason. By night I was usually awake on the couch, worrying. Often I thought of calling Palmer to resolve the matter, but from past experience I decided that would solve nothing.

I suppose what saved our family was the fact that I could sense negative spirits in my life and in our home during that period. They were busy infesting us all, and I'd drawn them into our home with my chronic fears. If this had happened to me a decade earlier, before my understanding of positive and negative spiritual influences on people's lives, serious troubles might have befallen our family. As it was, I eventually took the incentive to cleanse our family and myself—to draw Light into my life and into our home.

First, as a family we became closer to our church. Through the ages, churches have learned how to become havens of Light, and the church Regina had chosen for us to attend had a pastor and congregation who for the most part seemed happy, upbeat, and ethical, and also enjoyed a wholesome sense of humor. From what I had learned from my invisible ITC friends, these were qualities that raised the spirit. Our family made sure to pray several times a day in order to maintain strong bonds with God. Regina and I worked closely with Aaron on his Confirmation Class homework, supporting the moral teachings and encouraging right decisions among us all.

Second, I revived my old practice of breathwork. I'd lie on the couch in the middle of the night, breathing quickly and deeply, focusing on the troubled situation in INIT, especially the misinformation about me. Soon I'd feel a tremendous surge of panic well up from within, and then I'd release it. Troubled memories of childhood bullying came to mind, then drifted away. Flashbacks of tenuous moments in Vietnam overpowered me, and disappeared. When the fears seemed to be all gone, I'd slow my breathing, move to my heart, and soak up love and Light like a sponge. I'd let the Light fill me up at all levels of my being, then I'd envision myself spraying the Light out into the house, filling every corner of every room. Then, usually, I'd fall into a deep sleep.

The pattern of panic, breathwork, and heart meditation repeated itself for many nights until the fear seemed to shrink to a manageable level. Thanks to that process and to the support of a good church, I felt the presence of loving spiritual energies—especially of Timestream and my guides—move in closer. For the first time in my life I developed a deep appreciation for Jesus Christ and his teachings, and I was gratified with the bond I saw developing between our son and Christ's intercessors.

THE RIVER RUNS DRY, THE EARLY
SPRING OF 1998

As INIT's supporters and donors learned about the conflicts that were rocking world ITC, they began to withdraw their support. So while our contacts dried up in 1998, so did our sources of funding.

Early in 1998 I started to scrape together enough money for an emergency meeting which would be held in the fall. For a meeting site we chose Schweich, Germany, the hometown of Fritz Malkhoff, because most European INIT members lived close enough to that city so that travel expenses would be nominal. At Schweich we would try to pull INIT back together and set it on a firm foundation.

Meanwhile, I found myself in an unfamiliar position. Money had always come to me when I needed it, but now the money sources for INIT were drying up. It was as if a gentle and generous river had been flowing through my life and through INIT, but now that flow was blocked.

What formed the blockage? I came to realize later that it was, to a large extent, the raging doubt, fear, and aggressive behavior being stirred up in INIT. Regina and I were learning through the writings of Deepak Chopra and Emmet Fox, and the channeled materials from the entity Abraham (via Edith Hicks), that abundance was a birthright of all people, but that most people denied their birthright by succumbing to self-defeating mental and emotional patterns such as fear, doubt, insecurity, guilt, resentment, and craving. These negative patterns of thought blocked the natural flow of abundance to individuals and to groups of which they were part.

According to the books and audiocassettes from those folks, there is a fundamental law that governs the conditions of all life everywhere. It goes by various names, such as The Law of Abundance, The Law of Creation, The Law of Manifestation, The Law of Attraction, and The Law of Resonance. According to this law, we humans (and all beings) resonate with other beings on Earth and Beyond who are compatible with our thoughts and intentions, and through that resonance we create much of our reality. We draw into our life spiritual influences from Earth and Beyond which help us to form the reality of our choosing.

Our choices can be conscious or subconscious, and they can be beneficial or harmful to us. If we are happy and optimistic, we draw helpful spiritual influences into our life. If we are driven by fear or pessimism, negative spiritual influences move into our life. We are the composite of our thoughts, feelings, and attitudes, and we attract into our life spiritual influences which resonate with us, for better or for worse. These influences shape to a large extent our reality while we are alive on Earth.

At our innermost core we are a piece of God and we are one with all life. We not only have access to all that is, but we *are* all that is. Hence the ancient Hindu statement, "Thou art that." The closer we can get to our innermost core, through meditation, prayer, and right attitude, the more of that sheer abundance we will experience in our lives. There will be a generous flow of love, joy, material comforts, and much more through our lives in ways and from sources that we can't begin to imagine. All it requires is an attunement to our true nature.

However, it is not so easy here on Earth to become attuned to our inner core. It requires, first of all, that we neutralize our cluttered minds to find a quiet place within us, through such means as meditation. The clutter in our minds consists largely of random thoughts. It also includes negative emotions and long-held misconceptions that inhibit or undermine our birthright of abundance.

For INIT, that meant that as long as we members remained confident, enthusiastic, and optimistic after our first meeting in Dartington Hall in the autumn of 1995, our group would be blessed with abundant ITC contacts and generous support from sponsors. That was certainly the case throughout 1996, as miracles poured into our lives, and as large grants were received into our nonprofit organization's bank account to cover all meeting costs.

But as negative emotional patterns worked their way into our group, starting in 1997, the contacts and the financial support slowly, almost imperceptibly started to diminish. As the conflict raged in 1998, the flow of both ITC contacts and money dried up to trickles.

If you tap a delicate crystal goblet softly with a pencil, it emits a beautiful tone because it can resonate. If you grasp the body of the goblet tightly in your hand and tap it, there's just a dull "clunk." In 1998, INIT was in the tight grip of negative emotions, making resonance impossible.

From the perspective of our spirit colleagues, and especially The Seven higher beings, it became harder and harder to remain synchronized with our group as negative emotions stifled the vibration. As long as we were in harmony, they could attune to us and work their miracles; but once there was dissonance, it required an enormous effort on their part to make contact.

The troubles of INIT boiled over into the personal lives of its members. That was most evident in the shortage of ITC contacts, but there was much more happening behind the scenes. There were lost jobs and lost incomes which threatened members with having to sell the homes they loved and compelled them to scramble to find new jobs, maybe even to strike out in new careers. Dr. Ralf Determeyer fell into that position. There were serious illnesses; Fritz Malkhoff, for example, developed heart troubles and other maladies. Sonia Rinaldi was hospitalized for dangerously high blood pressure. My own digestive troubles began to return, including pains at the spot in my abdomen from where the tumor had been removed ten years earlier.

Also, the troubles of INIT created in my family a strange, new sense of financial insecurity. Regina began to apply pressure on me to contribute more money to the family, so I began to consider part-time employment. At the same time, INIT needed money, so I began to think about ways to raise funds for INIT.

One possibility was to get a job, but then I wouldn't have time to pursue ITC research to the extent I had grown accustomed. To me, that was out of the question unless the situation at home became critical.

Another idea was to start charging people a fee for publishing INIT's contacts in books and other media that they sold for profit. At least that would make money for INIT. I shared the details of my plan with some other INIT members, and no one expressed any reservations. I tried it on one occasion, and it quickly became obvious that the idea was a bad one. A gentleman named Frank Tribbe asked to use some Luxembourg contacts in a book called *Spirit Images* that he was assembling. I told Mr. Tribbe that INIT would probably request some compensation, perhaps a small percentage of the book's earnings.

"INIT's percentage would be on a sliding scale," I said, "based on how much of the book consists of our material." Naturally, a person who included only one or two INIT pictures in a book couldn't be expected to pay the same fee as a person whose book was filled with INIT materials.

Frank Tribbe said the terms were perfectly agreeable, but he made it clear there wasn't much chance for significant sales. If he received a publishing contract, he said, he'd contact me.

Meanwhile I received a note from Maggy Harsch-Fischbach, whose contacts would be included in Mr. Tribbe's book. She said that Frank had been a longtime friend and supporter of her work and by all means should feel free to use her contacts. Frank Tribbe, it turned out, was editor of a small journal of Spiritual Frontiers Fellowship International, a nonprofit Christian research group which had been working for many years to encourage deeper and richer spiritual understanding, not only among individuals, but within the Church at large.

When I realized all that, it seemed almost a sin to be charging such a person a fee. People who work selflessly to spread spiritual understanding in the world should be helped and encouraged, not charged. There had to be a better way to get funding for INIT's meetings and future projects.

THE ROAD TO ABUNDANCE VEERS OFF COURSE

Regina and I started to receive brochures in the mail about how to make money through the stock market, and we began to notice stories in the media of people making a lot of money in stock trading. Even friends of ours were reporting their successes. So I decided to look into the possibility. I started to buy books and tapes by such expert investors as the Gardner brothers, who call their flamboyant but highly regarded enterprise "The Motley Fool," and a rags-to-riches advocate named Wade Cook. I bought a one-year subscription to the *Investor's Business Daily* newspaper, published by a well-known investor named William O'Neil (no relation to the Bill O'Neil of Spiricom fame). Soon I devised a plan to get a comfortable routine going, so that I could spend two or three hours each morning trading stocks, and the rest of the day doing what I loved—ITC research. It sounded perfect, and frankly, I became rather excited about the idea.

Life on Earth is like a lesson book. We're here to experience the Light and the dark, and to spread as much Light as we can before we die. The most important lessons are put in front of our face time after time until we learn them. My big lesson in this lifetime seemed to be fear. As I was coming to grips with the fear instilled in me during the INIT conflict, and as I began to make plans for stock trading, a new source of fear emerged.

At the time of my phone call to Dale Palmer, I knew almost nothing about the stock market, but two short months later I felt knowledgeable and confident. Through intense self-study, I learned wise methods of picking good stocks and mutual funds for long-term investments, and I learned exciting methods of making a lot of money quickly in fancy ways. I could buy stock options, write covered calls, and trade stocks that rolled up and down in price—buying low and selling high.

I decided to test the methods to be sure they could not only supplement our family income, but also provide some basic funding for INIT. With some confidence, I started to make trades on paper, only pretending to invest money, and from early April to the middle of May, I had good results, making more pretend money than I lost.

In May 1998 I invested $10,000 of our nest egg with an Internet stock brokerage firm and began to trade over the phone and through the Internet, buying and selling stocks, and occasionally stock options, which are a great deal riskier.

I was not aware of an ominous pattern that was shaping up in the market. At the time that I began actual trading, the stock market, which had been rising almost steadily since 1987, was growing flat. Fewer and fewer stocks were going up in price; most were staying about the same or going down a bit. I had made plans to buy low and to sell high, but very often when I bought low, the stocks stayed the same or went lower. As they started downward, I sold quickly to minimize my losses. Each time I did that, a bit of our savings slipped away.

I grew nervous. Things were not going according to plan. I proceeded more cautiously and tried a variety of different strategies, but the results didn't improve. Through June and July the market remained flat, and our savings continued to dwindle.

Then, in July, the bottom fell out of the market, and in a span of six weeks the Dow Jones Industrial Average—the most popular measuring stick for the

U.S. economy—dropped about 1,500 points, its largest plunge since the 1929 stock market crash that had dragged our country into the Great Depression. I had studied methods of making money from a growing stock market, but now that I was actually involved in it, the market was collapsing very quickly, and most of my efforts lost money—a lot of money. Every time I lost, I was gripped by more fear, and the fear quickly turned to panic.

But the worst part of my entry into the stock market was not the loss of our money, though it seemed horrific at the time. The worst part was the fact that my entire life purpose was pushed to the back burner as I was immersed in stock trading. It was almost as though I were selling my soul for money, and not successfully at that!

Ever since childhood I had been a light sleeper, and many a night I would awaken with an irresistible compulsion to write down ideas that were pouring through my head. I had always been driven by a passion to understand things at their most basic level—things of importance. As a youngster I would write about teachers, friends, kids at school, and family members, about the noble side of human nature that brought love and happiness, and also about the injustices and cruelties in human relationships that caused so much pain. Years later, as a young man I would write about social, political, and economic systems that brought abundance, comfort, and peace to human lives, or that caused suffering for the people in them and stirred up conflicts with the other large systems around them—governments treading on the rights of individuals, racial and religious groups persecuting each other, economic powers vying with other economic powers to prevail, social systems encroaching on ecosystems, and so on. I would try to find the underlying forces that made such behavior occur.

After my cancer I lost interest in world affairs for a number of years, and I began to write with a passion about healing and spiritual reality. Night after sleepless night I would be typing at the computer or lying on the couch with a small, handheld tape recorder capturing the ideas that were pouring through my mind.

As I began to explore the eternal, multifaceted reality of spirit, my focus continued to narrow, and before long all the nonspiritual matters seemed less significant. Finally, in the late 1990s I was writing about the biggest passion of my life: the miracles of ITC. I felt that ITC was the reason I had come to

Earth in this lifetime. It was my purpose to learn all I could about this new field of research and to apply it to making the world a better place.

Then came stock trading. Now, in the middle of the night I would awaken to thoughts of stocks that should be bought and sold. I would toss and turn in bed, then move to the couch, and I would think about the way particular stocks were behaving. Unable to sleep, I would go to the computer, log on to the Internet, and study stock charts, trying to find some sense of order in their rise and fall, and in the larger rising and falling of the market.

The small voice in the back of my mind that had always provided guidance in my daydreams and meditations was now shouting at me at the top of its lungs to *knock it off,* but it was softer than an EVP voice; I couldn't hear it over the roar of the stock market.

It was impossible for me to "dabble" in stock trading. It consumed me. I was driven by the need to make money for the family and for INIT . . . but everything I tried only lost more money. I was creating my own hell. Why is this happening to me? I wondered over and over.

So, my initial plan was to make enough money through part-time stock investing to contribute more to our family, to support the ITC research I needed to do, and to help support the good work of INIT. I would develop a steady stream of incoming money with which to feed world ITC. The plans fell to pieces in the fear of the moment and my bad experiences with the stock market.

I believe I learned two good lessons from stock trading: (1) As the Bible says in 1 Timothy 6:10, money itself is not evil, but a love of it or an obsession with it takes you away from God and your mission, and it can present serious problems. (2) Fear is never a good driving force with which to conduct the affairs of your life. It will undermine your investment, be it financial or spiritual. Through it all, my purpose finally got back on track.

THE COLLAPSE OF CIVILIZATION

In a lengthy computer message received through Station Luxembourg (March 3, 1998), The Seven higher beings issued a not-so-subtle warning about science. They told us of a day, long buried in the sands of time, when a stubborn reliance on scientific methodology had led to disaster.

Again, *the italicized passages* are adapted directly from the ITC contact, while the other material has been added to fill in the holes.

In an ancient civilization, a panel of wise, old priests met in a temple called "Sothis," in a city named Shanidar sitting along the banks of the Euphrates River, centuries before the city of Babylon would emerge on that very spot. The birth of Babylon would mark the beginning of the second major epoch of human civilization on Earth. Meanwhile, barbarians from surrounding lands were breaking down the doors to the temple and walls to the city at that moment with intent to pillage and sack this final stronghold of civilization.

For years the priests had been working intensively to enlighten the masses in order to ward off a coming dark age, but they had failed. *The signs of impending collapse loomed everywhere—starvation, disease, indifference to death and suffering, city streets strewn by the homeless, widespread murder, and rampant use of drugs. Such conditions had not plagued the Earth so heavily since the previous dark age.*

The priests had been trying to develop a "space-time doorway" to higher levels of spirit that would allow the wisdom of the ages to pour into the world and enlighten humanity. *In hopes of accelerating and legitimizing "Project Sothis," they had forged an alliance with scientists who would be able to convince humanity of the importance of this project as the last chance for peace in a sick world.*

Alkbrat, the head priest, acknowledged that they had made a big mistake. While the scientists had become so intent on measuring things, dissecting them, and counting them over and over again, he lamented, the higher purpose of the project was lost. That higher purpose was to understand that the physical world was inexorably linked to the spiritual worlds, that the doors between the physical and spiritual worlds had been closed, and that it was time to reopen those doors. While waiting patiently for the scientists to prove the existence of spiritual realms, the priests had wasted the time necessary to complete the project.

And now, the walls of Shanidar were coming down. The following day would mark the beginning of the next dark age on Earth. All would be lost.

The priests took this tragic occasion to bid each other farewell, knowing that tomorrow they each would be dead or in hiding. They vowed to try to come together in another lifetime, in a future era when darkness once again was spreading on Earth, leading to another end time. They would not remember each other consciously in that distant day, but they would feel the sense of belonging, and they would devote their lives to spreading Light and spiritual understanding within humanity. This reunion would occur when voices could "speak from boxes," and when people could "move through light behind glass."

The Seven higher beings had been working closely with the priests, and they would return at that future time to help usher in the miracle.

THE CHALLENGE TODAY

Humanity now stands at a crossroads. Burgeoning technology is creating a global brain in the form of the Internet with its computer servers, cell phones, and satellites. In the course of a lifetime our world is being transformed into a society in which cultural and nationalistic boundaries are being erased. For the first time in the development of human life on Earth, we are creating the opportunity to find peace, prosperity, and oneness through open doors of communication around the world.

At the same time, we face serious threats. The rain forest—the lungs of the Earth—continues to disappear; the nuclear arsenals of Russia and the United States still possess the power to destroy world civilization in the course of an hour; addictions trap a large segment of humanity in dark patterns of thought and behavior; and millions of people starve every year as others enjoy unprecedented abundance and conspicuous consumption. Drugs abound. Violence and promiscuity abound, thanks to their rapid spread through movies, television, the Internet, and other mass media. Many sources of information outside ITC research suggest that difficult times lie ahead if we don't change the living conditions and behavior within and among the societies of the world.

Will we find a sustainable paradise on Earth, or will we enter the next dark age in the coming years, or will we simply continue to tread the thin, treacherous path between Heaven and Hell on Earth? I believe that will depend largely on issues involving our sciences and our spirituality. Allowing ourselves to be guided by love, faith, and trust can open the doors to miracles that can move us ever closer to the Light. Doubt, suspicion, fear, and other debilitating emotions will only pull us toward darkness, chaos, and a dim future. Much of conventional science at the present time, from my view, is anchored in doubt, suspicion, and fear, and that has to change.

Chapter 8

~~~

AN AMERICAN SEED TAKES ROOT

THE AFTERLIFE OF INIT

INIT was like a luscious melon filled with rich, sweet miracles. In 1999, however, the four-year-old international research panel was left to die on the vine, which seemed like a tragedy to most of us involved. Looking back on the situation now, though, I believe it was an evolutionary process typical of life on Earth. Cells split apart tumultuously again and again as tissues grow within the human body. Human groups also undergo turbulent growth—coming together (forming) and establishing their values (norming), then conflicts erupt as personal values of members clash with each other and with the values of the group (storming), and then, eventually the group consolidates into a stronger unit (re-forming). Then, usually, the whole cycle of norming, storming, and re-forming starts all over again, and it may continue for the lifetime of the group.

A world ITC association has tried to form several times since the 1980s. It succeeded in 1995 with the birth of INIT, and since then has developed the norms and survived the storms in several cycles, and as I write this final chapter, I believe we are ready to enter the next stage of re-forming. Efforts are already under way as this book goes to press. Nearly a dozen researchers from as many countries are in close contact via e-mail—discussing the viability of a new, three-pronged association to focus on (1) establishing a resonant research group through a co-creative process, (2) launching a scientific project, and (3) setting up a public information group to coordinate journals, websites, and presentations.

Meanwhile, the various members of INIT are like seeds. We were imprinted with miracles from 1995 to 1998, and now many of those seeds have spread to take root in various parts of the world. We're keeping the dream alive—germinating—mostly at the local level, through our writing, through our experiments, and through lectures, seminars, and workshops.

In Brazil, Sonia Rinaldi continues to experiment with computer and video, hosts an ITC website, and coordinates a network of several hundred experimenters. She has been writing several books which, hopefully, will be translated into many languages. Cristina and Luciano Rocha experiment as well, keeping in touch with Dr. Hernani Andrade, the aging Brazilian pioneer of ITC research. Dr. Carlos Luz analyzes ITC from an engineering perspective. Since 1997 he has worked with spectral analysis of spirit voices, continuing and supplementing the work of Carlo Trajna and Paolo Presi in Italy. Dr. Luz says his research "shows evidence that there is a basic residual frequency of the human voice which dislocates to the upper part of the spectrum."

In Finland, Irma Weisen continues to write and speak about ITC research.

In France, Jacques Blanc-Garin continues to host gatherings in which grieving families can hear from their departed loved ones. He publishes two ITC journals to spread the word of ITC through the French-speaking world and hosts an ITC website. Books about ITC by Father François Brune and Monique Simonet continue to sell. Father Brune speaks often at international conferences.

In Germany, Dr. Ernest Senkowski, Fritz Malkhoff, Dr. Ralf Determeyer, and Hans Otto Koenig continue to share ITC results in public forums. Fidelio Koeberle stepped down as head of the largest EVP association in the world and has been replaced by Theo Bleitgen, whose aim is to invite greater collaboration with other ITC groups.

In Israel, Dr. Adrian Klein stays in contact with various ITC researchers, keeping lines of communication open and testing the waters until the time is right to call a founding meeting for a new international ITC association.

In Italy, Dr. Franco Tellarini provides complete translations of a few ITC journals into the Italian language and distributes them at no charge to Italian researchers, keeping them abreast of world ITC. Marcello Bacci continues his radio experiments, Paola Giovetti writes books and articles about ITC, and Paolo Presi pursues ITC from a technical and scientific angle.

In Japan, Siyoh Tomiyama arranged for the translation and large-scale publication of *Conversations Beyond the Light,* a book by Pat Kubis and my-self, and hosts a website that contains ITC information.

In Luxembourg, Maggy Harsch-Fischbach continues to get occasional contacts from Timestream and The Seven ethereal beings. Some of the contacts are published in "Transdimenion" by Alfred Zogg in Switzerland. And I believe Maggy is writing a book about her miraculous experiences since the mid-1980s. When her book is published, I hope everyone in the world reads it. I have complete faith in her honesty and in the validity of her contacts, mind-boggling though they are. Her experiences embody the miracle of ITC at its best.

In Mexico, Yvon and Maryvonne Dray plan conferences and publish an ITC newsletter.

In Portugal, Maria Saraiva coordinates an ITC association.

In Spain, A. Cardoso publishes an ITC journal which she started with Carlos Fernandez with the collaboration of Sinesio Darnell (Spanish ITC re-searcher since 1973) and Pedro Amoros. Ms. Cardoso is Portuguese, cur-rently living in Spain for professional reasons.

In Sweden, Dr. Nils Jacobson coordinates a network of researchers who experiment and maintain an ITC website.

In Switzerland, Alfred Zogg-Meier publishes a journal for a Swiss associa-tion dedicated to ITC research.

In the United States, Alison van Dyk and Peter Ledermann hold weekly experimental sessions with a small research team near the border of New York and Connecticut. Erland Babcock conducts video experiments in Massachu-setts. An independent researcher named Bruce Moen, who took advanced training at The Monroe Institute, is also working in ITC, I have been told. In California, researcher John Klimo received funding for an ITC project. My team in Colorado has enjoyed some major strides, which I report in this chapter, and in October 2000 I participated in the founding of a new associ-ation called ITCP (the ITC Platform) along with seven other researchers from seven countries, whose aims include a strengthening of ITC contacts through resonance of members.

This is just a partial list of the serious ITC research under way as this book goes to press, and I apologize to those whose names I forgot to include. I'm confident that the miracles of ITC will not only survive, but will reshape our world in a most profound and positive way in the coming years, as a stable and vital new association comes together based on resonance and ethereal connections.

A GAIT PROJECT

In 1999, Dale Palmer, the principle founder of GAIT, tried to introduce into our field of research a new term: EDP (electronic disturbance phenomenon). Unlike EVP (electronic voice phenomenon) and ITC (instrumental transcommunication), both of which implied a collaboration with intelligent, invisible beings who were creating the voices and participating in the communications that were involved in our work, "electronic disturbance phenomenon" was an objective, impersonal term, and perhaps therefore a more scientific term.

On the other hand, in my view, it took away the sense of collaboration and personal rapport across dimensions, which I regard as fundamental to ITC research. In fact, I believe that scientists will have to build that premise into their worldview before they can hope to prove the existence of life after death. As ironic as it sounds, they'll have to collaborate actively and directly—perhaps with a sense of awe and wonder—with the folks whose existence they're trying to prove.

In the fall of 2000, Palmer announced in the AA-EVP newsletter that he and his associates in GAIT were fourteen months into an eighteen-month project to enhance the volume and clarity of EVP (or EDP) voices with computer technology.

PORTAL TO MIRACLES, THE SPRING OF 1999

"You two *really* have to meet," she said, as though she wouldn't take "No" for an answer.

A colleague of mine from Texas named Susan was a psychic, a chiropractor, and a longtime reader of my ITC journal, *Contact!,* as well as a member of ISSSEEM (the International Society for the Study of Subtle Energies and Energy Medicine), which held its annual conference in Boulder a few miles away from my home. Sue attended the ISSSEEM conferences almost every year, and if it fit into her schedule, she would stop by our house to discuss ITC research with Regina and me.

In the spring of 1999, Sue called me to say that another ISSSEEM member named Jack Stucki would be at the conference a few months later with a subtle energy device called a "Luminator" that might be very helpful to ITC research.

"All right," I said. "I'll mark it on my calendar, and I'll plan to see you and Jack in a few months."

On June 22, Susan called to report that Jack had his Luminator in a room at the Harvest House Hotel, where the conference was being held. He was talking to a number of people about the device. Sue was there too, so I grabbed a few copies of *Contact!* to give away, hopped into the car, and drove to the Harvest House.

In the hallway, as I approached the room, there was a strange, disarming sense in the air. It gave me a safe, pleasant, and unusual kind of feeling. The door was open, so I walked in. The feeling was stronger in the room, where a small group of people had gathered.

Susan greeted me and introduced me to Jack Stucki, a young-looking fifty-seven-year-old with wavy blond hair, weathered skin, and a boyish grin. I immediately felt a kinship to the fellow.

"Pleased to meet you," I said, extending my hand. "Sue told me a lot about your work and your machine. Is that it?" I pointed to the black tower standing a few feet from the window.

"That's it." Jack smiled as he shook my hand. Jack described the Luminator and showed me some blurry photos of individuals standing alone in a room with the device. At first glance they seemed to be photos taken in low lighting. Many of them looked like double exposures.

Jack assured me that was not the case. They had been taken with a Polaroid camera in good lighting, making it virtually impossible to produce a double exposure. Some pictures had been taken while the camera was mounted motionlessly on a tripod. Snapping the shutter twice to achieve a double exposure was not an option with a Polaroid camera, since a photo was ejected from the camera every time the shutter was snapped. I was puzzled. From everything I knew about photography and about "the real world," those pictures were impossible.

But what stunned me were the faces in the photographs. Part of the person's face was gone, and in its place was another face of someone else. If this was what it was purported to be—a picture of a spirit being superimposed over a physical human being—then humanity was on the verge of receiving a tremendous gift. For the first time in history, people would be able to see solid evidence of the multidimensional composition of their own bodies. A person would be able to see in living color how the human spirit and his or her own physical body can occupy the same space. This would be a major milestone in ITC research, confirming in a very dramatic way the diagrams developed by George Meek showing spirit bodies superimposed over the physical body.

Ten years earlier I might have assumed that the pictures were all a hoax, but my worldview had been broadened immensely during a decade of ITC research. It seemed the more my mind was stretched, the more difficult it became to reject new ideas outright, simply because they didn't make sense to me.

One of the most amazing things I'd ever witnessed had occurred at our 1997 INIT conference in Brazil. Jules Harsch had taken a Polaroid snapshot of a small group of INIT members, but when the picture had developed a few minutes later, it was not my friends and colleagues in the picture, but a dolphinlike creature swimming playfully in the water. We had been told later by spirit colleagues, via Station Luxembourg, that the picture showed living beings from another world in another dimension—a watery world. These dimensions can cross each other under certain conditions, allowing inhabitants of one dimension to perceive, and sometimes cooperate with, inhabitants of other dimensions.

Such an experience would have stretched my mind beyond the breaking point a decade earlier, but over the years I had been forced to change my way of viewing the world. After witnessing a succession of miraculous experiences, I had developed an attitude that I call "trusting discernment."

When I observed something that didn't make sense to me, I would not immediately discount it. First of all, I would think about the people involved. Did I know them? If so, did they have a track record of sincerity and honesty? If I didn't know them, were they known by someone whose opinions and judgments I trusted, and did that person regard them as sincere and honest? If someone was reported to be wielding miracles, and if my trusted colleagues or I regarded that person as sincere and honest, then I would allow those miracles into my view of the world. I would stretch my mental model accordingly, even if I couldn't understand right away exactly how the miracles were happening.

That was the case with those strange pictures of physical and nonphysical human beings posing together in front of a Polaroid camera. I didn't know Jack, but I knew Susan and trusted her intuition and judgment, so I would accept these miraculous pictures as legitimate while I tried to answer the obvious questions in my mind.

- How can nonphysical beings and forms register on film when we can't see them with the naked eye? (Some films can capture light and energies that are beyond the range of our eyesight, so it stands to reason that some things can appear on film that we can't see.)
- How does the Luminator facilitate the appearance of spirit beings on film? (Since the beings always show themselves sharing a person's body, maybe the machine alters the energies in the physical body—perhaps raising the vibration—in such a way that spirit beings are able to comingle with their brethren in physical bodies more easily.)
- Who were these invisible folks who were moving in close to smile for the camera? Were they attached beings? Were Jack's clients possessed? Were they guides and guardians of the clients—beings who were active in the people's lives, trying to help them out? Were they former incarnations of the same soul? Were they simply visitors—spirit beings who moved randomly in and out of the lives of people on Earth, and who just happened to be present for the pictures? Or were they a team of spirits who worked closely with Jack and his Luminator, showing themselves with the clients? (Although there was no way to be certain, there seemed to be different explanations that applied to different cases. If only the spirit beings could *talk* to Jack and explain their presence, that would eliminate a lot of guessing.)

For some time, an important goal of my ITC project had been to get images from the spirit worlds to supplement the voice contacts. Exactly how I should go about it, I hadn't decided, but these images of Jack's seemed like a good opportunity.

Jack's thoughts were moving along the same line. "You know, I'd love to talk to these guys on the radio," he said, referring to the nonphysical beings in his photographs. He told me that if he could communicate audibly with his spirit collaborators, they might be able to answer a lot of his questions.

It suddenly struck me what an effective team we could become—Jack and his Luminator working together with me and my ITC equipment. Ideally, images and voices could be delivered to us at the same time from beyond the veil. Our spirit friends could tell us who was in the picture and the nature of their influence, if any, on the person being photographed. They could show themselves while telling us all sorts of insightful things about their worlds.

"I think our meeting here today was planned by a lot more folks than just Susan." I smiled.

Jack laughed and replied, "I think you're right."

Our Spiritual Design

Soul

Light, Ethereal Bodies

Astral Body

Quantum Body

Physical Body

This diagram shows the spiritual makeup of a man and woman. When we die and shed the physical body, we live on in a quantum body for a few days or a few weeks. The quantum body is a template of the physical body—nearly identical in every way except composed of a substance so subtle that it cannot be detected by the physical senses.

Before long the quantum body is transformed into an astral body, which is subtler still and takes on the appearance of the physical body at the prime of life, between ages twenty-five and thirty-five. Physical bodies that had been ravaged during lifetime with disease, amputation, or paralysis are vibrant and complete in every way at the astral level, containing all organs and functions of a perfectly healthy physical body. When we die on Earth and take up residence in the astral world, our new body is whole and in the peak of health until we decide to move to the ethereal realms. At that time we go through another transition, relinquishing all form and structure to become pure consciousness.

Our ethereal body resides in the realms of angels. Many mystics say we have three of these Light bodies, or sheaths, around our soul. They have no form; they are like balls of living energy or clouds of pure love and wisdom. Light beings generally live closely together in clusters.

Everyone is a composite of all these bodies. Our physical form is just a temporary shell or vehicle which our higher self uses to navigate here in the physical world. That higher self is the soul, an eternal flame of pure, nonvibrating light. It is said to be a piece of the Source, or God—a spark of pure love and wisdom. At the soul level we are one with everyone and everything. The greatest reality exists at the soul level. Each level beyond the soul becomes increasingly flawed and illusory as the substance becomes denser and of slower vibration. Twin souls often come to Earth at the same time as identical twins or as individuals who will form an unusually close and loving marriage.

A BREAKTHROUGH FOR STATESIDE ITC, THE FALL OF 1999

After my initial meeting with Jack Stucki, we began working together, incorporating the Luminator into our group experiments once a month. I would drive to Colorado Springs on a Thursday or Friday, pick up the Luminator, bring it home, and let it run in my lab over the weekend to build up an energy field in preparation for our Monday meeting. Jack and his psychic friend Catherine Yeager would drive up Monday morning for the meeting, then take the Luminator home with them afterward.

It was at our second meeting in September when we received a miraculous picture that would lock our project on course. Jack took a photo of me with his Polaroid 600 camera, but when the image developed a few minutes later, it was not my face perched above my neck, but what appeared to be the face of my father. My forehead was barely visible, and it was up and to the left of where it should have been. I was overwhelmed at seeing my own head displaced from my body, and my father's face resting contentedly in its place. I sat down and studied the image for several minutes.

A few days after the meeting I left the picture on the kitchen counter. When Regina passed by and glanced at it, she remarked, "It looks like Willis Harman."

"No," I replied, "it's definitely my father." I took the picture to the kitchen table and studied it for a while in good light with a magnifying glass. Yes, definitely my father, I thought, although—I suddenly noticed something odd about the picture. The mouth, the eyes, and other facial features were not symmetrical. There were noticeable differences between the left and right halves of the face. I grabbed a sheet of paper and covered up the right half of the face, and there was no doubt: That was my father on the left.

When I covered up the left half of the face, however, I was stunned. That was not my father. Regina's words came back to me. Oh my gosh, I thought, it *does* look like Willis Harman!

I jumped into the car, drove to Mailboxes Etc., and had some enlargements made on a color copier. I sent one to Charlene Harman, Willis's wife in California. When Mrs. Harman opened the envelope a few days later, she took one look at the picture and exclaimed to herself, "Oh my goodness, this is a picture of Bill! He's found a way to come through!" She showed the picture to many close friends and relatives (all of whom knew Willis as "Bill"), and many of them recognized Bill Harman in the photo.

It was interesting to me that Regina, who'd never met Willis Harman but had seen pictures of him years earlier, had been the first to identify him. It was also odd that Regina had seen the image of Willis more easily than that of my father, whom she had known very well. I began to wonder if people's impressions of dual pictures such as this one were shaped largely by the dominant hemisphere of their brain. Perhaps Regina was "right-brained," and I was "left-brained," or vice versa, and that was why I recognized my father on the left, and she recognized Willis Harman on the right. When I reversed the image so that Willis was on the left and Dad was on the right, I saw Willis instantly, and it was more difficult to recognize my father. In any case, it was apparent that the two men had somehow come together for a most miraculous ITC experience in my lab.

This was truly an historic moment! Willis Harman, the late president of IONS, had spent the last years of his life carefully building a bridge between science and spirit, and now he apparently wanted to finish the job. I accepted the picture as an invitation for the two of us to collaborate from opposite sides of the veil on this project that we both deemed vital to the future of humanity.

Since then, my research team and I have received hundreds of spirit images on Polaroid film in living color in my lab. We have received pictures of our spirit guides, our departed loved ones, and beings unknown to us. Over Christmas vacation in 1999, many friends of our family stopped by for pictures, and nearly all of them came away with holiday souvenirs of spirit guides and/or departed loved ones. Throughout the year 2000 we hosted many visitors from various countries in the lab, and nearly everyone walked away with spirit faces posing with them on film.

When gifted psychics posed for pictures, I asked them to adjust their vibration for a series of pictures. Typically, when they "tuned in" to the light, ethereal realms of angels and higher beings, the faces of the psychics showed up clearly in the picture, with no spirit faces present. When they thought mundane thoughts—for example, what specific chores would be awaiting them when they returned home—very often there were spirits posing with them in the picture, maybe the face of their departed mother or father.

One of the most startling images appeared when I took a picture of Jack Stucki during our meeting on April 17, 2000. His face was replaced entirely by a very clear, familiar face. It was the face of Patrick Richards, the man who invented the Luminator, and who *was still alive* and living in Michigan. This was the first known case in which the image of a living person appeared in our experiments.

WHAT TO MAKE OF THE IMAGES

Exactly how and why we received an image of a living colleague—Patrick Richards, who at the time was at home in Michigan—we can only speculate. We assume it was his spirit body, projected as though in an out-of-body experience, which was present with us that day in the lab.

There's little doubt in my mind that the faces in the other pictures are of people in spirit. Many questions arise. For example: What is their purpose in the lives of the people with whom they are posing? Why are they here? In what levels of spirit are they residing? Do they have to "commute" to denser levels of spirit by lowering their vibration in order to work with us in ITC research? How can we get them to communicate more clearly through the radios so that we can get messages to supplement the images?

I've begun to realize that there are no simple answers to these questions.

For example, we're finding that different beings manifest in the pictures for different reasons. It's not necessarily a case of "spirit possession," as I had thought when first seeing Jack's pictures. Regarding my picture with Willis Harman and my father, for example, it is obvious to me that I am not "possessed" or "obsessed" by these two good men. I am certain that both men have gotten settled into very positive spirit worlds. I am also certain, based on ITC messages received in recent months, that they move in close to my life, especially when the radios in my lab are turned on, to help me out in my ITC experiments. They are very positive forces in my life.

The role of all these invisible folks will be one subject of our research here in Colorado in the coming years, as we expect to get messages coming through the veil with increasing clarity. We hope our spirit team will be able to identify the spirits appearing on film and to describe what effects they have on us, or what role they play in our lives.

MY OWN LUMINATOR, THE GT-21

When telescopes were invented around the year 1600, Galileo used one to see sunspots, lunar craters, Jupiter's moons, and other realities that were invisible to people, including scientists of the day. The telescope gave humanity a new, more accurate view of the world, but it was not well received by conventional scientists, who were aligned with the Church at that time. Many scientists refused to look through the telescope, saying, "God is perfect, and so his creation is perfect. Humans are imperfect, and so things made by humans are imperfect. It would be foolish for us to use an imperfect tool, such as Galileo's telescope, to try to perceive God's perfect creation." It was simply a convenient excuse by scientists, allowing them to preserve their familiar, albeit incorrect, view of the world.

We like to think that science is more open-minded today than it was back in Galileo's time, but that is not necessarily true. Every human being and every human institution has a version or road map or model of reality which they use to navigate through time and space here on Earth. We each see things a little bit differently from the way other people do. Mary Smith in America and Ali Abubakar in Iran see the world differently, and of course, science and religion see the world differently.

As more is learned about reality, most of us individuals and most of our institutions try to update our road maps accordingly, but if the new information is so radical that it would upset or shatter the existing road map, we will usually find a reason to reject the new information. That's what happened to Galileo and his telescope. They were rejected because the new view of the world they offered to humanity would shatter the conventional scientific and religious model of the time.

In April 2000, a new Luminator was developed for me and sent to my lab. It was custom-made for my research. I named the new device a "GT-21." That's short for Galileo's Telescope of the Twenty-First Century.

The images made possible with the GT-21 prove conclusively, in my mind, that our physical world is superimposed by other worlds, which I call the spirit worlds, and that those worlds are teeming with life. Will science, religion, and other institutions today embrace this new technology which broadens our view of reality, or will they find reasons to reject it because it will upset their road maps of reality?

Well, let's wait and see. The next few years should be very interesting.

Meanwhile, Jack Stucki will continue to work with my local research team and me. We have set up a radio configuration in Jack's office in Colorado Springs for ITC experiments as well. Our aim is to have twin ITC labs working in Colorado—one here in Boulder, the other in Colorado Springs.

Colorado Springs, by the way, was the town chosen by Nikola Tesla a century ago for advanced energy experiments that stunned the world. A room-sized cylindrical coil generated fifteen million volts that cascaded and crackled around the inventor's head in the form of thousands of wild, brilliant snakes of raw electricity. A sixteen-story tower antenna shot lightning bolts one hundred thirty-five feet upward, creating thunderclaps that could be heard fifteen miles away. One such experiment drew so much electricity from the public grids that the main generator at the Colorado Springs power station erupted in flames.

People walking a few miles from Tesla's laboratory could sometimes look down and see sparks jumping between their shoes as they walked. Horses grazing peacefully on the surrounding prairie would grow frantic and stampede during some experiments, as electricity shot through their metal shoes.

Tesla theorized that the Earth could be "split open like an apple" by achieving a critical resonance between his equipment and the planet itself, which vibrates at 8, 14, and 20 Hz. That experiment, or one like it, apparently was conducted on another planet in our solar system many thousands of years ago, leading to that planet's destruction. At least that is what we have been told through ITC contacts. Fortunately, an experiment of that magnitude has not been conducted on Earth.

According to more recent legend, which many people living today regard to be factual, the U.S. Navy employed Tesla's resonance theories in a secret experiment early this century in which a naval ship, the U.S.S. *Eldridge,* was dematerialized along with its crew at the Philadelphia Naval Yard. Books and movies about "the Philadelphia Experiment" suggest that the vibration of the vessel was raised, causing it to move from our physical domain into subtler dimensions nearby which are imperceptible to us. As the ship vanished from the physical world, the sailors could feel the solid structures around them becoming softer, and before long they could literally walk through the steel bulkheads of the ship. Several became fused in the metal, many died or were lost, and most of the surviving sailors were violently ill after their ship rematerialized. Some of the sailors who survived went insane.

These incidents surrounding the life of Nikola Tesla, whether true in part or in their entirety, indicate that the man was far ahead of his time. Even today they are discussed only in small circles beyond the fringes of mainstream science.

Our plans for experiments in Colorado certainly are not as radical as those conducted around the ideas of Nikola Tesla. Even so, we have some pretty exciting prospects.

Patrick Richards of Michigan is the inventor of the Luminator. He tells a story of the time he placed three of the devices in a triangular configuration spanning two rooms in his house. He turned them on, sat in the center of the triangle formed by three devices, and felt a very strange sensation. As he leaned his head against the wall, it went *through* the wall as though it were passing through a light beam rather than a solid object. He quickly withdrew his head, turned off the Luminators, and has not tried the experiment again since then. He says it was quite a frightening experience. Somehow the triangular configuration of the three devices seemed to have created a vortex to other dimensions, or at least it altered the molecular structure of things (the walls or the inventor's body) in this world.

If the incident can be replicated under controlled conditions in the coming years, our Colorado ITC experiments might evolve very slowly and carefully into the development of a space-time doorway through which we on Earth not only can communicate with beings in subtler realms, but can move back and forth between worlds.

When I mentioned that to Regina, she said, "Before you start walking into that doorway, talk to your wife."

We laughed, and I agreed.

As I've indicated elsewhere in this book, such notions would have been far beyond my boggle point fifteen years earlier. They would have shattered my road map of reality. But the things I have seen and the experiments I have observed and conducted in recent years lead me to think that we are on the threshold of a new era. We here in Colorado, along with other researchers elsewhere in the world, are beginning to gather the solid evidence that might persuade even confirmed skeptics (1) that intelligent life abounds all around us in worlds that are blocked from view, as though flourishing behind closed doors, and (2) that we have reached the point in human evolution when it's time to reach out carefully, in a decidedly positive frame of mind, to start opening those doors.

As our ITC efforts in Colorado begin to establish a stable footing with positive contacts received on a regular basis, I am rekindling ties with my colleagues around the world. My hope is to establish a lasting relationship with one another and with the light, ethereal realms of existence. I hope the overriding aim of the association will be to help wash away the darkness that has spread so widely in our world. I'd like to think we can help cleanse the world of spiritual misunderstandings and negative thoughtforms.

As we enter the twenty-first century, perhaps we can adopt the first words God ever spoke to our world:

"Let there be Light!"

TRY THIS

To achieve resonance with ethereal beings and with other people interested in attracting miracles into this world and into their lives, there is a useful exercise that can get us into the habit of raising our vibration:

1. Clear your mind and move your awareness slowly from the head to the heart. It might take some practice during quiet moments when you're alone before you can achieve this step, but once you succeed, it will feel as though your thinking and feeling are taking place in your chest. Your brain more or less closes down. You may feel wonderful surges of energy passing through your body.

2. At this point you have come as close as possible, I believe, to a direct connection between yourself and God. You can absorb immense volumes of love, wisdom, and grace directly from the Source. Let it swirl through your spirit bodies and physical body, cleansing and purifying you at every level. You can fill yourself with this Light like a sponge soaking in water, and then you can let it out into the world through your thoughts, feelings, words, and actions.

3. As the process becomes easy and natural, join with others of like mind and heart. Have meetings and discussion groups in which this process of going to the heart is part of the agenda. When you are all in your heartspace, direct your powerful group intentions toward healing individuals and healing the world, toward opening up a rapport with ethereal beings, toward sending lost souls—people who have died and are now trapped near the Earth—to the Light. These and other good efforts will quickly bring ethereal beings into your group and into your life for protection and service.

4. At that point, if you want to get involved in ITC and get good results, your chances are now much, much better.

EPILOGUE

As I was putting the finishing touches on this book in the summer of 2000, Regina and I enjoyed a visit by Louise Hauck, a talented and charming clairvoyant currently living in New York who has written several books about her experiences seeing beyond the illusion of time and death, helping grieving individuals to contact departed loved ones, the most recent book being *Heart-Links* (Council Oak Books, 2000).

I took a series of pictures of Louise in the lab that evening, and we all discussed them over dinner. Of the nine photos taken, seven had spirit beings posing with Louise. After dinner I turned on the radio system in the lab, and Louise clairvoyantly saw the late ITC pioneer George Meek working fastidiously from the other side of the veil with Radio #3. She said my late colleague was working with intensity to open a voice bridge through that radio with the help of a small team of spirit colleagues, including Willis Harman. Several ethereal beings were working with the team, providing guidance and protection. They were working on the same spiritside system that Bill O'Neil and Arthur Beckwith had been using several years earlier to try to contact me. According to Louise, George had locked himself onto the task of breaking through to our world through my radios, and his team expected success fairly soon. Louise saw all this very clearly in my lab that evening, and her insights locked my research on target more firmly than had been possible since the storm of INIT disrupted the lives and the work of so many of us. Since her visit, I have been focusing with renewed vigor on Radio #3 and the efforts of my spirit team, with encouraging results.

In her books, Louise emphasizes the importance of gratitude in making the connection to spirit. That message is especially appropriate as I close this book, deeply thankful to her and to all of our spirit friends who are making this miracle possible for our world as we step into a new century.

For more information about the author and ITC research,
please visit www.worlditc.org.